through

MW01633348

Other books by Caroline Jones

The Search for Meaning (four titles)

An Authentic Life: Finding Meaning and Spirituality in Everyday Life

CAROLINE JONES

through a glass darkly

A JOURNEY OF LOVE AND GRIEF WITH MY FATHER

FOREWORD BY MAL McKISSOCK

ABC
Books

Published by ABC Books for the
AUSTRALIAN BROADCASTING CORPORATION
GPO Box 9994 Sydney NSW 2001

First published April 2009

National Library of Australia
Cataloguing-in-Publication data

Jones, Caroline
    Through a Glass Darkly: a journey of love and
    grief with my father / Caroline Jones
    1st ed.
    ISBN 978 0 7333 2398 0 (pbk.)
    Includes index
    Jones, Caroline
    Television journalists – Australia – Biography
    Parents – death
070.92

Edited by Jean Kingett
Internal text and photographs design, and illustrations by Helen Semmler
Typeset in 12/16pt Celestia Antiqua by Kirby Jones
Index by Puddingburn Publishing Services
Cover design by Ellie Exarchos
Front cover illustration by Salvatore Zofrea
Back cover photograph by Peter Solness
Project management by Richard Smart Publishing
Printed and bound in Australia by Griffin Press, Adelaide

5 4 3 2 1

For my mother Nancy Rae James who gave me life,
love, encouragement and purpose. And for my father
Brian Newman James who showed me a way to live
with gratitude, patience, courage and humour. And
in loving memory of my stepmother Mary James
and her sister Win Purnell.

For now we see through a glass, darkly; but then
face to face: now I know in part; but then shall
I know even as also I am known.

1 Corinthians 13:12

Contents

Photographs

Acknowledgements

I acknowledge with gratitude all those who have supported me in the writing of this book.

The list begins with those who gave me a love of language: my grandmother Janet Pountney; my parents; my first teachers at Murrurundi Central School, Miss Lettie Lee (Mrs Watson) and Miss Beryl Read (Mrs Morrissey); Miss Phyl Bennett and Mr Carl Sundstrom at Gosford High School. Several people read and responded to the manuscript-in-progress: my thanks to Tony Barry, Maria Costa, Myree Harris RSJ, Hugh Mackay, Dianna Ridley, Joanne Rowe and Valerie Smith, who also suggested the famous quote from Corinthians as the book's title.

Patti Miller's critique was critical, as was the insight of psychologist Carmel Ross, who helped me to interpret my experience as I was writing. For details of family history I turned to my father's sisters, Melvie Tait and Gwen Bohlé and my cousin Jan Lindsay.

To those who were kind and generous in their care for my stepmother Mary James, and for me, my deep appreciation: to

Heather and Frank Bock, Susan Hammer, Jo Nelson, Sandi McCush, Julie Phillips: to the doctors and staff at Yallambee Lodge; to the staff of Phillips Pharmacy, Frangipani, and Instep Footwear, Gosford; to the staff of Gosford District Hospital and Woy Woy Rehabilitation Hospital; and to Professor Peter Lipski, Conjoint Associate Professor, University of Newcastle, a champion of wholistic care for aged patients.

For their encouragement and care for me I am grateful to Catherine Bayliss, Stella Cornelius, Lee Carmody, Jenny and Peter Coleman, Paul Coleman SJ, Kate Cadell and Sayed Hamed, Dr Gabrielle Casper, Dr Len Fabre, Stephen Godley, Garth Harris, Ray Hourigan, Barbara and Patrick Lewis, Meryl Litherland, Sr Bridget O'Halloran RSJ, Dr Marcia Manning, Liz Millard, Rosemary Moir, Judy Purdon, Gordon Nicholls, Louisa Ring Rolfe, Roula Spiropoulos, Fr Robert Walsh SJ and Trudy Zipf.

My gratitude to those who cared for my father, especially Dr Ray Raper and the Intensive Care and Cardiac Ward staff at North Shore Private Hospital.

I offer thanks to the following poets, writers, publishers, copyright owners or estates for allowing extracts to be used from their works: Peter Alexander, Peter Kocan, Les Murray, David Rowbotham, Kenneth Slessor, *The NSW Doctor*, Harper Collins, Spectrum Publications, Random House, and Oxford University Press.

Some events described in the book have previously appeared as part of a regular column entitled 'The Search f or Meaning' that I wrote for *Madonna* magazine from 1998 to 2002. My thanks to editor David Lovell and Jesuit Publications for permission to use this material.

For photography my thanks go to Peter Solness for the back cover portrait, and to Shawn Connell, Heather Bock and Howard

Harris. Ron Mills made the glazed earthenware doves in the back cover photograph.

Salvatore Zofrea graciously allowed a detail of his *Illawarra flame tree and bower bird 2008* to be reproduced on the front cover of the book. The work, a hand-coloured woodcut on Japanese Kozo paper, is one of a gloriously exuberant series entitled 'Days of Summer' which is touring Australian regional art galleries. The printmaker is Trevor Riach.

Special thanks to my publisher Richard Smart, and to all those involved in the project at ABC Books, including Brigitta Doyle, Jane Finemore and Louise Cornege; to Helen Semmler who designed the book so beautifully; to Ellie Exarchos for her creative work on the cover design; and to Jean Kingett for her sensitive editing of a difficult manuscript.

I am delighted that Mal McKissock OAM has written the Foreword. He is widely respected for his wisdom in the care of dying people and in bereavement counselling and teaching. He was one of the founders of the National Association for Loss and Grief and, with his wife Dianne and others, established the Bereavement Care Centre in Sydney. His participation in the book will lead you to his own insightful writing, including *Coping With Grief*, which has become a classic.[1]

The Gardener

I watched my father digging in his garden.
His spade, with a sound like the palm of a huge hand
Against a huger tree, struck through the soil,
Lifted, turned, let fall. He pounded with care
Each stubborn clod and broke it into earth
That flowed between his fingers;
And the peewit came from the nest in the
    camphor-laurel
And, with a bird's simplicity, like a child's trust,
Stabbed for worms in the shadow of his knees.
You can not know the kindness of a man
Till you see him in a garden with a spade
And birds about his feet.

David Rowbotham

Foreword

In my professional experience of working with bereaved people for over three decades, I have found the most helpful thing any of us can do is to create an environment in which grieving people can feel truly understood, and safe enough to share the passionate intensity of their experience without fear of judgement or interpretation.

If we ask genuinely interested questions we provide precious opportunities for the bereaved person to bring the deceased *to life*, to reconnect through memories, through sharing hopes and dreams that will not now be fulfilled. Through this process we stimulate biochemicals which promote healing, slowly and gently facilitating the bereaved person's ability to learn how to live with grief, to build new life around painful emptiness.

Grief, for all of us, is influenced by many factors. We grieve as we have lived and loved, the intensity and duration of reactions largely determined by the degree of centrality the deceased person held in our lives, the meaning they gave to our sense of wellbeing.

Learning how to live with grief is a challenge, a struggle, and one which takes far longer than is commonly believed. Much of

Caroline's struggle was focussed on religion and spirituality, on relationships, including her relationship with God. Many will identify with her, but whether the bereaved person is religious, agnostic or an atheist, it is the process involved in finding meaning that is wholesome and helpful in the long term.

Initially, most of us protest about the seeming unfairness of being forced to exchange the comfort and pleasure of the deceased person's tangible reality for the elusive power of memories and dreams to bring them back *to* life. Once we accomplish this ability, as Caroline says, 'Grief is not all there is'.

Caroline brings her father *to* life in a way that allows the reader to get to know him intimately so that he becomes part of *our* story. Our connection with him changes and deepens as she weaves the story of their relationship from past to present, and eventually to the future—the future she hoped for, and as it will now be. Many people talk *about* significant experiences in their lives, but few take us *into* the experience with the degree of honesty, passion and vulnerability that Caroline expresses in her book. We are left in no doubt about the depth of her love for her father, for her parents. But this is not a 'Pollyanna' story—anger, self-doubt, despair and feelings of abandonment are expressed as openly and honestly as feelings of love, commitment, duty and respect.

There is an invaluable universality in Caroline's story. I hope many bereaved and their carers will embrace the details she shares, stay with the intimacy and passion she expresses, understand the normality of the prolonged nature of grief. In doing so, the difference between passionate sadness and depression will be more clearly understood; there will be less need for the medicalisation of grief.

Mal McKissock

Introduction

My father died in Sydney's North Shore Private Hospital on 30 July 2000, eight weeks after open-heart, coronary bypass surgery, at the age of ninety-three. The final eight weeks of his life were a terrible ordeal for him, and for me.

It seems to me that suffering presents the greatest challenge of human life. And to witness the suffering of someone I loved was unbearable, yet I had to find a way to bear it.

It is not unexpected that someone will die once they reach their nineties, and I believe now my distress was more for my father's suffering than for his dying. But, because of the circumstances, the two causes became intertwined.

I have read a good deal about suffering and bereavement and many people have told me their experiences. Yet I was unprepared for the intensity of my own grief and for the extent to which it disabled me. I am an only child, and maybe that fact deepened my attachment to my parents and my reaction to their deaths. I have heard that when your second parent dies you feel orphaned, even if you are an adult, and that you are confronted—perhaps for the first time—with your own mortality. I don't think that was my problem, but I won't be dogmatic about it because the main quality of my condition at that time was uncertainty. It was difficult to make decisions. I found it hard to know what mattered. My sense of meaning was shaken and I was unclear about my purpose. I put on a good face and I made myself do everything as usual, but my heart wasn't in it. I felt very sad most of the time and sometimes I was angry. What most people talked about seemed very trivial. I felt that I was behind a pane of glass on the other side of which people's lives went on. But I was not part of that life.

I now have come to think of grief as a sort of severe illness, bordering at times on derangement; an illness that dislocated me physically, mentally, psychologically and spiritually.

In time it also made me grow, changing me into a different person who had to find a new perspective on life. It forced me to go where I did not wish to go, to discover new aspects of my character and to re-examine a faith in God which lacked the maturity to see me through the crisis.

Suffering, loss and grief are facts of life for everyone, although I am sure people experience them in very different ways. I have noticed that some people accept the death of a parent as a sad event but one which is acceptable in the order of things. While they may feel sorrow, they soon resume the business of their lives without suffering any deep trauma. People who experience a parent's death in this philosophical manner would, almost certainly, find this book a puzzling over-reaction to a natural life event.

I have also pondered the possibility that a subconscious fear of abandonment may have accentuated my own experience of grief.

As an enlisted soldier in World War II my father was largely absent from my early childhood.

At the age of twelve I felt painfully abandoned by my parents when I was sent to boarding school. Confused, too, knowing that they did this at some personal sacrifice and for my good.

When I was seventeen my mother first attempted suicide. When I was thirty she took her own life, by drowning. This was the loss of a most deeply beloved and influential person in my life.

These several life-altering events have heightened my sensitivity to being 'left behind' and to saying goodbye. They have also given me an acute awareness of the fragility and unpredictability of life. While such awareness brings a sense of vulnerability, it also adds to the treasuring of life because of its impermanence.

I think my father's death revived my grief for the loss of my mother and that probably I was grieving for them both. After my mother's death, now forty years ago, I buried my grief in relentless work. It was not until I told the story to a counsellor twelve years later that I began to find my way through the devastating loss. So, I hoped that telling the story of my father's suffering and death might help me rediscover some meaning, understanding and equilibrium.

My father's death also left me with increased and sole responsibility for the welfare of my stepmother, Mary, aged eighty-seven, a testing role for which there was no manual. Dad and Mary lived in the coastal city of Gosford, eighty kilometres north of Sydney.

During his last eight weeks in hospital I made detailed notes in my diary, at home each night, or sometimes during the long hospital days. When he recovered, I wanted to be able to tell him exactly what had happened to him. I felt sure he would want to know.

I have included those diary entries in the book in an expanded, more fluent form so that readers can appreciate his struggle and his courage. I have also used excerpts from his unpublished writing about his life so that he can be known as a man, not only as a patient.

In the course of my long working life I have listened to the stories of hundreds of Australian men and women. The candid recounting of the milestones of their lives has been enlightening and encouraging both for me and for large radio and television audiences—how they've come through their trials; where they've lost and then regained their faith in life; what really matters to them; and the wisdom they've won along the way.

Through many years of listening, and through audience response, I have come to believe in the healing power of sharing stories; it is in that spirit that I offer this challenging seven-year chapter of my life. I consider that the honest telling of my life experience is the most authentic gift I have to offer.

In Australia we have the privilege of healthcare beyond the dreams of most people in the rest of the world. My father's ordeal, and my grief, cannot be compared with the excesses of their suffering and deprivation. Yet the experience of every individual has its own validity, and I think my painful time has heightened my awareness of the suffering of others and increased my capacity for compassion.

Before deciding to publish this account I wanted to place my story into a wider context that could be useful for anyone else confronted by a traumatic life event. To this end you will find, in Appendix 1, a response to the manuscript from psychologist Carmel Ross which contains insights into the questions I have struggled with.

I also gave the manuscript to Dr Ray Raper, Head of Intensive Care at North Shore Private Hospital. I wanted him to know that I was publishing a confronting account of Dad's period under his care. Dr Raper graciously invited me to see him and has written a candid and clarifying response for which I am grateful. I have his permission to publish it in Appendix 2.

Because it documents a very challenging time, this book will not suit every reader. But if this is a stage of life you are ready to explore, I hope it will offer you company on your journey.

Caroline Jones

PART ONE

Reclaiming the Past

I'm trying now to recapture some memories of my father as he used to be, to displace the tormenting images of his suffering. I'm thinking about him doing some darning. Mary, his second wife, is willing to do it for him but, at ninety-two, he does his own washing and mending, as he has always done.

He fetches my mother's sewing basket. She made it fifty years ago by lining a yellow-painted wire plant basket with printed cotton and threading it with a drawstring. By now it resembles an archaeological dig but everything it contains will come in useful one day. He sorts through pieces of elastic, cards of press-studs, hooks and eyes and cotton reels of many colours.

Then he unearths a square tin which once contained assorted chocolates. It's decorated with a picture of a serious boy in a tweed cap, posed with a fishing rod and a retriever. Inside are packets of sewing needles and a piece of flannel folded and threaded with darning needles.

The socks he plans to mend have been darned many times before, with various colours. Not the neat weaves that my mother used to achieve by sewing the heel stretched over a wooden mushroom. These socks are cream and gaping at the heel, ready to be thrown out. But he doesn't throw things out. He chooses a bright blue embroidery cotton for the job and holds the needle up close to his glasses to thread it. He drops the needle on the floor.

'Fall down, you bastard,' he says mildly and searches for it by running his hand over the carpet near his feet. Finds it. Threads it again. And, with a bold approach, cobbles the hole together effectively. Patiently. He repeats this on all four socks.

I tell him, 'You're pretty good at darning'.

'Yes, I've been doing it for years … except when I was in the army. Then my batman was supposed to do it for me.'

'And did he?'

'I can't remember.'

He holds his handiwork up to the light for examination. Pleased, he folds the socks into pairs in a particular way. First they are turned inside out. Then the right hand is plunged down into the sock to grasp the toe between thumb and forefinger, while the left thumb and forefinger pinch the heel. The toe is then withdrawn while maintaining a hold of the heel. The sock is now conveniently ready to slide your foot inside. The procedure is repeated with the second sock of the pair. The socks are then rolled into a neat ball secured with the cuff of one of them. Anyone my father's age will be familiar with this method and of course I cannot put a pair of socks away in a drawer without doing the same.

Next, he puts all the sewing kit away in the tin, replaces it and puts the basket back exactly where he found it.

At the top of the stairs, he lets the socks fall to the floor and drop-kicks them down to the next landing, on the first leg of their journey back to his room.

'You've got to get gravity working for you in this life.'

He's quite pleased with himself and about to head for the kitchen to pour a whisky but suddenly he goes quiet and stands very still, his buoyant mood deflated. Taking small, careful steps he makes his way back to his chair. His face is ashen. He slumps like a rag doll and spreads his left hand protectively over his heart. With his right hand he waves feebly towards the little spray bottle of medication nearby. He has these nitrolingual pump sprays of glyceryl trinitrate strategically placed around the house. He takes the bottle from its box, removes the lid, tips his head back and squirts the spray under his tongue, taking a sharp breath in. Then he lies back to wait for the angina pain to pass. He looks exhausted and helpless, his head turned away on the back of the chair. His legs are sticking out in front, yellow, thin and scarred in their brogues and short socks. His arms, mottled with big purple bruises, are lying still along the arms of the chair. For the next fifteen minutes he's got no energy to speak or to move. Eventually, 'Sometimes you wonder if you're going to come out of it. Or if this is it.'

'How do you feel about that?'

'Oh, I'm not frightened of dying if that's what you mean. We all have to go some time.'

He rests for a few more minutes, then adds, 'You know how you can see thousands of dust motes in a shaft of sunlight? I sometimes wonder if that's how we'll all end up. Afterwards.'

'Do you reckon there is an Afterwards?'

'Maybe, but I can't work out where everyone will fit. Think of all the people who've ever lived. Millions and millions. Billions. How could you fit them all in? Unless we all end up as dust motes.'

He appears to think about this for a while, with his eyes closed. Or perhaps he's just getting used to the strong headache caused by the medication.

Then he gets up and goes to the garage, takes the big shears out the back and prunes the plumbago.

'Do you think you might be overdoing it a bit?'

'A man's not a wimp. I'd like to put in a new lemon tree up the back but I don't seem to have the energy just now.'

I wonder if Dad has some idea of how long he will live but I don't like to ask. He's not talking about planting some more annual flowers but planting a new tree. Is this just the instinct of a gardener who will never stop gardening? Or a wish to grow lemons for whoever comes after him? Or a belief that he might still be alive to enjoy the lemons himself?

Dad has green fingers. And he's the one who makes sure there are always flowers around the house—from small exquisite posies to big sweeping arrangements. If there are no blooms available in his pocket-handkerchief-size garden, he brings in fern fronds and leaves and berries. The highlight of each year comes when he harvests his hydrangeas. Dad is very masculine, even in his nineties, and it's touching to see him immersed in this creative domestic art.

He grows the hydrangeas in his compost heap and they reward him with rich colouring. On the day he picks them, he carries them into the laundry, cuts the stems at an angle with the secateurs and squashes them with a hammer. Then he brings them carefully upstairs on an old towel and chooses a vase to receive them. He doesn't want to drop any bits because that only makes housework for him.

The heavy blue, pink and mauve heads are difficult to manage. He places them, one by one, then steps back to see the effect and returns to make an adjustment. He is patient and utterly concentrated on what he is doing. This is the culmination of a long process. He has watered the hydrangeas, pruned them, watched them, picked snails off their leaves and waited for their flowering. He has cultivated beauty and now it is rewarding him. He is in a reverie; it would be sacrilege to interrupt him, to call his attention back into time. He has escaped into the eternal—and all in the modest art of arranging flowers.[1]

The rain has stopped for a while. My father is feeding five magpies on the wet lawn. They take scraps of yesterday's sandwiches from his fingers. They're standing on long, cautious legs in a half-moon around him, throats extended, carolling, taking it in turns to stalk forward for a morsel. He is in his morning dress of sandshoes, shorts held up with an old necktie around the waist, and a cotton shirt. The veins stand in cords on his outstretched hand. His thin skin is mottled with the dark spreading bruises of age. He bends his knees to reach down to the birds' level and waits patiently for them to approach.

'They know me by now,' he explains with a modest smile, just in case I may think that he is proud to have won the trust of wild creatures.[2]

In the early evening, after he's done all his jobs and finished writing for the day, Dad heads upstairs to the kitchen to pour a whisky. One for himself and one for Mary. This marks the unofficial start of the evening. As he goes, he mutters in pleasant anticipation, 'A man could die of thirst …'.

He talks to himself quite a lot in the last couple of years. Perhaps it's because Mary has become deaf and conversation is disappointing.

'By the time you've had to repeat something three times you've lost interest in it and you don't care about the reply, which could easily be, "I can't hear what you're saying unless you speak up".'

Mary likes her whisky poured to very exact specifications. He shows her how much he's poured. 'Too much.'

He tips a bit into his own glass. He presents her glass again for inspection. 'No, a bit more.'

Rolling his eyes and muttering, 'Half a millimetre more, third of a millimetre less, once a teacher, always a teacher', he tops it up again and then goes through the same tortuous procedure, adding water to the required level. I wonder how she feels about this well-worn jibe at her lifelong profession but she remains inscrutable.

He puts an ice cube in her drink and carries both glasses on a tray into the sitting room, exactly in time to switch on *As Time Goes By*.

They both enjoy it very much. It's a situation comedy about Lionel and Jean, a middle-aged couple who've met up again years after a brief wartime romance when they were both in the services. I think Dad and Mary like it because it's their story too. And perhaps they relate to the prickly characters who get on each other's nerves, have misunderstandings and make up again as they explore the possibilities of becoming a couple when both are set firmly in their own idiosyncratic ways. Mary misses most of the show because she's in the kitchen getting dinner. She comes in to watch intermittently, which drives Dad mad. On the first occasion, it's to remove the ice cube from her whisky with a dessertspoon. She does this every evening.

On her second entrance she offers savoury biscuits, standing in front of the screen, and asks Dad what's happened so far. His exasperation is a reflection of Lionel's expression on the television.

It's possible that both Dad and Mary get something out of this ritual whereas to me, as a bystander, it looks like purgatory.

But he doesn't have angina pain this evening. His face even has a bit of colour and he tells a couple of good stories at dinner. Mary hears enough of one of them to laugh at it, which pleases him.

Dad has slept badly for years.

'I've got no idea how to have a good sleep. I'm hopeless. It's not as though a fellow was worried about anything. I go to bed. I'm warm. I've got a roof over my head. I'm tired. I'm so tired but can I go to sleep? Twelve o'clock, one o'clock, two o'clock … I suppose I must get a bit of sleep, at some stage … otherwise you'd go mad, wouldn't you?'

Sometimes he goes to lie on his bed after lunch. In a few minutes I look in. He's lying on his right side, with his shoes on and both arms sticking out over the side of the bed. He's snoring. An hour later, he's out the back in his tiny garden, checking to see if anything's getting at his tomatoes.

'Did you have a bit of a sleep?'

'Oh, no, I'm hopeless. I might have had a doze for a minute or two.'

I paint the tiles of the shower recess with a non-slip solution. Mary comes in to inspect. She looks amazed and disapproving as though she has found me making mud pies in the bath.

'What on earth are you doing that for?'

'So none of us will slip and fall in the shower.'

She looks even more mystified. 'I never slip and fall.'

I suppose it's good that she has no recall of the frequent petit mal episodes which stop her in her tracks, grinding her teeth, and then drop her to the floor in a dead heap. Dad recalls. He sometimes catches her as she falls, or discovers her with a cut head or other bruises and picks her up. She's small but very heavy as a dead weight. So he's on round-the-clock caring duty, at the age of ninety-two.

One morning when I arrived for the weekend, Boy, one of the kind neighbours, was helping them to clean up a flood. Boy is not young himself but very handy. Mary had left the tap running over the kitchen basin. She has a short-term memory loss which leaves saucepans cooked dry on the stove, and things constantly getting lost and found and lost again. The condition seems more poignant in someone who was always efficient and precise to the point of being pedantic. Years ago when they were first married she rearranged all the washing I had hung on the Hills hoist so that the garments were more compatibly classified, socks with socks in graded sizes and towels likewise. When I set the table for a meal, she would replace various items and reposition everything to her liking. I never got the knack of selecting the right salt and pepper shakers for the occasion.

⎯�〟⎯

I follow Mary into her bedroom to help her with the bed. She's got two antique underblankets under the electric blanket. We position the two narrow single sheets a few times until they satisfy her exacting requirements. The sheets could be the result of a double, cut in halves and hemmed. Thrift is second nature to a generation who've survived two world wars and a depression.

Next, one old single blanket is placed low down and tucked under the mattress, but only at the bottom of the bed, not at the sides. The second single blanket is placed higher up the bed with the sheet folded neatly down over it.

'Don't tuck anything in at the sides,' she tells me, as she always does. Finally the bedspread goes on. It all takes quite a long time. I used to hurry her but now I've learned that causes distress so I go at her pace and accept her directions. Sometimes I swear to relieve my impatience, but only when I'm sure she can't hear me.

By the time we finish, Dad's done his washing, hung it out to dry, made his bed, cleaned their shoes, swept out the front and back, hosed the garden and climbed the ladder to remove the filter from the airconditioner and wash the lint out of it.

'A man's work's never done,' he says agreeably to himself. It's not a complaint, just a statement of fact. 'I used to think that when I retired I'd sit around with my feet up, reading the *Herald*.'

I find Dad in his little study, sitting on a straight-backed wooden chair at the card table, writing. Whenever he can find a bit of free time, he's writing his life story. He writes in an almost illegible longhand, which would be a credit to any GP, on lined writing pads or scrap paper.

His favourite subject is Grattai, the property outside Mudgee in New South Wales where he was born on 5 January 1907 and where he lived with his family until 1918. He was the eldest of four children. Grattai has remained his spiritual home throughout his life and he has made many pilgrimages back to the old home.

Every few weeks he allows Mary and me to read what he is writing but only if we ask. He's doing it mainly for himself, I think. It's a work of art and identity, a record of his life and of his family and what made him who he is.

 BRIAN NEWMAN JAMES

By the age of ten, in 1917, I was a station hand. I had been instructed in all the jobs on the place and tackled most of them. What I enjoyed most was mustering and least, milking the cows.

In between there was a multitude of interesting jobs: tar-boy at shearing time, ploughing and harrowing behind a team of four heavy draughthorses, lamb-marking and feeling ill seeing a station hand remove a lamb's testicles with his teeth, chaff-cutting and helping in the blacksmith's shop.

Less demanding was riding on the horse-drawn poison cart to combat the rabbit plague—no myxomatosis in those days; accompanying Dad on fox and kangaroo shoots over the hills of Grattai, he with his 32 Winchester and I very proud and very careful with a .22 rifle.

Aged eight, my first foray into business was somewhat on the nose. For various reasons—drought, dogs, old age and crows—sheep die in the paddocks. My father suggested that I bring in what was known as 'dead wool' from the carcasses when they had sufficiently matured. So I would ride out on Bobs, my pony, with a chaff bag and gather the wool with bare hands and fetch it back to the wool shed. Dead wool had a low commercial value, fixed by the wool, skin and hides dealer in Mudgee. The modest returns were quite out of kilter with my efforts but it was rewarding to have something in return for thorns in my fingers and the stench in my nose. I was oblivious to the dangers of anthrax but I was lucky to escape it.

While they were both healthy, Dad and Mary enjoyed some adventurous travelling. Their long motoring tours often included a return to Grattai.

But in the last few years I've been concerned about how to arrange a holiday for them in compatible accommodation adapted for frail guests. They need a holiday but each time I've made a plan, the recurring illness of one or the other has thwarted every attempt to organise some respite from the daily struggle of their lives at home.

Then a breakthrough. I was invited to present a weekend of reflection at the Star of the Sea Retreat Centre at Yamba, New South Wales, run by the Grafton Sisters of Mercy. Tentatively I asked Sr Rosie Carroll RSM if she would consider not just one visitor, but three—and could we stay not just two days but a week.

'By all means, come,' she said. No doubts, no questions.

From the moment we arrived at the end of the long day's drive north, we were made welcome in the generous Mercy tradition of hospitality. There were comfortable chairs on a sunny verandah out of the wind, books to read and home-made biscuits for afternoon tea. There was always a thoughtful arm for support on the stairs, or a walk along the clifftop; always the company of a sister at mealtimes. We were not in silence on that retreat and Dad delighted in stimulating conversation with the sisters.

Neither Dad nor Mary is Catholic and I heard him announce this to Sister when he arrived. Next morning she asked him how he'd slept in a Catholic bed.

'Pretty well,' he admitted, and they both laughed.

From every window there were views of the sea or the mighty River Clarence. The Grafton Mercies are deeply involved in the life of their district in many practical ways. We learned about life for the sugar-cane farmers and one evening saw the great flare of a cane crop being burned in preparation for harvest.

We saw a woman come to seek the sanctuary of the convent. We met a youth working for the sisters on community service instead of going to jail. We heard about the risky lives of the prawn fishermen and watched their boats leave the harbour at dusk and return to the shelter of the breakwater at dawn.

And each night there was the sound of the ocean to put us to sleep. With deep gratitude, I watched the elders relax into the loving, carefree atmosphere created by busy women who somehow always made time for us, as though that were their pleasure. Star of the Sea is a popular retreat centre, but they don't let you see the effort that goes into running it.

When the time came to leave, all the sisters saw us off as we drove away reluctantly, hoping there might be a next time. For me, it was a deep spiritual refreshment to have others recognise our needs so sensitively and to answer them.

One corner of my study is filled with memories of Dad. Where I am writing, I look up to see one of his paintings, of gum trees on a hillside. It was the result of an exercise in composition, using only white, grey and black oil paints, probably designed to explore light and perspective, and the texture of bark and leaves. It is painted with acute observation and feeling. It is completely convincing but I remember him dismissing it as being just a bit of an experiment. I found it propping up a jar of nails among the tools in his garage. I rescued it, along with several other discarded paintings, and framed them, much to his chagrin. He may have been a bit pleased as well.

The trees are solidly rooted in the earth, leaning at a slight angle, determined by the prevailing wind as they grew. He has succeeded in portraying the unmistakeable great hanging clusters of eucalypt leaves. Light and shade suggest the undulation of land rolling away towards a hillside. The painting is not signed of course—that would have been pretentious.

'It's just an exercise the teacher gave us to do but I'm hopeless, haven't got a clue.'

I wish that he had made the time to do more painting. He had a real talent for it as he did for writing. I think of all the long years he spent disliking accountancy but doing it anyway, to make his living, and ours. All that artistic desire buried under the tedium of making figures balance. In the way of his generation, he made a sacrifice in duty to his family.

Even as a child I remember Dad made anxious and sometimes cranky by the dockets and disorganised papers of his clients, the woolgrowers made suddenly rich by their wool clip fetching an unheard-of price ('a pound-a-pound' in the old system of currency and measurement) in the 1950s. Some of them had little formal education. It was up to him to make some sense of their shoeboxes of receipts for the Taxation Department and to keep them out of trouble. And he was good at it. He was honest, always straight, conscientious, but I remember his worried expression—not happy as an accountant, ever.

Beside the gum-tree painting there is a framed photograph of my father aged about twenty-seven, very handsome in a tweed jacket, well-ironed shirt and a tie that could be silk, with a single diagonal stripe. The long points of the shirt collar are tethered with a tie pin. He'd probably spent more money than he had on this outfit.

There's a story that he was in debt to a tailor at the time of his marriage. He probably thought it was worth it. Some people always look good in their clothes. He was one of them. Like my mother, he had a flair for putting things together effectively and wearing them with a casual grace that was pleasing to look at. It was a question of style rather than expense. Perhaps that was something they found attractive in each other: no money but a bit of style.

Above that black and white portrait, there is a sepia photo of the old homestead at Grattai, settled under its deep corrugated iron roof among gum trees and orchard, with the shearing shed away to the right and wooded hills up behind. In the foreground, a well-kept post-and-rail fence. There are Scotch thistles between the boundary fence and the road, and horses grazing in the home paddock. It looks like home, settled, familiar, beloved, and I can well understand his heartache at leaving it—and the longing he carried for it all through his life.

Next to that, a small, framed photograph of the house extended by a subsequent owner, with a wide, sweeping lawn sloping down to a long rockery planted with daisies.

I remember Dad dreaming of going back, the creases of disappointment becoming more deeply etched in his handsome face as the dream remained unfulfilled … Dad drinking a beer, too much sometimes, telling stories with perfect timing, enjoying the nickname 'King', laughing happily in the company of his men friends, generous in conversation with both men and women.

The next frame holds a certificate awarded to Dad when he hit a 'hole in one' at his golf club on 10 April 1965 (my third year with the ABC in Canberra, just starting out, Mum very excited by my prospects, Dad more quietly so). The certificate is in the form of a big cartoon showing the triumphant, haloed golfer surrounded by rejoicing colleagues and buxom admirers and inscribed 'Know Ye All Men and Be Ye Hereby Warned that Mr B James Did This Day

Hole Out in One and Did Receive Among the Plaudits of his Fellows this Corio 5-Star Old Whisky Award'. Underneath the inscribed date Dad has added 'And again on 1 Feb'y 1985' and underlined it.

Dad has framed the hole-in-one certificate himself, with a brown paper surround on which you can see the pencil lines drawn to cut it straight. He then put it behind glass, tacked into a shiny wooden black frame that once contained one of his accountancy qualifications. It makes a good contrast to a professionally framed certificate proclaiming him as a Life Member of the Australian Society of Certified Practising Accountants. The golfing one would have meant most to him.

At the time of Dad's second hole-in-one, I was working as a trainer of teachers for Elizabeth Campbell's wonderful leadership and communication initiative for students, the Peer Support Program. We travelled Australia-wide and to New Zealand, spreading the program to many thousands of teachers and their students. In the course of two years working with Elizabeth, I learned a great deal that I would use later, travelling the country offering days of reflection, to gather people together for the sharing of their stories and the wisdom of their lives.

Dad is very interested in peer support. He had a hard time at high school himself and likes the idea of older children taking responsibility for younger ones. And Mary is keenly interested in it as a teacher because she can see the benefit for students.

I try to bring news of my wider world into their smaller orbit. And I encourage Mary to talk of her interesting life so that she remembers it and so that her deafness does not isolate her from conversation.

With Dad, Mary represents a generation which believes in fairness and honesty and caring for the weak and disabled. She has donated blood to the Red Cross more than seventy-five times and is generous to many charities. Now she is weak and disabled and in need of care but she doesn't acknowledge it.

In the last ten years I have been spending weekends with them regularly—now, once a fortnight. It allows me to be part of their lives and to keep an eye on their increasing needs as they become more frail. Gradually, I've introduced the idea of more practical support. As we take each new step, Dad resists, but, when it's in place, he's glad of it. His angina is getting worse and his poor old body is worn out. I suppose he acknowledges, at some level, that he can't go on being the main carer forever.

Hospital Diary

5 June 2000 – 30 July 2000

It's my goddaughter Kim's birthday today: she is turning thirty-five and in the prime of life, with her partner and four young children. She tells me, with some excitement, that they're thinking they might even get married soon. When I suggest that there is no need to rush into anything, she laughs kindly, recognising my attempt to be with it. She's the third of my four goddaughters. Between them, I have six grand-godchildren.

For me, today is a normal working day, in my fifth year of presenting *Australian Story* on ABC Television. But for my father, at the age of ninety-three, it is his day for open-heart surgery.

Less than a kilometre away from the hospital, I go through the professional motions of speaking to the camera to introduce this week's program. It is very cold and we are filming in an outdoor location so I leave my dark brown overcoat on.

With every nerve on edge in anxiety for Dad, it is a relief to have something so prosaic to do. I concentrate on memorising my lines and delivering them with meaning. The film crew know what's happening in my life and I am steadied by their familiar Monday-morning banter, a bit funny, a bit melancholy, as they lug awkward, heavy cases of gear out of the back of the station wagon.

I am with two men I know, good workmates, but Dad is alone among skilful strangers, taking his last gamble on life in an operation that pushes medical science and human endurance to the boundaries. I have read something about the operation and am very unhappy about my father's agreement to have it, at his doctors' suggestion. He's too frail, too exhausted, to have a fighting chance of survival, let alone recovery.

A week ago I brought him to Sydney to have an angiogram, a procedure in which dye is injected, via a cannula inserted in the groin, into the blood vessels of the heart. X-ray photography reveals where the vessels are constricted or damaged. Although I tried not to communicate it, I was upset about him having the angiogram. It is very invasive and it carries a risk of stroke. I thought it would be very stressful for him. But as the angina worsened over the months and was no longer alleviated by drugs, he decided to explore the drastic options offered.

In his usual patient, courageous, stoic, intelligent way he went through the long day of angiogram and recovery without complaint. He was hoping that some angioplasty—the use of balloon-tipped catheters to widen the constricted blood vessels, permitting a free blood flow once again through the heart—would be possible. But the angiogram revealed that there was already too much damage to allow this. He was very disappointed.

In the late afternoon the professor who had carried out the angiogram procedure brought a heart surgeon to see Dad where he was recovering in the Day Surgery Unit. Together, they explained his situation as they saw it. They thought it was well worth doing open-heart surgery, in which blood vessels could be taken from his legs to put into his heart, bypassing the damaged sections of coronary blood vessels. They told him there was no guarantee of success and warned him of the risk. I assumed they meant risk of death.

Most unusually, he happened to have a good colour in his face and I wondered if his alert awareness and lucid discussion of the subject gave them a false impression of a fit man in his seventies whereas, in fact, his body is very thin, frail and depleted from years of stress, pain and insomnia. And he's ninety-three! As he says himself, everything is past its use-by date. But I assumed they had studied his records in preparation for the angiogram, and no doubt their offer was made in the light of their skilled experience.

It wasn't a long conversation. He agreed to their suggestion. I wish that he had decided against it but the alternative is to continue suffering angina until a heart attack kills him. Without any further consultation, he decided to give it a try.

He wanted to go home for the few days before the operation. I suppose he must have had a sense that these might be his last days in his home. He was quiet as he put his affairs in order, did some writing and walked round the house looking at things. He spent a good deal of time in the garden.

It is early afternoon by the time I get to the hospital. I find my way to the Intensive Care Unit (ICU) visitors room. Several tired and anxious-looking people are already waiting, someone else's relatives. There is a big, half-eaten plate of sandwiches on the table, with the day's newspapers in disarray. I suppose they have been reading to distract themselves.

Someone explains to me that you have to dial the extension number of the ICU receptionist to see if it is convenient for you to visit. I do this and am asked to wait … someone will come to get me.

When I go in, everything is strange to me. In the centre of the unit there's a large administration desk. Around the perimeter of the ward, eleven cubicles, each accommodating one patient. One nursing sister is allocated to each patient. The patient is never left unattended. There's an Intensive Care specialist doctor and an intensivist registrar on duty or on call round the clock.

The IC nurses are all sisters. There are both men and women. They wear long, white, cotton gowns tied with strings at the back. They move back and forth between physical care for their patient and their individual desks, where they write up the story of the patient's progress, as displayed on a bank of monitors and from their own observations. At frequent intervals the patient must be turned to a new position and this requires two people, not only for strength, but to ensure there's no disconnection of the myriad of lines and tubes attached to the patient's body.

The curtains of Dad's cubicle are open and his nurse is standing beside his high bed, watching over him, one gloved hand resting kindly on his forearm. He is unconscious. His body is hugely swollen from the surgery. He looks like a beached whale, utterly helpless, uncomfortable, out of his element. A row of fresh, raw stitches runs from his throat down to the base of his breastbone. Beneath the skin, his breastbone, which has been split open and retracted to allow access to the heart, has been rejoined with wire.

There are lines running, via cannulas embedded in the side of his neck, up to bags suspended on crooks, dripping medication slowly into his veins. Cannulas in the backs of his bruised hands and forearms lead lines up to bags of blood transfusion, sustenance and sedative. Draining tubes empty into containers beside the bed, as does a urinary catheter. His legs and feet are encased in white pressure stockings inflated with air.

A wide, white, concertina tube leads from the respirator into a narrow tube leading into his open mouth and down his trachea into his lungs. It's held firmly in place by white cotton ribbons retracting the corners of his mouth in a mirthless smile, and tied at the back of his neck.

Each line measuring blood pressure, oxygen levels and cardiograph has its own electronic monitor. Coloured numbers alter constantly on the digital displays, mapping the struggle of his body to survive. On one, a continuous horizontal line leaps into peaks and troughs to monitor heartbeat. Another screen measures intake of oxygen through a peg clipped onto Dad's finger. At regular intervals the shrill, repetitive beep of one monitor or another sounds the alarm that something needs attention.

The ventilator is virtually breathing for him. It has its own display screen, revealing the extent to which his breathing needs support.

My dear father seems mortally wounded and I cannot imagine him ever recovering from such an onslaught. I am utterly shocked by the sight of him but it seems vital not to show it. Everyone is moving quietly and efficiently about their business of patient care. There is no sense of alarm, no sign that anything unusual is happening. It seems important to adopt a similar manner, to pretend to be calm and accepting.

Sister is smiling at me. She introduces herself as Linda.

'He's doing pretty well. Isn't he marvellous for his age?'

Obediently I agree. When confronted with a fearful situation I do my best to repress the fear and present a calm and rational exterior as though I am quite under control. The effort is very costly. I pay for it in a reaction that can be long delayed.

One of my first intuitions is that I must be here, as much as possible—to protect him. I must be his eyes and ears. I must try to sense what is happening with him and be his voice. And to achieve that, I assume I will have to be acceptable to his carers, friendly, deferential, showing no sign of the panic I am feeling and barely able to suppress; no sign of the fury I feel that they have subjected him, in his frailty, to such an ordeal.

The hours wear on and gradually I begin to learn the routine—what to expect, what story the monitors are telling, what constitutes progress, what warns of trouble.

I sit beside Dad and hold his hand and, although he is unconscious, I tell him I am there. I read somewhere that patients can sometimes hear, even when they can give no sign of response.

I am surprised by Linda's bright cheerfulness. She has years of experience in ICU nursing. She is happy to answer any of my questions. She is constantly checking the monitors. Regularly she undoes a valve where the breathing tube is connected to the respirator and feeds a sterile suction hose through the tube down into Dad's lungs, to draw out any liquid gathering there.

There is a lot to do for a patient in Intensive Care. Linda has everything she needs to nurse him set out in an orderly display on the chest of drawers in the corner. She also has his spare pyjamas and his clothes neatly stowed and his teeth in a labelled container. Dad would give her full marks.

At seven o'clock the night staff arrive and are briefed by the head nurse and the doctors, and allocated their patients.

Our night sister sits beside Linda as she tells the story of Dad's condition from the charts she has been entering all day. Dad would approve of all this meticulous record-keeping. He keeps a diary and is diligent in keeping his books of account and home and health records detailed and up-to-date for himself and for Mary. When they returned from each of their round-Australia travels, Dad would make another illustrated entry in a series of scrap books. He would draw a map, freehand, with highlights marked in and pictures cut from appropriate brochures to tell the story of their latest journey. He remembers the names of places, old family names and connections. Wherever he goes he always knows which direction is north.

Together the two nurses stand beside him checking his lines and drips. They know nothing of the man himself. They are two professional strangers who have come to his aid.

When it is time for Linda to go I ask if she will be caring for Dad tomorrow. She is not sure and that makes me feel very insecure. I am surprised that, now she has become so familiar with his condition, anyone else would be assigned to nurse him.

I stay another hour and a half, to befriend the night nurse and tell her something about Dad. I want to make sure that she is interested in him.

Suddenly a loud alarm buzzer sounds in a cubicle opposite. A doctor arrives fast and two flying sisters manoeuvre a trolley to the patient's side. My scalp crawls at the urgency of their response. It is a cardiac arrest; they are working to restart a heart that has stopped beating.

Dad's sister does not leave him but stands watching from the entrance to his cubicle. The tension is palpable.

I feel sick. In my stress I have been breathing shallow for hours and holding my muscles clenched. I have not eaten and am not hungry. Having established that little change is expected in

Dad's condition overnight, it seems best to go. I leave him very reluctantly.

In the ICU visitors room a woman, her face bleached with anxiety, is sitting, waiting. It is her husband whose heart stopped. In our mutual need, we talk together easily. She is exhausted, on the edge of panic, but trying hard to hold onto some calm. Her name is Genevieve. After a while she is called to go in to see him. I leave like a sleepwalker, wandering along the corridors past the operating suite, past the Cardiac Recovery Ward, past Day Surgery where Dad was a week ago, and into the lift.

My heels tap loudly on the floor of the pink, mock-granite foyer as I pass the magnificent, tall floral arrangement in the centre. A tired-looking cleaner is pushing his humming vacuum cleaner slowly back and forth across the expanse of floor. The automatic doors open and I step out into the shock of a very cold night.

Day 2, Tuesday 6 June 2000

At the hospital, I have to wait a while in the visitors room. When I go into the ICU I am amazed to learn that Dad has had a bleed in the chest cavity and been taken back into theatre for surgery once again.

I find it difficult to believe that he could have survived this second invasion of his exhausted body. I still feel angry at the original decision to perform bypass surgery, even though he agreed to it, and this second round seems an outrage. But once you take the first step there seems to be no turning back. You have entered a process in which you lose all autonomy.

Dad looks pale and defeated as he lies unconscious in the narrow, high, white hospital bed.

They explain things to me and the explanations sound reasonable but I think we have entered into a nightmare in which everything is utterly beyond our control. Today seems very long.

By evening Dad is still unconscious but his face shows more colour.

I talk with Mary on the phone. She has decided not to make the eighty-kilometre journey until she is able to speak with Dad. I'm glad to hear her decision because I don't think I can leave him to make the round trip to get her and look after her, as well as being with Dad as constantly as possible. She rings the ICU each evening to get news of Dad directly from the staff.

I keep my vigil with him and speak to him and try to learn and to understand what is done for a patient in the various stages of recovering from such massive surgery. It's a timeless other world which bears no relationship to everyday life. I wish that my father was anywhere else. I wish that somehow I could save him, get him out of hospital, but of course I can't. I haven't even thought to pray. We seem beyond rescue. I wish that I had a brother or sister to support us, to be with us in our powerlessness. I'm sure my dear friend Val would come but I think only family or ministers are allowed.

DAY 3, WEDNESDAY 7 JUNE 2000

When I wake the sky is a cold clear blue, and for an instant I feel happy, before the memory of Dad's plight overwhelms me with a feeling of sick dread. I cry helplessly for a few moments and then realise I should be with him. I have found out the schedule of the doctors' rounds and I can time my arrival to coincide. After the first round of the day they make decisions and are prepared to talk.

Their readiness to take responsibility for the survival of a patient is awe-inspiring. I am grateful, but I also feel that somehow they have stolen him or kidnapped him. They are patient in explaining the extremity of my father's condition and how they plan to help him. They use words that I can understand. They speak of him with respect and use his name when they are attempting to speak to him, even in his unconscious state. With me, they are frank about the danger, but firm in their insistence on a positive attitude. In my long vigils I watch their calm professionalism with gratitude and even enjoy them sharing a moment of fun.

But this is the worst day yet. Dad is regaining consciousness. He is agitated and restless but not strong enough to move. With his body flooded with painkillers and drugs to inhibit infection, it must be desperately confusing for him as he tries to work out where he is and why he is so constrained, why he cannot move or see or speak or swallow. Because he is gagged with the breathing tube he can't make any sound. They told me he wouldn't be in pain but clearly he is distressed and utterly helpless and it is anguishing to see him like this. The sister speaks to him often, calling him by name, and I try to reassure him as best I can, explaining that he has had surgery, that it was successful and that he is now recovering; that he has a tube in his throat into his lungs to help him breathe and that's why he cannot speak or swallow. I try to imagine myself into his situation. It seems to me that explanation is crucial for him to try to make sense of what is happening, and also to reassure him that he has not been abandoned.

His mouth, forced permanently open by the ribbons tying the tube in place, must be feeling parched. I ask if he can have some drops of water on his tongue but it is not allowed in case it should choke him. The sister puts vaseline on his lips and in the corners of his mouth which are beginning to split. It is terribly distressing.

I ask how long the breathing tube will be needed and am bewildered to learn that there is no immediate prospect of its removal because Dad still needs breathing support.

It's demoralising to see patients who arrived in the ICU at the same time as Dad having their tubes removed the day after arrival. The man in the next cubicle is sitting up in bed today, eating ice cream. I feel intensely resentful and cannot look at him. Most heart patients stay only a day or two and then graduate to the Cardiac Ward to have regular nursing for a week before going home. Clearly that is not going to happen for my father, but we were given no warning of an outcome like this.

Were we supposed to know? Should we have asked more?

At home again, I almost forget to watch the *Australian Story* go to air. I have lost my usual routine. It features Syd and Les Howard, brothers and rivals in one of the world's most spectacular industries—fireworks. The Howard dynasty has been in the business since 1922 but the brothers haven't spoken for fifteen years. Their bitter duel is just one of the dramas that have beset the family. If only people realised how fragile life is and how easily it is lost.

Under normal circumstances I would appreciate how well this story, produced by Caitlin Shea, has come together, exploring both the technical challenges of their inspired displays and the complexity of the family relationships. But tonight I feel that I am watching it through a closed window. It is so far removed from my current reality. Yet I'm grateful that my professional role claims my attention for part of the time, shifting my focus from this present anguish back into the steadying discipline of work.

I can't relax. I worry about Dad every minute and keep him company in thought. I identify as closely with him as I can imagine, as though I can somehow share his agony. In this process, I seem to have taken on his insomnia. I don't think about praying. It doesn't seem relevant, which is peculiar and disappointing. Some time in the early hours of the morning, after sleeping for a while, I wake with my mouth open and so dry I feel I cannot take the next breath. It is terrifying. I sit up, swallowing and gulping convulsively to get some saliva into my mouth. And then I sit on the side of the bed, shivering, as I realise that Dad can get no such relief. How can anyone be expected to endure that? I hope that he is asleep or sedated to a point where he is not suffering.

Day 4, Thursday 8 June 2000

I ring the hospital early to talk to the night nurse about to go off duty. She has given Dad a wash and a shave and tells me they have just moved him into a new position. She says he does not seem very happy this morning and has been restless overnight. My heart sinks. I feel the awful, helpless dread known to anyone who sees someone they love suffering. I ask her to tell Dad that I will be there soon, just in case he can hear.

It is bitterly cold and a sneaky wind channels through the bleak, asphalt wasteland of the carpark. By now I have worked out where the ICU is from the outside of the hospital and have identified Dad's window.

Inside the main front doors, it is warm and I feel stifled in my overcoat. It takes another ten minutes to get to the ICU and go through the entry procedure to get in. I take my coat off, fold it inside out and put it under the chair in Dad's cubicle. There are a few pale stripes of sun coming in onto his wall through the venetian blinds. The head has fallen off one of the white camellias I brought in yesterday.

Dad is agitated. I think he is conscious to some extent. I stand by his bed and talk to him. Although his eyes are open, they do not seem to be focussing on me. He lifts his bruised hands weakly, each trailing its intravenous lines. He seems to be fending off something looming above him. His expression is haunted, fearful. The sister explains that his system is full of drugs and some of them can cause hallucinations. Gagged by the breathing tube, he can make no sound, cannot tell us what he is seeing, what is disturbing him, how he is feeling, what he needs us to do.

Before now I had no idea that someone would be kept on a ventilator indefinitely after they became conscious. It seems to be a terrifying experience and I think it unacceptable. But they say it is vital—that he would be unable to breathe on his own. As well, Dad's heartbeat is not satisfactory. It is showing an irregularity they want to correct. The doctor explains that they want to try an electric shock procedure which sometimes succeeds in tripping the heartbeat back into a normal rhythm.

I listen carefully to what he is saying. I try to keep calm, to hide my alarm. To me it seems that Dad is enrolled on a spiral of increasingly aggressive technological interventions that may be life-saving—but at what cost in terms of suffering? The doctor goes on to say that there is a risk attached, that I will need to give signed permission. He thinks it is worth a try and he will come back when I have had time to think it over.

I feel very alone and very uncertain. The worst aspect is that Dad cannot make his own choice. We are in a foreign place, out of our depth. I don't know how to go about making the decision. I don't think it is right for me to make it. The only logic I can find is that he trusted them to do the open-heart surgery and so it probably makes sense to continue to trust them in the aftermath and take the gamble. The procedure will be done under sedation. Another onslaught on his body.

I sign the paper and then I have to leave. They suggest I come back later. I put my coat on and go out into the cold wind. I sit in the car, tense and miserable, not knowing what new horror I have given permission for, through ignorance. After a while I drive home and sit watching the water. I can see that it is beautiful but, for once, the beauty does not touch me. It is in some other dimension not accessible to me now, yet it is the view of the water, dappled like beaten lead by the westerly, that triggers a vivid emotional memory.

Suddenly I picture the wide, sluggish, green river at Morriset. Dad and I had sat looking at it together, in silence, after he reluctantly signed the paper giving permission for my mother to receive electric shock treatment, forty-five years ago, in the psychiatric hospital crouching behind us on the hillside. The shocks left her injured and with loss of memory. This situation has the same sense of helpless treachery, the same feeling of being manipulated into doing something one does not wish to do.

When I get back to the ICU, they tell me that the shock treatment has not worked. Dad's heartbeat remains irregular, unsatisfactory, and now there is another threat—his kidney function is failing. The end of Day 4. It feels like a life sentence.

DAY 5, FRIDAY 9 JUNE 2000

A terrible day. Dad is restless and has hallucinations which give him the horrors. There is no prospect of the breathing tube being removed. His mouth has split further at each corner. The sister finds a new way of dressing the splits in an attempt to do less damage. Sometimes she increases the level of sedation to give Dad a period of relief from his distress. It's easier for me when he is lying quietly and apparently more peacefully. I am ashamed of thinking about what is easier for me. Sedation is not like catching up on sleep or rest; in a way it sets his recovery back.

Sometimes, as I sit with Dad for hours, I wonder if it's alright to be watching him so closely or if it's an invasion of his privacy, even though he's unconscious. For the last thirty-one years there has been so much pain between us, so much grief unspoken, unresolved, over the death of my mother, because she ended her own life. As Les Murray wrote, in his poem 'The Steel', of his mother's tragic death:

and on Friday afternoon
our family world
went inside itself forever.[1]

Dad and I have not been able to discuss it, yet it has created a bond between us. We have not been able to look each other in the eyes for more than a few seconds in case either glimpses the question not far below the surface, the mutual disbelief that she is gone, the terror of the manner of her leaving. I feel so protective of him now, as I always have. We understand each other far too well and cannot talk about it. I feel his pain, his loss, his disappointment, his shame. Or am I projecting my shame on him? Shame that we did not save her.

Saying goodbye has been almost impossible for us. After every one of my frequent visits to his home, his eyes fill with tears. He grabs me hard by the shoulders. Our eyes meet fleetingly but slide away from the encounter after a piercing moment of recognition and acknowledgement of all that has been. I remind him of my mother.

He always packs a little parcel for me from his garden: fragrant tomatoes ripened on his vines, mignonette lettuce leaves and a bunch of mint and parsley, with damp paper pressed around the stalks to keep them fresh. The gift is unbearably moving, too deep for me to feel at that moment. I save my crying for the journey home in the car. I have started my grieving early so as to expend some of it before he goes, as though to avert a flood. The car is perfumed with mint and tomatoes. Their aroma stirs even deeper filaments of memory like fronds of seaweed swaying lazily in the current on the ocean bed; when I was a child my mother soothed my sunburnt back with the cool flesh of a tomato cut in half.

On one visit I offered him an up-to-date photograph of myself for his dressing table. The one he has is from 1969, the year my mother died. But he said, 'No, I like this one. I like to remember you as you were.'

Driving away from his home, I see him in my windscreen mirror, standing uncertainly, watching until I am out of sight, waving slowly. There is so much pain in leaving and yet I must. We cannot stay too close too long. We must always keep our emotional distance, for safety's sake. We may admire the sunset on the water but we never mention that she drowned in that beautiful view. Always, as I drive away, I feel like a rag doll, spent from the suppression of all that could be said but may not be spoken. To insist on it would be to plunder him, to pierce the protective shield he has built around a terrifying event to keep it under control. And perhaps I have done the same.

Another close encounter, another family day safely negotiated until the week after next. We relapse into the relative safety of regular phone calls, short and treading safe ground: the weather, how he played golf, the need for rain, our health, how Mary is, perhaps a sentence or two about my work. It's all we can manage. It's the best we can do.

As the hours go by, the intermittent high-pitched beeping of all the monitors is grating. Each time one begins I watch for the sister to move quickly to make the necessary adjustment so that it will stop and Dad will not be disturbed. But sometimes she doesn't come quickly. I think the staff are so used to the sounds that they tune them out to some extent. But it gets on my nerves.

The cleaner comes at the same time each day and pushes the vacuum cleaner round the floor. Sometimes she bumps the bed and it makes me wince for Dad's sake. Her name is Lin. Her blue-black hair has been permanently waved which looks unusual on a Chinese woman. She wears yellow gloves. She pushes a cloth slowly over the windowsill and along the metallic venetian blinds. She asks how is father today and looks down at him with pity. I ask her about her own father. He is not too well and very old, back in China. So we have something important in common. She has two jobs, very long hours. She is always tired. She always has a smile for me but in repose her face is sad.

Every two hours, Dad needs to be turned to a new position. A second nurse is called to help, often one of the men. I'm not sure how conscious Dad is, but they talk to him, and explain what they're going to do. They lower the side-rails on the bed and use the drawsheet under him to heave his six-foot frame higher up on the slippery, rubber mattress. Then they pack him around with pillows. He has to have his head, shoulders and chest raised and to be tilted, so that he is lying for two hours facing left, then two hours facing right. He doesn't seem to find either position very comfortable. He would rather lie on his back but he must be propped up so that his lungs will not become congested. They keep shifting the pillows under his back and head slightly until he seems to accept the new position. Then they check that none of his lines have become tangled or blocked.

I am always watching. I watch every detail.

The pillows are hard and unyielding and all the same size. They look uncomfortable, especially as he prefers a low pillow. When I go out for a while in the early afternoon I find a babywear shop and get him a small pillow. I also bring in a feather pillow from home.

I find my way round to the Angiography Suite to take a small gift to Maria. She was very good to us when Dad had the angiogram. Was it only a fortnight ago?

Now that the gargantuan swelling of his body is going down, Dad looks pale and haggard. I am surprised how quickly all the incisions in his legs have healed, where they took lengths of six blood vessels to bypass clogged vessels inside his heart.

～⌒～

I haven't been going to dancing school because I don't have the heart for it. Usually it's one of my best pleasures in life, completely absorbing, artistic, life-giving, spiritually sustaining. When I'm dancing, I think of nothing else and that gives me release from any stress. It would do me good in this situation but it seems to belong to another dimension which is not accessible to me now. Like God. I seem to have forgotten about God. A week ago I would have said with confidence that I have faith and trust in God but now I can't give it any attention. And that's a shock. I thought that faith was at the centre of my life and would see me through anything.

This evening, Petrea King of the Quest for Life Foundation comes to visit me and they give permission for her to come in to see Dad. I am surprised. She is a friend and we have worked together. She has been with hundreds of people dying, or living with life-threatening illness. She sits quietly beside Dad for a while, meditating and praying, I think, and tuning in to his condition. He is unconscious or sedated during the time she spends with him. She has never met him before.

Afterwards we talk in the visitors room. She says I should try to stop worrying—that Dad is a great spirit, with deep reservoirs of character, strength, determination and humour, as demonstrated by his care of Mary. She says that he has a rich inner life and is capable of rising above his physical condition. She says that we are not only our bodies; that, in extremis, we come to know this and to move beyond body into spirit.

I hope that this is true. I am grateful for her visit and try to be reassured by it. Perhaps I have made the error of assessing Dad's capacity by my own relatively weak standards, underestimating the courage he has forged through his long experience of life.

I have recently borrowed his diaries and memoirs to read, some for the first time. And I turn to them now for evidence. As I scan through the pages of the several bound but unpublished volumes my eye is caught by his memory of a shattering setback he suffered in 1914 as a small boy. He had jumped out of a gum tree on Grattai. As he landed he jarred his right leg, causing severe pain. I have seen the long, deep scar on his leg and here he had written down the story:[2]

Sir Charles Percy Barlee Clubbe,
Sydney, 1914

It was raining in Sydney when the overnight train from Mudgee arrived at Central. I remember the clup-clop of the horse-drawn cab along shiny Macquarie Street. My father carried me in his arms from the cab up some stone steps into Dr Charles Clubbe's rooms. Mother, Father and I were ushered into the presence of the famous surgeon. It was the year when a single gunshot in Sarajevo started the catastrophe of World War I. But I was only seven and I had my own private battle to fight.

For some months I had been in hospital in Mudgee. I was suffering from what was later diagnosed as osteomyelitis (diseased bone) in my right leg. I had been in the care of two local doctors who had opened up my shin in four places. Their procedures had been disastrous, my pain agonising. I can still smell the choking chloroform. 'Try to count to a hundred,' they said. Finally they gave up; they told my parents they could do nothing more and would refer me to a Sydney specialist.

And here we were, at great inconvenience and expense, and a long way from Grattai. I was terrified. Anyone called doctor meant chloroform and pain. 'So you're the boy from Mudgee,' was the kindly greeting from a tall, elderly man; in fact he was sixty-two. His manner was reassuring enough as he gently undid the bloodied bandages. Then some misgivings when he exclaimed: 'What a mess!'

Dr Clubbe arranged for my immediate admission to the Children's Hospital at Camperdown. My parents returned home, Mother to care for my two younger siblings, Dad to cope with the drought then ravaging the country west of the Blue Mountains. They left behind a very lonely and unhappy little boy.

Dr Clubbe operated three times over several weeks, gradually excising the diseased bone. I'll never forget his kindness. He understood my emotional as well as my physical problems and I appreciated his role, in loco parentis. He appeared at the hospital nearly every day, always with encouraging words for me. I cannot recall any other visitors (although there may have been some). But I do remember a call one evening by a young house doctor doing his rounds. He was in military uniform, Sam Browne belt and all. He asked me how I was. I complained of pain. He turned to the sister, 'Well, Sister, the only thing left to do is to cut off his leg'. No doubt it was intended as a joke but it was a very sick one. Next day I sought reassurance from Dr Clubbe who convinced me that amputation was not on the agenda. (I imagine he would have 'had a word' with the thoughtless warrior.) A one-legged station hand would not have been much use for my Old Man!

After what seemed years, in reality probably five or six months, I was allowed to go home—on crutches. My leg gradually strengthened and I am forever grateful to Dr Clubbe for saving it. I was fortunate to have been put in his care.

Charles Percy Barlee Clubbe was born in Buckinghamshire, England, in 1854, the son of an Anglican clergyman. He graduated in medicine in 1877 and came to Australia in 1882. His work as a surgeon and a physician soon became widely recognised, especially in the paediatric field. He has been described as 'the great pioneer of paediatric surgery in Sydney'. His special interest was the development and administration of the Royal Alexandra Hospital for Children at Camperdown, now relocated as the New Children's Hospital at Westmead. Dr Clubbe was a member of staff of the hospital for forty-eight years and chairman of its board for twenty-eight years.

In 1927 he was knighted for his distinguished service to medicine. He died in 1932, aged seventy-six. I quote briefly from a lengthy obituary in the *Medical Journal of Australia*, 14 January 1933: 'Sir Charles will be remembered as a great surgeon and a very distinguished member of the medical profession but, above all, as a lover of children and a healer of the sick'.

How lucky was I! However, at the age of ninety-one, I have one regret. In 1931, I was living at Rose Bay where Dr Clubbe also resided. I was on the Woollahra golf course one afternoon when an elderly gentleman took a short cut across the fairway. I recognised him as Sir Charles Clubbe. I hesitated but did not approach him. I should have made myself known and shown him the result of his skilful work so many years before. I think he would have been gracious and pleased. Alas for the things we ought to have done!

Day 5, Friday 9 June 2000 (cont'd)
Later in the evening Bridie comes on duty. She's a cheerful Irish sister from the agency. She is upset by Dad's restlessness and misery and she increases the sedation drip.

'I'm not having a patient of mine in that condition.' The brogue is unmistakeable.

I see the sedative kick suddenly into his body and he lies still as though pole-axed. The manipulation of it is chilling. Bridie looks pleased. Dad looks at peace but it is a false peace.

It is difficult to leave. But, as I put my jumper and overcoat back on and go down the corridor to the lift, across the deserted foyer, past the depressingly perfect floral arrangement and out into the biting cold, I try to compose a litany of gratitude: Dad has his own nursing sister to care for him and watch over him all night. He is safe.

We are lucky to live in this time when there is sophisticated intensive-care nursing and the benefit of well-educated, good, caring doctors, nurses, physiotherapists and other health professionals. We are fortunate to have modern hospitals. We are privileged, luckier to be in Australia than anywhere else. And, as a war veteran, Dad's medical care is provided for him without cost. And so on. I can register this gratitude in my head but it doesn't make me feel better.

Back home, I think about how I can give the staff a picture of Dad's character as he really is—rather than as the speechless, dependent patient they are caring for. Probably it's not important for them but it matters to me.

After talking with Mary on the phone, I find a photo of them both. It's not a very good one but they look happy. And I write out a one-page story to describe him. It's difficult to reduce him to a succinct summary. I write that he was a country boy, then a soldier, that he has worked for most of his life as a reluctant accountant, that he writes, reads, loves golf and a drink and good company, that he's a great conversationalist, very alert and aware of current affairs, that he cares for his elderly wife, has a cynical view of most politicians and people in authority, and a strong sense of humour. It feels good to be doing something positive. I will put this in his file tomorrow so that each new person who cares for him will see it as they read up his notes and know him a bit better. I only wish they could read his diaries and memoirs as I am doing now.

RABBIT-TRAPPING

I hated rabbit-trapping but it was a year-round job. In those days it was simply a matter of us or them. In Mudgee there was a ready market—the freezing works. They bought the carcasses, bled and gutted but not skinned. A rabbit trap, made of steel with chain and steel peg attached, weighed about two and a half pounds (more than a kilogram). I know that a dozen traps carried over the shoulder was quite a load for a small boy. Professional rabbiters would set up to one hundred traps each night. My limit was about twenty, set late afternoon after school, just below ground level, at the entrance to burrows, hollow logs and holes in netting fences. During the evening you would go round the traps in darkness, aided by a low-flame hurricane lamp, and of course again before breakfast.

It was not an occupation for a small boy. I can still see those squirming, doomed, wretched animals in the flickering light of the lamp and feel the bloodied chaff bag over my shoulder and smell those rows of furry carcasses hanging on the road fences.

They were hard days and nights, but still I was relieved to be able to walk again and do all my jobs after the shattering experience in the Children's Hospital.

DAY 6, SATURDAY 10 JUNE 2000

The beginning of a long weekend. I'm writing this at the hospital. There's a different feel about the ICU today. Fewer staff and all people we haven't met before, mostly from nursing agencies. As well, a new team of doctors comes on each weekend. It makes me nervous. All these new people don't know Dad. But it soon feels alright. They read his file which is a detailed record of everything that's happened since he arrived and they have been briefed by the team going off duty. I had put my one-page description of him onto the sister's desk and I'm pleased to see it's been incorporated into Dad's increasingly thick file. I stick the little photo of a smiling Dad and Mary up on the glass partition between the nurses' desk and Dad's cubicle. I throw out the flowers from yesterday and put a new one in the vase I've brought from home. It's only a tall drinking glass to hold one or two flowers. Not that Dad can see them, but perhaps they're nice for the nurses.

Mary rings each morning to ask after Dad. She's decided not to come down from Gosford to visit until he's a bit better. Selfishly I'm relieved, because I don't want to leave him to drive up and get her and then take her back. But I will, as soon as she asks. I ring her later each day. She seems detached and self-absorbed, which is a help. She sounds as though she's managing well, with the support of her regular community care visitors—and meals delivered.

Dad keeps his eyes closed. He is lightly sedated, I am told, but sometimes conscious.

The day seems very long and very sad.

It's little Sam's birthday today, my goddaughter Kim's eldest boy. I hope he's having a happy day out in the country where his parents work on one of the great grazing properties of the central slopes— in the Crookwell district where Dad had his first accountancy practice after the war.

COUNTRY CLIENTS

In Crookwell in the late 1940s I had inherited two clients who had been pampered by my predecessor. One was Mrs Bustard, licensee of the Tuena Hotel some fifty miles north of the town. Each of these clients insisted on an annual visit from the accountant to straighten out their affairs for income tax purposes. Some months elapsed before I could afford to buy a car, so these trips out of town meant bus travel and overnight stops.

On my first professional visit to Tuena, by bus, the weather was bitterly cold; it was almost snowing. The bus arrived just before lunch. Mrs Bustard greeted me with enthusiasm and a large hot rum. After lunch I was confronted with her books and records. They were in disarray. I worked through the afternoon, interrupted now and again by my hostess and client with hot rummy 'afternoon teas' but with scant recall of several substantial debits and credits. However, we made educated guesses and by nightfall I reckoned I had a good enough idea of the state of her financial affairs.

Tuena is an old gold-mining area, long since abandoned except by the odd fossicker around the mullock heaps and along the creek and the steep gullies. There were several outlying properties, a public school and a post office store. The pub was the focal point. It was a long, low, rambling building with its ambience enhanced by several warming log fires in the various rooms. After dinner I finished off my work and, abetted by another hot rum, had no problems in the enjoyment of a sound sleep.

Next morning after breakfast it was freezing. I and several locals were waiting in the parlour, warmed by a great log fire, for the bus to convey us back to Crookwell and beyond. Mrs Bustard introduced me around and we shook hands as was the custom. The grip of my handshake is apparently similar, not intentionally of course, to that of the Masonic brethren.

On the bus, I sat with a gentleman to whom I'd been introduced. We talked of various innocuous matters when, apropos of nothing, he said, 'Are you going south?'

As the bus was lumbering along the dirt road in a southerly direction towards Crookwell, I replied that I was.

After a pause he asked another question, rather enigmatic, but designed to elicit a reply which would satisfy him as to my credentials. I've forgotten the question but I remember my answer: 'I think you've misunderstood me. I am not on the square (as in square and compass)'.

'You've made a bloody good pretence then,' he said, as he turned his back to me and gazed steadily and silently out the window.

When I got off in Crookwell I was waved a cheery goodbye from all the passengers proceeding onwards, with the exception of the irascible old craftsman.

In the 1950s, when we moved to the Central Coast of New South Wales, many of my clients were orchardists and poultry farmers.

Arthur was a citrus grower who, like most of them, ran some free-range chooks on the side. His financial records were kept in his packing and machinery shed which was also a shelter at night and on rainy days for his poultry. He arrived for his first visit to our office with a large cardboard box which contained, in disorder, his cheque butts, bank statements and invoices. The box had also been used as a roost; interlarded with his records were several dollops of encrusted chook manure. When I handed the job over to my senior clerk, she was not amused.

Another new client arrived one day, obviously nervous, rustic, thin, fortyish.

'I'm Ernie 'odges from Wyee,' he said.

'Yes, how can we help you?'

'Well I 'ave all these 'ens. I took 'em over when me Old Man died about seven years back and I've never put in a tax return.'

I was puzzled. Was this a case of Steptoe and Son, collectors and dealers in rural odds and ends?

'How many of these 'ens have you got?'

''Undreds and it costs a lot to feed 'em.'

The penny dropped, rather slowly, I'll admit.

In due course Ernie unearthed some primitive records and from these and Ernie's memory we prepared tax returns for seven years. I must admit to some creative accounting and some guesswork. Eventually his returns were processed without penalties. The returns disclosed modest incomes and attracted very little income tax.

I was satisfied with the result; Ernie was happy and showed his appreciation when he paid my account by presenting me with a dozen large, brown, free-range eggs.

DAY 6, SATURDAY 10 JUNE 2000 (CONT'D)

At seven o'clock I turn on the television news and put the remote control volume on the pillow next to Dad's ear, in case he can hear it. But I'm not sure that he can. At home he always pours himself and Mary a whisky in the evening and watches the news. It's a ritual. But he shows no sign of hearing it tonight.

At home he always watches *Australian Story* too. Only two weeks ago, comfortable in his armchair, he appreciated the program about Aboriginal sprinter Patrick Johnson, produced by John Millard. Patrick is one of our great hopes for an Olympic medal in Sydney, in three months time. As a child, he lived with his father on their fishing boat and was rowed ashore for school in whichever town they were near. His father believed that education was vital for Patrick's future. It paid off. Patrick is training now for a diplomatic career, as well as making his remarkable achievements in athletics. That story is an encouragement for any young Australian, to show them what is possible. And it is important to portray a young Aboriginal man in a positive light, as a counterpoint to the frequent negative press coverage.

After our story, people will have an extra enthusiasm for cheering Patrick on in the Olympics.

DAY 7, SUNDAY 11 JUNE 2000

Queen's Birthday weekend. It seems very long. It's also Pentecost Sunday. Instead of going to Mass I come to the hospital. It seems more important.

In the hospital we are caught in a sort of time warp. It's another world, away from real life and all the everyday things we take for granted, like fresh air and birds carolling, and having a potter in the garden.

Waiting in the ICU visitors room, I have a few minutes to talk with Genevieve. She looks pale, strained and tired. Her husband is still terribly ill. He's been back in surgery, his chest opened up once again, just as happened with Dad.

I think she knows he may not live. They're only in their fifties. We compare notes and exchange news in this new idiom of medical emergency which we have had to learn. We are both given confidence and comfort by the staff. We both live in hope and trepidation. After a while there's not much more to say and we just sit together, in sympathetic silence. Like me, she doesn't seem to have other family to come with her.

When we are allowed to go in, I have to walk past her husband's cubicle. He looks very still and very low. During the day I see her sitting beside him, watching him, or talking with his nurse or the doctors as they come and go. Their cubicle is diagonally opposite Dad's. Sometimes she rearranges the flowers which her husband will never see because he is unconscious.

During the day Dad is sometimes half-awake. I tell him again the story of what has happened—that he has had heart surgery, that it was successful, that he is now recovering. He watches me and seems very surprised by what I am saying. He's not himself. I can't be certain he knows me. I'm not sure how well he can see me, nor quite how much he understands. I explain about the breathing tube, why it is there, how it helps him, but I feel like a traitor as I hear myself rationalising something which must be so appalling for him. I have a horror of any interference with my breathing and I feel panic as I imagine what it's like for him to have that tube tied into his mouth and down his throat—unable to speak, to swallow, to eat or to drink.

I am careful not to show the panic I feel lest it demoralise him. I feel a terrible anger on his behalf and every day I ask the doctors when the tube can be removed. I am careful to conceal my anger because I want to keep them on side. I want them to be very interested in Dad. I want them to like him, to pay him the closest attention, to give him every relief as soon as possible. And I want to be helpful and co-operative so that I am allowed to stay closely involved as his advocate, his voice. It infuriates me that they think it's acceptable for a person to be restrained like this, but of course it is normal to them. That's what they do here. They have the technology to support a patient's breathing while he's still in recovery and they use it. And they have great success with it. It saves lives. But I wonder if any of them has actually experienced and known the terror of it, as they become increasingly conscious and aware that there is no escape from the terrible gag, and that, worst of all, they cannot speak to plead for its removal? They cannot speak to protest at the invasion when a suction tube is introduced frequently down the inside of the tube into the lungs to cause coughing and to remove fluid. Each time this is done—and it has to be done—Dad turns purple in the face from the forced cough and his eyes look panic-stricken, like those of an animal caught in a trap from which it knows there is no escape.

I come home feeling emotionally exhausted, defeated that I cannot save him from this ordeal, that I leave him there, hour after hour, day after day, to endure something that's very close to unendurable. I hope they help him to sleep tonight. I'll never forget this Queen's Birthday 2000.

QUEEN'S BIRTHDAY 1994

Today we celebrated the birthday of Queen Elizabeth II.

It is also an occasion for awards to worthy citizens whose names and claims for recognition have been put to some obscure committee comprising no doubt other worthy personages.

With no expectations I marked the day modestly with a walk into town to buy a newspaper. The way took me through a small park where our cenotaph overlooks the lovely Brisbane Water. The sole occupant of the park was a middle-aged, respectable-looking woman, seated in a shady, secluded corner. She seemed to be enjoying an alfresco lunch. The day was clear and fine but quite cool. I wondered why she had chosen a seat in shade rather than a sunny spot with a view of the sparkling waters.

Twenty minutes later when I returned through the park, she had finished her lunch. As I came closer I heard music. Then I saw it was the woman playing a mouth organ, producing softly and faithfully the haunted strains of 'Waltzing Matilda'.

I was intrigued. Firstly because, in my experience in town and country, the harmonica has been the exclusive preserve of the male musician, amateur or professional. Secondly because of the oddity of the occasion.

I wondered, was she protesting the honours system or was she perhaps registering as one of prime minister Keating's republicans? I will never know.

DAY 8, MONDAY 12 JUNE 2000

As I arrive at the hospital I feel as though I am crossing into some parallel dimension, another time zone in which it is always present tense.

Queen's Birthday holiday, but not for us. The hospital has the deserted air of any institution on a public holiday. The doctor on duty has decided that Dad's lungs are in trouble and need draining. He has made incisions between the ribs on both sides into the lung sac and inserted tubes to drain fluid from the base of the lungs. The tubes drain down into tall glass containers on the floor beside the bed. They are filling with reddish liquid. It's hard to credit there could have been so much fluid in Dad's lungs. He is still pretty groggy after the insertion of the tubes and I hope he doesn't know much of what's going on.

How can they inflict more suffering on him in the name of life-saving? What an appalling situation. How will we ever escape from this chamber of endless horrors?

A welcome visit from Sr Monica, a Sister of Mercy in a windjacket. Like a small, kind, weatherbeaten angel, she has travelled a long distance to visit patients today. She is on the team of the nearby public hospital and has come in response to my request for a chaplain. I am amazed that this private hospital has no pastoral care team. She has a prayer printed on a small green card. She gives me a copy and we stand beside Dad and read it together, aloud:

Every day I need you Lord
But this day especially,
I need some extra strength
To face whatever is to be.
This day more than any day
I need to feel you near,
To fortify my courage
And to overcome my fear.

By myself, I cannot meet
The challenge of the hour,
There are times when humans help,
But we need a higher power
To assist us bear what must be borne.
And so dear Lord I pray—
Hold on to my trembling hand
And be near me today.

It's a good prayer. I can't really take it in but I hope that God might be in this awful situation somehow. And I hope Dad hears us; I think he might. Anyway, I always act as though he can hear so he knows he is not abandoned, not alone in this terrible plight. I wonder if that makes any difference, provides any solace, when one is in extremis?

I am very grateful for Sr Monica's visit, after feeling so alone this past week. Of course people are ringing to ask after Dad. His sisters ring every day and my cousin, and my friends leave messages. But it's not the same as having someone who actually comes with me and sees what is happening and keeps me company and helps me to make decisions. Sr Monica promises to visit us again and I could weep with gratitude.

In the evening the doctors start Dad on renal dialysis to help his failing kidneys. Another machine is wheeled up to the bedside and two more tubes are attached to the lines inserted into veins in Dad's neck. One will carry the blood out of his body and into the dialysis machine, to do the cleansing which the kidneys are failing to do. The other line will bring the cleansed blood back into the body. This process will go on for several days.

Dad is sedated and it's always easier to leave when he is unconscious. Each evening I wrap a box of chocolates to leave on the day sister's bag, with a note of thanks for her care. And when I go, I leave another small gift for the night nurse. I have no idea how to thank them adequately—these strangers who take care of my father, round the clock, in his great need. I spend many hours with them. We talk as they work. I listen to the stories of their lives and discover what has led them into nursing or medicine. They work very long hours, twelve-hour shifts. Many of them are young men and women juggling family life with their demanding profession.

Today is the deadline for my article for *Madonna* magazine. I can only write about what is happening in my life now. It's pretty raw but it's truthful and I explain to the editor, David Lovell, that I will understand if it's not suitable but it's all I can manage.

I'm up to the part in Dad's memoir where he's writing about his forebears, recognising their resourcefulness and strength of character. I must remember that Dad has their qualities in his blood and try to find their courage in myself.

GRATTAI

The first white settler in the Grattai district was my father's maternal grandfather, William Reeves, who was granted initially about 1000 acres, around 1836.

William Reeves was born in England in 1798. Aged nineteen, he 'took the King's shilling' and became a soldier. His regiment was posted to New South Wales. When he received his honourable discharge, he went, with his wife Marianne (Clarkson), to live over the Blue Mountains, at Mudgee in New South Wales. There he was manager of the estate of Captain William Cox, who had been his commanding officer and was his friend.

Family history has it that William Reeves, searching for some straying cattle, came upon a valley, well grassed and well watered, twelve miles south of Mudgee. Its Aboriginal name was Grati, meaning 'deep hole', a name later altered to Grattai. When the rains came, Grattai Creek was a fine stream—and afterwards a series of waterholes, some of them home to crayfish—and all a bonus for thirsty livestock.

The small local tribe of Aboriginal people were friendly but must have been dismayed by the white newcomers moving onto the land to which they belonged, without any invitation or acknowledgement of its prior occupation.

With the help of his assigned convict servants, William Reeves built a house. He acquired a small flock of sheep and a few cattle, including milking cows. My great-grandfather and his men cleared trees and built fences, ploughed several acres and sowed them to wheat, oats, barley, potatoes and other vegetables. As time went on, William employed three shepherds to protect the increasing flocks from dingos, and the crops from kangaroos and wallabies.

Grattai Station became almost self-sustaining. Great-grandmother Marianne, with the help of her daughter Ann Elisa, set the milk, and skimmed off the cream to make butter and cheese. They made soap, tallow candles in moulds, and bush lamps (tins of fat with a wick inset). They baked bread in a camp oven and later a fuel stove or brick oven. Ann Elisa (later to become my grandmother) reared any motherless lambs and, in time, built up a flock of her own. They made drip safes to keep their food cold. They washed their clothes by boiling them in four-gallon tins over an open fire. For news, they depended on travellers. They fought bushfires, floods and droughts. Sometimes they came into conflict with the Aborigines. They also made some Aboriginal friends.

They had to combat grass seed which spoiled the wool and blinded the sheep, which were also subject to blowfly strike. In the early days, all the sheep were washed before shearing. A good, clean waterhole with a sandy bottom, in a running stream, was selected, sufficiently shallow to allow the washers to stand up to their middles. The sheep were penned close by and supplied to the washers who scrubbed them with soap, rinsed them and released them on the opposite bank, onto clean pasture, in the charge of a shepherd. The yards at the shearing shed were swept of all dust and, after about three days of fine weather, the sheep were delivered to the tender mercy of the shearers who took off their wool with blade shears—machine-shearing with combs and cutters being unknown in those days.

The five sons helped with all the work, including the harvest. Wheat was cut by hand, with reaping hooks, tied into sheaves and stacked to await the visit of the threshing machine. If there was a late frost, the men went out early to draw long ropes, a man at each end, over the crop, to dislodge the frost before the sun came up.

But great-grandfather William still needed to work for Captain Cox. This included taking bullock teams over the mountains to Sydney and back, with wool and wheat on the down journey, returning with supplies—

flour, sugar, tea, tools and woolpacks. The 200-mile journey took about six weeks. The drivers were mainly 'ticket-of-leave' men, some of them unreliable and very fond of rum. Great-grandfather William made his last trip with the bullock teams in 1846 when he was forty-eight. He was killed near Cox River, not far from Lithgow, when a heavily laden wagon ran over him, through the negligence of a driver under the influence of rum.

Great-grandmother Marianne decided to carry on, with her family of five sons and one daughter—the eldest child was then sixteen years old. She built another house, with the help of her servants, among whom were a stonemason and a carpenter. It was a cottage of four rooms at first, with stone walls two feet thick, and door and window frames made of cedar, carted from the coast. The home, known as Grattai House, has been added to over the years. Today it occupies fifty-four squares and stands as a tribute to those fine tradesmen, involuntary though they were. Alas, the house and property are no longer in our family but I've always thought of Grattai as home.

Great-grandmother's house was always open to travellers, including ministers of all denominations. Services were held there, with neighbours, shepherds and servants invited to attend.

On more than one occasion, William Browne, the Gold Commissioner, broke his journey at Grattai and did some of his writing there. His pen-name was Rolf Boldrewood and he was author of the classic *Robbery Under Arms*. He presented Marianne with a first copy of one of his other books, *Ups and Downs of Australian Life*. There were also many swagmen on the roads and none was denied a feed and some food to take on the road.

Marianne's death in 1871 was recorded in a lengthy 'In Memoriam' article in the *Australian Churchman*, in which she was described as 'much-respected … with an honourable reputation for hospitality and Christian kindness. Calm and full of hope she patiently resigned her soul with faith in the One All Wise'.

The year before her death, Marianne Reeves saw her only daughter, Ann Elisa, marry my grandfather, John Hart James.

Brave Marianne, if only it were possible to give your great-grandson Brian some of your courage now. And perhaps you have. He seems to have inherited it in his character.

DAY 9, TUESDAY 13 JUNE 2000

I did my introduction for *Australian Story* this morning. I was operating on automatic pilot. It amazes me that I could concentrate well enough to do it, even to memorise what I wanted to say. It's a marvellous story on the pianist Gerard Willems, who has made a career of performing Beethoven around the world for the last thirty years.

The story was well titled 'Grand Obsession', produced by Helen Grasswill. It's good to be able to feature one of the Australian-designed and hand-crafted Stuart & Sons pianos, now highly regarded internationally for their technical innovation and aesthetic qualities. There surely are some wonderful Australian stories to tell. And our production team is working so well. After five years, I give most credit for the program's success to our executive producer, Deb Fleming, who seems to bring out the best in everyone. Somehow she keeps us all in touch with what's happening, no easy matter, with the team scattered between Brisbane, Sydney, Melbourne and on the road.

Dad is still on kidney dialysis and the lung-draining continues. He is sedated and yet I have an idea that he can hear. Sr Monica makes her faithful visit and says a prayer for him.

I feel a nagging dread. Dad is so terribly ill that I wonder if there will come a time of decision soon about whether or not to continue treatment. I ask the doctors and they say we will face that if it happens, all of us together, but the situation now is just normal treatment to aid recovery. I feel clearer about that but the miasma of anxiety comes home with me.

DAY 10, WEDNESDAY 14 JUNE 2000

The drains have been removed from Dad's lungs today, having allowed the escape of a great deal of fluid. One lung is infected. The dialysis continues, the reels whirring rhythmically on the machine which is acting as an artificial kidney so that blood is continuously removed, cleansed and recycled into the body. Dad lies still, trapped, his handsome face disfigured by the breathing tube keeping his mouth constantly open in an unnatural, joyless smile. I feel sick and frightened and I desperately don't want to be here. I feel trapped with Dad in this awful situation.

Sr Monica visits and so does the Anglican chaplain, Rev. Ross Weaver. He's a big, masculine chap in a jumper. He prays, standing beside Dad's head, and I have an idea that Dad can hear him.

On the phone Mary announces that she has booked herself into their local hospital for a cataract operation. I am instantly defeated. I cannot be here, and eighty kilometres north, to support her, at the same time. She says she does not need me to come.

DAY 11, THURSDAY 15 JUNE 2000

The routine of another day unfolds. An early phone call from home to see how Dad is before the night nurse departs.

Once at the hospital, I take up my vigil. The physio comes to exercise Dad's arms and legs and listen to his chest with her stethoscope. Portable X-ray comes and goes. An injection to thin the blood, to guard against clotting. Careful inspection of the toes which are developing some necrosis. I think that means gangrene or dying. I have bought a beautiful lambswool mattress cover which I hope may make life more comfortable. Dad's left heel is becoming sore from pressing on the bed. One of the night sisters fills rubber gloves with water and ties them at the wrist, to fashion little buoyant balloons to put under Dad's ankles, raising the weight of his heels off the mattress. Clever. They keep Dad's body very clean. His hair has grown long and it knots under his head but he is clean-shaven except for his moustache.

Dialysis is completed today and Dad looks a bit healthier as a result, I suppose. Sr Monica visits. Also Rev. Ross Weaver. God bless them. I don't know where my own faith is but they are praying for us and that means something to me.

As Dad becomes more conscious and aware of his situation, the constriction of the breathing tube in his throat becomes more tormenting and incomprehensible to him. The nurses and I explain the reason for it but for him it must seem like a terrible gag from which we will not free him.

We end the day with Psalm 121. It seems to give him a bit of peace, although I can't be sure.

I lift up mine eyes to the hills
from whence comes my help
My help comes from the Lord,
who made Heaven and earth.

I wish the psalm could carry him back to the hills of his beloved Grattai, the hills of home.

Pioneers

On my father's side of the family, John Hart James, born at Hinton, New South Wales, in 1840, was the eldest son of Samuel James and Harriet (Wood) who were married in London in April 1839. The story goes that they eloped to Australia, arriving at Morpeth, New South Wales, in August 1839. My great-grandfather Sam and his family lived near Hinton and later Clarencetown. He was in the business of cutting cedar and hardwood logs, hauling them to the Hunter, and later to the Williams River, and floating them to Newcastle, some to be absorbed by the local mills and others to be loaded onto ships for Sydney and overseas.

The discovery of gold at Hargraves, New South Wales, in 1851 dramatically changed the lives of thousands of people, including the James family. With several other families from around Maitland, Sam and his brood set off for the goldfields. After many weeks and some adventures, they arrived at a point on the Meroo Creek about six miles from Hargraves. They named it Maitland Bar. I drove down there last year and returned to the main road, over the rough tracks, with a strange feeling—an eeriness tinged with sadness and yet some pride.

There are no records to show that Sam enjoyed any great rewards for his gold mining. But his decision to cater for the large numbers of people trekking to and from the goldfields was a wise one. He leased a portion of the Grattai estate from Mrs Marianne Reeves. Here, he built a large hotel. The publican's general licence granted to him on 25 April 1857 shows he named it 'The George and Dragon'. He employed a butcher, baker, blacksmith and bootmaker to complement the services of his hotel. Later he built another hotel on forty acres adjoining Grattai Station and called it the 'Grattai Hotel'.

Sam prospered, opening shops wherever gold was found in the district.

He and Harriet had four daughters and seven sons. The eldest, my grandfather John Hart James, married Ann Elisa Reeves in 1870. One of their sons, George Frederick (1877–1962), was my father.

Great-grandfather Sam gave up the ghost in 1889 aged seventy-one and there is an imposing headstone in the Mudgee cemetery to prove it. Great-grandmother Harriet died at Grattai in 1902 and was buried beside her husband. I wish I had met them, pioneers in the true sense. I missed him by eighteen years and Harriet by five.

But I think about them and about all my forebears, especially my parents. They had to struggle to keep afloat but they were rich in character with a deep lode of integrity, an abundance of good humour and a fine sense of fun. As small fry we were subject to plenty of church and Sunday school which I believe influenced us less than the splendid examples set by mother and father at home. We were reminded that, although financial stringency is a great inconvenience, it is not a disgrace. Dad tried to instil in his sons the virtues of fortitude, perseverance and persistence. I hope I've inherited some of them.

Mum and Dad were products of the pioneers of this great country and true pioneers themselves. Conditioned by hard work and tough living, they lived long, useful lives. Honourable and industrious to the end, they did their very best.

DAY 12, FRIDAY 16 JUNE 2000

How much longer before they decide Dad can breathe on his own without the ventilator? Apparently the machine has to show that a certain level of unsupported breathing is happening. Dad has to demonstrate that he can cough strongly enough, on his own. Each day there is talk that the tube might come out tomorrow, but tomorrow never comes. Just the same, this is the first day that he seems a bit better, and much more conscious.

It's the first day I feel he might live. I tell him the sequence of events again, trying to help him understand where he is and why he is so weak and so constrained. He looks surprised to hear that he is in hospital in Sydney. The sedatives and all the other drugs have made him forget, I suppose. But it worries me because it means he has no memory that he agreed to come here to undergo this operation. That must make him feel that he has no control over events and that others are deciding for him. I know that would be very frustrating for him.

Since he is unable to speak, we are exploring other ways of communicating. I have brought in small writing pads, pencils and pens. And the nurses produce a board with the letters of the alphabet printed large, to see if he can point out a word. His attempts to print don't succeed. It's difficult for him to hold a pencil and to form any letter on the page. He tries again and again and the page fills with sliding lines and scribble.

Again and again, the writing pad slips out of his hand. His attempts are hampered by the position in which he is lying, the lines attached into his forearm and an oxygen monitor clipped, like a large clothes peg, to his forefinger. He often manages to remove it. I also think that he cannot see very well. The nurses are good at guessing what he may need. Sometimes he achieves what looks like a slow nod of assent.

It's Friday and I am dreading another weekend because things slow down; the doctors are less visible; agency nurses are called in to augment the core of hospital staff. The lack of continuity is disconcerting.

At evening doctors' rounds I ask the doctor on duty if she will spend a bit of extra time with him, explaining his situation again.

She tells him his whole story slowly and kindly, describing his recovery process, the need for the breathing tube, the hope to remove it soon. She promises that he will be given something to help him rest tonight. He seems reassured by her careful explanation and becomes calmer.

A wonderful surprise tonight. Fr Robert Walsh SJ arrives. Someone has told him of our situation and he has come. No one could have been more welcome. Father was a doctor of medicine before he became a Jesuit priest and as a result understands Dad's situation and is not frightened by what he sees. He stands close beside Dad's head and looks down on him with great compassion, gently stroking his forehead. Dad has drifted into what might be sleep—or sedation. Fr Robert remarks what fine character he sees in Dad's face, now at rest, how handsome he is. Then he gives Dad the blessing for the sick and I feel very greatly relieved and comforted, just by his presence.

Fr Robert suggests that, if it's about the time I usually leave, we could have a cup of coffee and a talk. Having visited as a chaplain in the public hospital, he knows his way round the rabbit warren of corridors. We end up in a gloomy staff canteen with a cup of tea-bag tea and a biscuit. Not until then do I discover what sort of day he has had, presiding at two funerals. It sounds impossible to me but he is not complaining. His visit is like a tonic because he listens, he understands and he is not in a hurry.

It is very cold when we venture out into the night air to find our cars. For the first time, I drive home without the sense of doom to which I have become habituated. I think about how many people Fr Robert must help in the course of each week, as he has helped me tonight. He's a modest man, humble, quiet, human, warm, possessing the gift of kindness.

I sleep soundly for the first time. Thanks to Fr Robert, for the first time I have given the care of my father into the hands of God for the night. Up to now I have hardly thought of God. Maybe Fr Robert's visit means that God has not forgotten us.

When I became a Catholic I wasn't sure what Dad would think. His reaction came in a handwritten letter. He had cut out and pasted onto his letter a clipping from the newspaper:

Old Irish Blessing

May the road rise to meet you
May the wind be always at your back,
The sun shine warm upon your face
The rains fall soft upon your fields
And until we meet again
May God hold you in the palm of His hand.
May the Lord bless you and keep you,
May the Lord cause His face to shine upon you
And give you peace.

To which he added his own message: 'What ho! Begorrah now if these ain't foine sentiments. I'm not sure of the first line but my guess is it means may the way you go be easy. So there you are and so be it. Amen.'

I took this to be an acceptance that I had found a faith and that it has Irish connections which do not belong in his and my family history but which are valid nonetheless. Such was the cryptic manner of our communication. A few years later he was more expansive, commenting, 'I think it was a good move'.

At the dancing school tonight, they held the tango and cha cha competition. Normally I would have been there but it seems a world away and I cannot imagine that I will ever take part in anything so carefree and frivolous again.

DAY 13, SATURDAY 17 JUNE 2000

I've bought an audiotape of natural bush sounds recorded in Kakadu National Park. Dad's been indoors for so long that I hope it might give an illusion of freedom and fresh air.

He is more conscious today, aware of his helplessness and discomfort, the gag of the breathing tube and the violent coughing spasms produced by regular suction of his lungs. He is very frustrated by a plight which he cannot understand or communicate to us. When he reaches feebly to try to pull the tormenting tube out of his mouth, the nurse ties his arms to the side of the bed to stop him.

To see him restrained in this way and to see the look on his face is the worst moment yet. I am beside myself. I feel helpless with a rage that I cannot show. I know that I am betraying him, that I should be able to make them free him from this horror, yet I cannot, because they have the knowledge. They say the ventilator is essential and I do not have the knowledge to countermand them. I don't remember ever feeling so bad about anything. I don't want to be here and I am ashamed of having such a selfish thought, but it doesn't go away.

I ask the doctors if they are considering a tracheostomy and they explain the pros and cons. Yes, it would be more comfortable for Dad and might allow him to speak, even to swallow. But it means more surgery, another shock to his system. They will wait a day or two and see if they can wean him off the breathing tube instead.

In his situation I am sure I would be panicking but Dad is incredibly brave. He even continues his attempts to write but they still result only in illegible lines and squiggles. Mostly we rely on basic sign language and try to anticipate what might make him less distressed. It's a comfort to know that Fr Robert said Mass for him today.

~

Eighty kilometres north, Mary seems to be managing the aftermath of eye surgery, with visits from her regular community carers. I should be there, of course, as well as here.

DAY 14, SUNDAY 18 JUNE 2000

I go to Mass and, although I pray for Dad, I do not believe God can get him out of his predicament.

As usual, the days seem longer—interminable—at the weekend. I've written out a schedule of radio listening that Dad might enjoy and put it up on the nurses' desk. I've brought in a portable radio so he can listen to the news in the morning. But sister says he doesn't seem very interested.

I'm trying to think of ways to give Dad something else to focus on, something to free his imagination to take flight from the prison of his physical suffering, into his memory perhaps, his own inner place of understanding and sensibility, as John O'Donohue describes it, in his book *Anam Cara*.[3] I've been rereading the book in an attempt to find another way to think about suffering.

I know Dad has strong inner resources and I hope they carry him into the sanctuary of his soul, in order to escape, even temporarily, his utter dependence on others, in this little hospital room. I hope that, as his body becomes weaker, his soul is becoming a richer and more spacious dimension for him to inhabit.

Sometimes, with his eyes closed, he takes hold of the bed rail and I hope that he may have the reins of his pony in hand and be cantering across the paddocks of Grattai, or riding proudly in the sulky with his father on the way into the saleyards at Mudgee.

THE SALEYARDS

Some of my happiest recollections of those early days are associated with sheep. Attending the Mudgee stock sales with Dad during school holidays was a heady adventure. Whether we were buying or selling or merely observing, it was a great day for a small boy. The rapid-fire performances of the auctioneer and his offsiders, disposing of a large yarding of sheep, were entertainment enough. Add the plaintive bleats of hundreds of sheep destined for fresh pastures or the abattoirs, the yapping of sheepdogs and the colourful yarns of their masters. All these were bonuses, to be savoured for days afterwards.

I remember well one occasion when, for a couple of reasons, Dad had bought a mob of sheep at auction, through the stock and station agents, Crossing and Cox of Mudgee. At the conclusion of the sale, about noon, Roly Crossing, the auctioneer, invited Dad and me to join him for refreshment at the Woolpack Hotel. The Woolpack, alas no longer there, was within walking distance of the saleyards, and one of Mudgee's twenty-two pubs. It was a watering hole well patronised on sale days. Through the thick mist of nearly eighty years, I have a hazy recollection that mine host was Tom Underwood. But whoever he was, it seems that anyone, old or very young, was welcome in his bar. It was my first visit to a hotel bar so, when asked what I'd like to drink I had no idea, probably hanging my head in a dumb and shy fashion. Anyhow, the busy barmaid recommended 'a barmaid's blush'. This exotic beverage was a mixture of lemonade and sarsaparilla. It was delicious then, and maybe still is. Perhaps I should have persevered with it for the rest of my bar-visiting days!

The other reason for remembering that day was the trip home. Dad and I had driven into Mudgee in our sulky, bringing with us Darky, one of our sheepdogs. After slaking our thirsts, and not forgetting to water our horse and Darky, it was time to get the mob of sheep moving. It was a fair-sized mob, around six hundred. The stock route was known as the Old Grattai Road which branched off the main Mudgee–Hill End Road about two miles from the saleyards. When we reached the turn-off, Dad said, 'You and Darky can carry on now. I have some business in town. Keep them moving as we must reach Glen Gowan before dark.'

Well, there I was, aged nine, on foot, with a hungry mob of sheep that had been penned up overnight, grazing greedily from 'the long paddock' and reluctant to be hurried along. Glen Gowan was part of Grattai Station but separated from the main area and some eleven miles from where I was left in charge. It was then about 1 p.m. so I had approximately five and a half hours before nightfall. Dad caught up when we had covered about half the distance. His laconic, 'Well done, son', was approbation enough for the proudest and probably the youngest drover in the district at that time.

In those days sheep stealing was considered in some quarters to be a worthwhile enterprise. When I was a youngster a certain police sergeant enjoyed a deal of success in having a number of these rustlers convicted. Sergeant Small was a master of disguise. Sometimes as a swagman, sometimes as a hawker, he was tuned in to the bush telegraph, a potent source of communication, even to this day. His information and his disguise enabled him to turn up at places and times very awkward and frustrating for the moonlighting boys. Sergeant Small became a household name in western New South Wales.

DAY 14, SUNDAY 18 JUNE 2000 (CONTD)

Later in the day Dad seems a lot better. I think he can see a bit. He is tolerating the breathing tube, I don't know how.

In the brief biography I put into Dad's file, one of the doctors has read that Dad is a golfer. The kind young man comes bustling in to turn on the television so Dad can follow the play in the US Open. From time to time he darts back in to see if he can enthuse Dad about Tiger Woods' latest shot. I could hug him for the effort he's making to treat Dad as a fellow-golfer rather than a patient. And Dad tries to respond with a weak nod or a lift of the eyebrows.

Later, he has another go at writing. Today he has a bit more strength to control the pencil on the page. 'B' takes shape, followed painstakingly by a rough letter 'o'. It's too soon to guess the word but it's exciting to see that he can write. It must be incredibly frustrating for such an alert, articulate mind to have to struggle to write one word.

After about twenty minutes the word is legible. And it's such a relief to see it's not a cry of despair, that the nurse and I start laughing. Dad can only widen his eyes, pleased, no doubt, that we've got the message—at last. But he must wonder what seems so funny to us because the word he has written—his first message to the world in fourteen days is 'Bowels'.

I go out for a while. I feel grateful for the attentive nursing care Dad is getting. It will take two of them to manoeuvre him onto a bedpan without disconnecting the many lines and catheters to which he is attached. They will have to support him; he's too weak to sit up alone. It will be embarrassing and unpleasant for all of them. And how humiliating it is for Dad who is so clean and careful about his personal hygiene.

I have a talk with Genevieve in the ICU visitors room. Her husband is still in a critical state but a daughter has arrived from overseas and it's good to see her with some support at last. Two other new families are waiting. As old hands, we try to reassure the newcomers about the excellent standard of care and to give them confidence.

When I come back to Dad's cubicle, all his lines have been changed. I wish I could ask him about it. It must be painful to have cannulas fed into your neck and the back of your hands, when your whole body is sore and you cannot protest at this new, unwelcome invasion.

He makes another laboured attempt to write. The lines and scribbles don't form a word but I can make out three letters among the hieroglyphics—T U B. Of course he wants to get rid of the tube. I ask sister to explain it to him again and feel treacherous that we are talking about it, instead of doing something to free him from it.

Dialysis is resumed in the afternoon and he takes on a much better colour by evening. He seems patient and accepting. Perhaps they've boosted his sedation to give him relief.

Shift change at 7 p.m. As usual I stay for an hour after the night sister comes on duty, to see Dad rearranged for the night and to get to know her and assess her approach. Another agency sister tonight, new to us. She's calm and focussed and interested and I feel alright about leaving. I read Psalm 121 with Dad, as usual, last thing before I go.

The Lord will keep you from all harm.
He will watch over your life;
The Lord will watch over your coming and going,
Both now and for evermore.

I wonder if it's any help to him.

Thank goodness this long, long weekend is almost over. I hope Dad gets a decent night's rest. It is always problematical. The cracks at the corners of his mouth, where the tapes tie the breathing tube in place, look terribly raw and are widening. It must be so painful. I hope he has a way of escaping into his own thoughts and memories of the world outside the hospital, beyond his ordeal.

GOLF

'Golf is a game whereby one endeavours to propel an extremely small ball incredible distances with the aid of instruments singularly ill-adapted for the purpose.' I read that definition in a Melbourne newspaper, *The Argus*, in July 1927 when I was learning the rudiments of the game. I managed the elementary essentials of achieving a satisfactory shot but I'm damned if I can apply them consistently.

It's a maddening game, addictive, but not always a happy experience. I've seen men in utter despondency after a bad round. I've shuddered and turned away from a torrent of profanity engendered by a luckless shot at a vital stage. I've witnessed clubs hurled with exasperated anger, to be lodged high in trees and low in lakes.

The affinity between a golfer and his caddie is interesting. For two or three years before my need for a motorised cart, I enjoyed the services of a laconic lad of fourteen years. He preferred to be called Anthony, not Tony. He had a good sense of anticipation and generally led me to the destination of any wayward shot. I appreciated his taciturnity and any advice, sparingly offered. He attempted to curb my curiosity with a curt 'head down' or if confronted by a water carry: 'There's no water there'.

At a recent game, I played a poor tee shot at the dog-leg seventeenth hole par 4. Anthony was not impressed but made no comment. When we reached the ball, we found a good lie but the line of flight to the green was interrupted by a stand of tall turpentine trees with a lake on the right to claim any other errant slice.

Prudence and percentage suggested the choice of an 8 iron to chip back onto the fairway, with loss of distance but with some hope of a bogey.

Anthony said nothing and handed me a no. 3 wood. The game, with a few dollars at risk, was at a crucial stage. Surprised but silent, I gritted my teeth, kept my head still and drove the ball through the timber with a slight fade.

It reached the green, thereby ensuring an almost certain par.

Anthony replaced the club and with a slow smile said, 'I'm proud of you'. A rare tribute.

DAY 15, MONDAY 19 JUNE 2000

A new intensivist team starts today. The doctor in charge says that, since Dad's breathing is not yet sufficiently strong to do without the ventilator, he will perform a tracheotomy. This means that a hole will be cut in Dad's neck to allow a breathing tube to be introduced into his trachea or windpipe. The breathing tube in his mouth will no longer be needed.

I have longed for this decision because I see other patients with tracheostomies looking much more comfortable than my father. But, of course, it is another assault on the body, another anaesthetic, another risk. The doctor explains to Dad what he wants to do. Dad listens carefully. I still don't think he can see too well. As soon as the doctor finishes, Dad indicates that he needs to write. He starts his painstaking attempts to form the letters. After several frustrating false starts and fifteen minutes of effort he produces 'A second opinion?', in sprawling, angular letters. I am amazed again by his courage, by his intelligent insistence on retaining some control over his destiny. I take it as a very good sign. And suddenly think that I have been underestimating his capacity to cope.

I go looking for the intensivist registrar with Dad's request. When he can, he comes to Dad's side, and explains in detail the pros and cons of the tracheotomy. He concludes by confirming the first opinion—that this is the way to go.

Dad reaches for his writing pad and pencil and takes a long time to print: 'The op—sooner the better'. He then reaches out to shake the doctor's hand.

I could cry with gratitude to see his brave dignity and the respect shown to him by the young doctor. Mostly I am relieved to know that Dad will be free of the gag and the tapes that tie the tormenting tube into his throat, cutting ever deeper into the red-raw flesh at the corners of his mouth. It is strange to feel almost happy again— because my father is to have yet another operation.

Now in the writing mood, Dad takes another fifteen minutes to print out some letters scattered, sliding across the page: 'Where watch?'

I have been wearing his watch to keep it running, so I put his hand on my wrist so he can feel where it is. His grip seems a little stronger.

The physiotherapist arrives and I leave for a while.

When I come back, sister and I are talking just outside his cubicle and, as we watch, he raises one leg off the bed and holds it for a few moments, then lowers it. Then he does the same with his arms. These are the exercises he usually does each morning at home, before he gets out of bed. Does this mean he's feeling stronger, more like himself? I am amazed by his attempts to retrieve everyday normality in the midst of a nightmare.

I want to know about the pain he must be feeling from the massive open-heart surgery, from the cutting open and retraction of his breastbone and wiring it together again—twice in two days. In the booklet we read to prepare for surgery, there was a warning about this. But sister says he would be through that pain by now. I hope she is right. He's got so much else to put up with.

In the evening I put some piano music on the tape player and we enjoy a period of calm. After a while Dad seems to be sleeping, as opposed to sedated. It's wonderful to see. Sleep must be healing, after all that he's been through. He is utterly exhausted. Later he wakes and attempts to put one leg over the side of the bed, trying to get up. We tell him the story again—where he is, what has happened, the surgery successful, how he's recovering and so on. But he seems miserable. The drip is increased slightly to give him a greater degree of sedation. Tomorrow the tracheotomy promises a small step in the right direction. I feel a bit easier.

I never feel like going to my dancing lesson now. Somehow it seems selfish to do something so free and enjoyable while Dad is suffering and cannot move. But he wouldn't see it that way, so I make myself go. The dancing school is nearby. Once I'm there, the concentration of it gives me a rest from feeling so upset about Dad.

I love dancing. As usual, it's physically demanding and that's good. It brings me into another reality, away from the sadness and frustration of every day. The various dances allow the expression of different feelings—from the wistfulness of the waltz to the sensuous rumba and bolero and the fun of cha cha, mambo and salsa.

Dancing makes me feel alive. I end every lesson with aching feet and a lighter heart. And it's sheer pleasure to dance with a top professional dancer who knows how to help you find your own style.

My teacher Chris Michaels and his dancing partner and wife Joanne Middonte run the Arthur Murray School. They are clever, artistic, modern young people and we know each other well after ten years. They are very family conscious and sympathetic about what's happening in my life now. Rather than talk too much about it, they focus on making my dancing experience interesting and enjoyable.

I will sleep better tonight. I've been told I can ring the night sister any time but I don't ring during the night in case the sound wakens Dad.

DAY 16, TUESDAY 20 JUNE 2000

The day begins well enough, with some expectation of relief for Dad. Rev. Ross Weaver comes in the morning, after doctors' rounds. He is a reassuring presence. It's good of him to come—he's fitting us into his visits to the nearby public hospital. He talks to Dad, tells him he's looking better. Dad rolls his eyes in disbelief. Ross says a prayer and shakes Dad's hand before he leaves. The man-to-man gesture is just right, giving Dad the dignity so difficult to maintain as a dependent patient in a hospital gown.

The lack of a pastoral care team came as a rude shock to me. It represents an appalling failure in professional care, especially in an acute unit like Intensive Care, dealing with life-and-death issues.

Kind and caring as they are, medical staff cannot be expected to provide psychological, emotional and spiritual support for patients, relatives and staff. Pastoral carers are specifically trained to do this and are widely recognised as being a crucial element in the hospital healthcare team, so why has that been neglected in this prestigious hospital?

The scheduled time for the tracheotomy approaches. I leave, promising that I will be back later. I'm surprised to learn that they will do it here, in Dad's room.

I go out to shoot an introduction for this week's *Australian Story*.

I ring Gosford Library to explain why I have not been able to return Dad's books on time. I ring Dad's neighbour to tell him that Dad will not be back soon and will not be able to do the end-of-financial-year work for the body corporate, as he has done for years.

On the way back to the hospital I buy a new pillow from the baby shop because the first two have got lost—thrown out when they changed the sheets, I suppose.

I have felt some lightening of my spirit in the last few hours but the day ends in disappointment. When they make the incision for the tracheostomy, Dad starts to bleed too much and they have to abandon the operation. They keep him sedated for the rest of the day.

In the evening, a visit from the doctor who did the heart surgery. He says he will do the tracheotomy tomorrow, in theatre, with a general anaesthetic.

Go to the dentist at 9.30, then straight to the hospital. Dad is in theatre. I sit in the waiting room and, after half an hour, I hear a bed being wheeled along the corridor.

I get a look at Dad as he goes by, still unconscious, but a good pink colour and, at last, his mouth free of the tube and the ties. It's a while before they get him settled and I'm allowed to go in. It's a long while before he starts to wake and, when he does, he is confused and tearful. We explain to him what has happened, that he is now breathing through a tube in his neck but I think he cannot take it in. For him it is yet another in a long series of painful, difficult invasions.

At regular intervals, sister disconnects the breathing tube from the valve embedded in his trachea, through an incision in the base of the neck. She feeds a finer tube down through the tracheostomy tube to suction fluid from the lungs. As always, this makes Dad cough violently and go purple in the face; he must dread it happening over and over again, as it has, every couple of hours, for the last seventeen days.

The full extent of the damage to his mouth is now evident. Terrible, raw, sore splits at each corner of the mouth—and what looks like severe ulceration inside his mouth. It must be so painful, yet another torment. Sister paints his lesions with cotton buds dipped in solution. Then she raises him a little, in order to clean his teeth gently with his toothbrush. It has to be done very carefully so that no liquid goes down his throat. He is still not allowed to swallow any drink or food. He is fed through a naso-gastric tube which leads up his nose and down his throat into the stomach. He does not seem to be in pain but he seems wretched and I wonder how much more he can endure, and why his suffering cannot be alleviated more effectively.

Day 18, Thursday 22 June 2000

Today Dad is more conscious but keeps his eyes closed. They are attempting to wean him gradually off the respirator. They vary the amount of oxygen according to how much he can breathe on his own. The machine measures his breathing capacity and produces, on a monitor, figures which change from minute to minute. He is preoccupied by shortness of breath which he has to indicate with sign language. He is not happy today but, during periods when the breathing is satisfactory, he attempts writing. One tortuous message, with many false starts, reads eventually: 'Why can't I talk?'

I ask them to explain to us. It seems that the breathing tube, leading from his mouth through the trachea to his lungs, has been pressing on the vocal cords for the last eighteen days and the cords have to learn to work once again. Apparently this requires the insertion of a different valve, and the help of a speech therapist, and will not be attempted for a few days. I'm not sure why. It is a big disappointment and perhaps he feels they have let him down because he was told that a tracheostomy would allow speech and we both assumed, wrongly, that meant it would happen right away. Surely it would have been better to explain to him, beforehand, the likely sequence of events, to save causing unrealistic expectations and distress?

The tracheostomy also presents a new problem. The breathing tube protruding from Dad's neck is attached to the tube leading to the ventilator itself by a joint. Each of the tubes is inflexible and unwieldy and any movement of the head, neck and torso puts a strain on the joint so that frequently it disconnects, causing a noisy rush of air, and has to be reconnected. I am amazed that it is such a primitive, unsatisfactory arrangement—that it has not been streamlined years ago. The disconnection happens time and time again. It is startling and adds frustration and aggravation to all the other suffering.

There is a moment when we all stand around Dad's bed—the specialist, the registrar and the nursing sisters. Tethered to the ventilator, still unable to speak or eat, in every way helpless, Dad's eyes move from one to the other, questioning, waiting for answers, for liberation, to be allowed to breathe for himself, to speak, to move, to eat, to smile, to regain some independence. But no one can give him any satisfaction. They all seem like big, inept, well-intentioned children. They are doing their very best for him with their technology but still it is dreadful for him.

He is still alive but they don't seem to know what to do next—how to get him out of the predicament into which their sophisticated intervention has led him ... how to make his life tolerable, comfortable. They have invented a cornucopia of mechanical and electronic marvels but seem to lack the common sense to make the marvel bearable. They've demonstrated that it's possible, with massive surgery, to postpone or even to thwart death—but at what cost? Who is monitoring the psychological and spiritual effects of all this cleverness on the patient and on the medical staff themselves—or do they become, in self-preservation, emotionally desensitised to the human impact of some of their interventions?

Dad approached open-heart surgery trusting in the judgement of the specialists who suggested it. But to what extent did he make a fully informed decision? I believe he accepted it as a gamble, but naturally he hoped for success. I was with him when he agreed to the surgery and, although there was a warning that success could not be guaranteed, there was no description of the myriad of complications that could follow and that are now eventuating. He could not give consent in advance to what's happening to him now because he was not informed of all these possible outcomes. No one described what his post-operation challenges would be like, for him.

I am not seeking to blame anyone. But I do question the degree to which a patient has anything like fully informed choice in making a medical decision of this kind.

My father has the stoic courage which is the emblem of his generation. Like others of his great age, he was raised not to complain. He does not like a fuss. He and so many of his contemporaries had Spartan childhoods. They have lived and fought and struggled their way through two world wars and a catastrophic economic depression, as well as the personal challenges that come in the course of a long life. In a manner that is unusual today, they accept that suffering is part of the experience of being human, to be endured with dignity, patience and not much discussion.

'Everyone gets their turn.' 'Kindness in another's trouble, courage in your own.'

I recall that, the night before the surgery, he was holding my hand tightly and I thought that he must be feeling apprehensive. I told him that sometimes, when I feel anxious or frightened, I have a cry and it's a relief. He replied that, if he did cry, he hoped it would be in private.

Most of the time Dad is wonderfully patient. He appreciates what seems to be his only pleasure—having his teeth cleaned. The split corners of his mouth remain open wounds. Dad is managing a hard situation with courage, as ever, and poise, which takes some doing, in his dependent situation. I feel despondent that I cannot stop his suffering, but also proud of him, learning from his bravery, and, in a way that I do not understand, exalted by his acceptance and dignity.

His urine catheter is changed today and he is started on some treatment for thrush which is causing him terrible irritation— yet another unforeseen torment as anyone will know who has experienced it.

Tonight he indicates that he wants to write. His hands are weak, his eyes unfocussed. His efforts to write put tension on the tracheostomy tube joint, causing it to disconnect, time after time, so that it has to be reconnected, time after time. It is maddening and stupid. Dad is half-sitting up at an awkward angle. I put the writing pad into his left hand and the pencil into his right hand and try to untangle the lines bringing a blood transfusion and painkiller into the cannula on the back of his right hand.

He keeps rearranging the angle of the writing pad, turning it over and over, and trying to close his swollen fingers around the pencil. It is frustrating for him but he perseveres in silence, since he can make no sound. I am crying inside for him, in a rage of inadequacy, as I watch his effort. I don't want to show him how I am feeling because I think it won't help him. If I portray calm, it might give him the solidarity to bear this unbearable detention that seems to have no prospect of ending. If I let him see my horror at his plight, he might be undermined and doubt whatever reservoir he is drawing on to bear this ordeal. My intention is to keep him company as best I can, to be there, to support him, to question the medical staff, to get them to explain things to him, to win some meaning from this agonising situation in which we are caught.

I will never know if I was right or wrong. It is what I have decided is best at this time, today. More likely it is all I can manage to do. There are moments when I want to run away and I am ashamed of that cowardice.

This is the cruellest test of love and I am finding something new in myself to make me stay. Or is it the grace of God that's helping Dad to endure and me to stay?

It takes him about half an hour to write his message, one slow, poorly formed letter after another. Some of them I have to guess at. I read each one out to him as he writes it. Finally he lets the pencil slip from his fingers and turns his head away, exhausted. As he does, the joint disconnects yet again, with an infuriating, noisy rush of escaping oxygen, and when the nurse has put it back in place, yet again, I read his message back to him: 'Please take me out back and shoot me'.

There is no response I can make. I know he means it, that his life in this condition is not worth living. I feel a wretched sense of failure, that neither I, nor they, can stop his suffering. His message seems more a cry for help than for death. Neither he nor his father would have let an animal suffer so long without putting it down. Sometimes I do wish he could have the peace of death, rather than this suffering.

A TOUGH LIFE

Dad could be tough. I remember one occasion when we were out shooting rabbits and foxes, he instructed me to shoot my own dog. The hound had no kelpie in him and was quite useless about the place.

I found it difficult to keep a steady barrel.

Dad could be a softie too. When my pony Bobs, a long-time favourite with us kids, went missing, we mounted a search. Bobs normally grazed in the homestead paddocks and not far from the stables where a feed of chaff was available.

At last Dad and I came across his body. His legs were tangled in a five-wire fence, a section of which was partly down. There was evidence enough that he'd thrashed about to escape, but in vain. He had died of thirst and hunger. I could not restrain my tears and I noticed some moisture in the Old Man's eyes as well.

DAY 19, FRIDAY 23 JUNE 2000

When I arrive, I am surprised to see Dad sitting up in a big chair beside his bed, with his various lines and tubes attached. He looks extraordinarily frail and insecure but it's wonderful to see him upright. It takes a minute or two for me to see that his mouth is brimming with blood. He is trying not to spill it. I tell the sister but she doesn't seem to have a solution. The nurse from the next cubicle, Gerard, has come to call on us. He offers a suggestion, a mouthwash, and they order it from the pharmacy. They call the doctor to come and see if Dad has bitten his mouth or has a jagged tooth. Eventually the mouthwash helps but it can only be used if Dad's head is tipped forward so that he doesn't swallow and can spit out the blood and the mouthwash. He waits patiently for us to help him, although he must be astonished by how long it takes.

Rev. Ross Weaver comes to visit, and Sr Monica, as she does faithfully each day. The physio is here, a doctor, two nurses and the technician has just arrived to do his daily chest X-ray. The professional opinion is that Dad is quite a bit better today but he doesn't seem to agree. He is very low. The doctor explains everything to him. It helps. The more awake he becomes, the more aware he is of his condition.

With a phone call to Gosford I establish that the wonderful community care people have taken Mary to the eye doctor for a check-up after the cataract surgery. I should be there to support her but I cannot do it.

In the course of the day Dad takes a very long time to write us a few messages, 'Why I can't talk?', 'I can't see too good', 'I like a shower' and 'I want back to bed'. I am misled by his readiness to communicate and take it as a sign of improvement. So I am very disappointed when, in the early evening, he writes his last painstaking message for the day, in a shaky hand.

'Sometimes I despair whether ever better.'

At the end of this mighty effort, he drops the pencil and, as he turns his head away, the ventilator joint disconnects with a noisy rush of air. His message is not a request for reassurance but a statement of fact. And I can well understand it. The obstacles to any return to normal strength, health and independence seem insurmountable from here. He is very ill, very weak. His privacy is gone; he is constantly the centre of attention which he does not like. And he is always having something done to him—the dreaded lung suction and coughing spasm or an injection or enforced exercises or a dressing changed or the awkward, humbling discomfort of using a pan.

It's seldom peaceful as the monitor beeps are a constant aggravating interruption to any rare period of quiet. One of the male nurses, Phil, is patient and kind and explains to Dad that soon he will be able to have a shower and to talk. He knows how to make him more comfortable.

I have accepted an invitation to go out to dinner tonight and to hear a talk. Everyone says it's a good idea. I wonder if I am spending too much time with Dad and getting on everyone's nerves. I ask sister if I'm overdoing it. She says that, while it's not a problem for the staff, they think I'm getting overtired and there's a long road of caring ahead.

The evening out is not a success. I don't hear a word of the speech. And I feel mean eating out when Dad hasn't had a meal for nineteen days. I worry about him all the time—whether he has a night nurse he knows, whether he's getting any sleep.

When I arrive, Dad is sitting out in his chair, with his feet propped up in white, pressure, knee-high stockings. He is calmer today, more conscious but seems to be accepting. He tries to follow the exercises suggested by the physio but has little strength. When she's gone he writes 'Glasses' and I hand them to him. We experiment with his reading glasses and then his long-distance pair. He can't put them on and off unaided. He seems to have trouble seeing but takes twenty minutes to write a message which might say 'Long-distance OK for TV'. After an hour in the chair he writes 'Fed up. Back to bed.' But they want him to stay up for longer, to bring into play muscles that are very weak from too much lying down.

Late in the afternoon his nurse is helping him and talking to him: 'Mr James, I'm just going to give you this injection in your tummy. Is that alright? It's the one you usually have at this time.'

She is Chinese, a little difficult to understand. But suddenly he manages a tentative smile, as though he's just remembered how it's done. I could weep at his courage. I feel like crying out: 'This brave man is my father. He's teaching me the lesson of my life.' But I just smile too.

We listen to an episode of *As Time Goes By* on audiotape. There are frequent interruptions for treatment or monitor checks so it's not very successful. He likes to hold my hand, like a child, but not for long.

When he reaches for his writing pad, it's a plea for air: 'Some fresh please fresh air'. I can't imagine what it's like, breathing through the tube, not through your nose. It must be strange, especially in this transition period where his lungs are getting stronger but the ventilator machine still supports his breathing. He probably finds the airconditioned atmosphere too still, claustrophobic. He's a great devotee of fresh air and open windows. It's unnatural to feel no movement of air on your face, to hear no sound of a bird.

When it's time for the change of shift at 7 p.m., Dad is still troubled by his poor eyesight. The two sisters ask him some specific questions about what he can see. He looks from one to the other and holds up three fingers and they all laugh at the joke, although in Dad's case the laugh is silent.

The doctors and nurses are telling him that he is much better but his written response conveys his dissent: 'I am dumb and I cannot see'. At least it is encouraging that he does not write 'I am choking' or 'This tube in my throat is unbearable'.

This evening I have a surprise for him. I have kept it till now to make a small, pleasant break in his dreadful routine. His sister Gwen has sent a beautiful wooden cross, carved in a soft wood by Sr Angela, whom he knows from the mud-brick monastery at Stroud. It is curved to fit comfortably into the palm of your hand. It is a holding cross threaded onto a leather thong and, as soon as I give it to him, he tries to put it over his head, to wear round his neck. But it's not possible because of the tube leading to the ventilator and the ties round his neck that hold the tracheostomy in place and the lines embedded in the veins in his neck. So we loop the thong around his forearm and he holds the cross in his hand. He looks comforted to have it. We have never discussed religious beliefs or faith, so I don't know what his views are. I'm just guessing but as I start to read Psalm 121, his body seems to relax a little. When I kiss him on the forehead to say goodnight he doesn't open his eyes but lifts the hand holding the cross slightly off the bed. I pray that he will get some sleep tonight.

With the Lord at your right hand
The sun will not harm you by day
Nor the moon by night.

DAY 21, SUNDAY 25 JUNE 2000

It's Val's birthday. We have decided to take lunch up to Gosford to see Mary. She seems fine, recovered from the cataract surgery and pleased to see us. She doesn't ask much about Dad. She rings the hospital herself each day and talks to the sister on duty.

It's late afternoon by the time we get back to Sydney and I get over to the hospital. Dad is sitting up in his chair. He is depressed. He indicates he wants to use the alphabet board. His head is turned to one side—he seems to see better out of one eye than the other. With a pencil, he points slowly to one letter, then the next, to spell out a message. As he selects each letter with the pointer, I write it down on a pad. The pointer slides too easily across the laminated board and we have quite a few misunderstandings about which letter he is indicating, especially as he is not seeing the letters clearly. At last the message is plain: 'I want to end this sorry farce'.

I don't know what to say to him but I feel that I should let the doctors know, in case they want to take his wishes into account when making their treatment decisions. It takes a while for a doctor to come because he's helping other patients. In the meantime Dad gets to work with the writing pad and pen. It takes him a long time to write: 'It must be bleeding obvious that I want out. Some money for a gun and anonymity.'

I suppose he means oblivion. It's very understandable but still it gives me a bad shock. We've all been encouraging him and wanting him to fight for life and recovery. But maybe he's only trying so hard in order to please us when, in fact, he's had more than enough. Dad has never sought special attention, nor resisted the inevitability of death, which he expresses as 'putting down your knife and fork'. And I wonder if he disapproves of all this technological intervention to keep a man in his nineties alive while people in other countries have so few medical resources. I don't think he would approve. I wish we could talk about it.

The doctor arrives and I show him Dad's messages. He sits beside Dad and goes through everything with him—his condition, the treatment, the prospects: soon he will be able to speak and maybe eat some ice cream and gradually he should feel stronger and better.

As the doctor speaks Dad looks at him with trust and two slow tears run down his dear old face. He's at the end of his tether. When the doctor has finished, Dad motions to the alphabet board and points out 'Thank u doc'.

One of the male nurses, Steve, has asked to care for Dad tonight.

'I know what makes Mr James comfortable,' Steve says. 'The other night he woke up and I turned him and gave him a back rub and he was straight off back to sleep. Not a problem.'

Dad seems to feel secure with Steve and I feel alright leaving after a long day and an emotionally painful evening. Thank God another interminable weekend is over. It is three weeks since Dad's surgery.

Day 22, Monday 26 June 2000

Dad is restless. It must be terribly disappointing, at the end of another long, exhausting, hospital day not to be able to escape into sleep.

The splits at the corners of his mouth are slowly healing. How astonishing the body's capacity to regenerate is. Dad is onto a new phase now in his relationship with the ventilator. Sometimes he spends periods when he is not attached to the machine but receives a constant spray of oxygen through a mask placed over the tracheostomy in his throat. It creates a constant rush of air and is quite noisy. At other times he is reconnected to the machine for extra support. It is a process of weaning which may take some time. Obviously this is a source of confusion because Dad writes one of his laborious messages. His writing is all over the place. Big, angular letters trail into each other and pile one on top of the next. I decipher 'If heart now OK why tube?'.

It's a good question. The challenge of the breathing problem and the poor state of his lungs almost make me forget this all started with heart surgery. That now seems the least of the problems.

Today we have a new intensivist to get to know. He'll be here for the next seven days. He's a professor. He's nice and very interested but he's a bit inclined to talk to me and the staff about Dad, rather than explain directly to Dad. I have the sense that technically he's very experienced but that he cannot imagine himself into the patient's situation. Of course I may be wrong.

Without explaining what he's going to do, he removes a valve from the tracheostomy and places two fingers on Dad's throat near the vocal cords.

'Try to say something, Mr James.'

Dad tries but no sound comes. He tries again and only a strangled sort of gargle emerges. Dad looks up from the chair, puzzled and alarmed at the sound he has made. The professor replaces the valve and says they'll get a speech therapist to come and help Dad get his vocal cords working again. It's disappointing but Dad takes it patiently. Perhaps the one sound he did produce gave him a glimmer of hope.

The professor and his caravan move on. Dad gets back into bed and we are left with sister to get on with the many routine procedures of the day. The physio comes. She's a tall, young, animated Englishwoman called Nea. Dad knows her and likes her. He rolls his eyes as she coaxes him into breathing exercises and movements of arms and legs.

After she leaves Dad, I am standing outside his cubicle talking to her, finding out all I can about how he's progressing. He's unaware that we are watching him as he lifts one leg a good height off the bed and holds it there. Then he lowers it and raises the other one. He does a few of these. It's quite a comical sight since his thin legs are encased in white support stockings. Next he moves on to raising his arms. We're both impressed that he's found the energy and the determination to persevere with the exercises on his own.

Things improve during the long day. He is weary but trying very hard. In the early evening we listen to an episode of *As Time Goes By* on tape. It's not so funny just hearing it but he manages a wan smile or two. The sister who comes on duty at seven o'clock is very organised and brings a comforting air of calm into the ward. I feel relieved by her presence and her serene expression and go home in peace. I hope he will sleep and perhaps have pleasant dreams of happier times.

Schooldays

We generally walked to school, joined by other kids along the way. Sometimes we were driven by pony and sulky and, when the creek was up in flood, we rode our ponies. The little one-teacher public school was located down the creek, about one and a half miles from our homestead. Here, my father and his brothers, and much later, my sister and brother and I received our early instruction. The enrolment at any time would not have exceeded twenty pupils.

In those days, most kids were barefoot and complaints of kicked toes were many and tearful. Mum was sympathetic enough as she comforted us with kind words and Zambuk ointment. Dad sometimes was not so patient and would say: 'Don't be such a big calf'. But I don't think we howled as loudly and plaintively as calves do, in need of their mothers. Sometimes the mail coach returning to Mudgee from Hill End would coincide with our homeward trek from school. It was a big coach, drawn by four horses. This was an opportunity for a lift, if you were quick and nimble enough to clamber onto the back of the moving coach. It was a precarious exercise. The coach driver, Bert Spratt, wielded a whip, long enough to flick his leading horses. If the afternoon shadow of the coach revealed a couple of non-paying passengers clinging on desperately at the back, he would increase his speed and then flip his whip around the back of the coach to dislodge us. Bert won most of these contests as we stumbled off onto the dusty road, bruised but at least well ahead of our pedestrian mates.

I guess we were happy, playing along Grattai Creek; pelting down the mud nests built with such ingenuity by swallows (what barbarians we were then); skinny-dipping in the ponds on hot days; eating the unripe quinces growing along the banks, then complaining to Mum of bellyache, to be promptly cured by a large teaspoon of castor oil from the blue bottle. Now, eighty years on, living urbanly, I know we were lucky too, running free and close to the natural order of things.

I did not know it then, but there were tougher times ahead. In 1918, Dad sold most of Grattai. Factors necessitating the sale included drought, rabbits and the not-so-gentle insistence of the bank. What a wrench and a heartbreak it must have been for my father and his father whose family home and property it had been for eighty years.

DAY 23, TUESDAY 27 JUNE 2000

Dad had another bad night and is exhausted when I arrive. Madeleine is nursing him today. They get on very well. She's excellent with him, really interested and intuitive. We have talked together quite a lot. She can imagine herself into what he is enduring and respond with sensitivity. She is firm and competent.

He manages an occasional smile. He accepts the ventilator by now, how I don't know. The split corners of his mouth are almost better. We try an episode of *Dad's Army* on tape. It's silly but I am trying to find distractions for him and ways to pass the long, difficult hours.

I have to leave quite early because I have a speaking engagement at the New Children's Hospital. I was invited months ago to spend the evening with a support group for parents who have lost their children. It's raining hard and I'm not sure of the way. I feel a bit exhausted and wonder if I have anything to give them, anything of value or relevance. As it turns out, the evening is a gift for me. They are just the right company, because of their experience of suffering.

I begin by telling them what's happening in my life. It's all familiar to them. We are immediately on common ground. I have planned the evening to include short inputs from me, interspersed with time for private reflection with music, and conversation in pairs or in small groups. My purpose is to facilitate the sharing of each other's stories; and an opportunity to describe their situation and how they are finding a way to endure—or not. When you are suffering, nobody can understand and listen to you better than a person who knows their own suffering.

People tell me it's rare to find someone who listens. I agree. When it happens it helps—not because the listener can stop your sadness or heal your hurt or tell you what to do. I think the value lies in just being with a person, being prepared to hear their hard experiences, providing a time and space for the wounded psyche to express its suffering and for that pain to be accepted as legitimate. I have an evocative collection of black and white photographs[4] depicting many and varied situations in nature and the human condition. I spread them out on tables so people can browse among them and choose one or two of the powerful images as symbols of what's happening in their lives and how they are feeling about it. One which is often selected shows a parachutist falling before the 'chute has opened; another is a solitary climber; there's one of a masked face; another of miners carrying an injured workmate. Many people choose pictures of railway lines criss-crossing in confusion or skid marks running off a road. Some identify with the new tendrils of a fern or sprigs of fresh growth after a bushfire. Apparently the appeal of a photographic images lies, not in the literal scene necessarily, but in what chord of recognition it strikes in the imagination of the observer. It's almost as though the pictures choose the searcher.

I invite people to take their time, to wander round without talking and to respond instinctively rather than to make it an intellectual exercise. Then they sit with their pictures and, only if they want to, tell two others sitting together in a group for fifteen minutes what their chosen pictures mean to them.

The photographs and the structure of the exercise provide a way into the possibility of conversation in a more acceptable way than an invitation to sit down and talk straightaway. I always present it as a choice—to take part or not; some may prefer just to sit and reflect on their own. Most people join in.

I generally take part myself and find tonight that it helps me. This is one of the few occasions when I've had a chance to tell someone about what's been happening these last three weeks.

Their stories are harrowing. How can anyone endure the suffering and loss of their beloved child? And yet, that's what they are enduring. There is no remedy for it, no answer that satisfies or gives solace. There is only companionship. Indeed the only gift of suffering I can think of, at the moment, is the gift of knowing how to be with another suffering person. And perhaps how not to be, as well. In meeting these parents tonight, I hear they don't want to be told that it's God's will or that time will heal or that they are still young and will have more children—or that their dead child is mercifully free of her suffering now.

It doesn't sound very significant but I see tonight that bereaved people value their experience of a support group like this one. I've heard others say they find solace or distraction in the unquestioning devotion of a pet or in taking the risks of a challenging sport or in gardening or sewing, music, prayer or swimming.

The two social workers who've organised this gathering have also provided a home-made supper. Some of the participants have brought a plate as well. It's exactly the right way to round out our evening together. During the long, rainy drive home I feel uplifted by their company. And not for the first time, because this is what I've been doing, as well as my *Australian Story* work, for the past three years. I've been invited all round the country to gather groups together for a day or an evening of reflection—in clubs and homes and outback community halls, to share our stories, our experience of life, our hard-won wisdom. It's been a wonderful journey.

DAY 24, WEDNESDAY 28 JUNE 2000

When I get to the ICU Dad is sitting up in his chair and has done a rough sketch which he presents to me with a smile. It shows him under the shower. How Madeleine could have kept him upright on a chair in the shower I cannot imagine, but she has and it's the first really good thing that has happened for him in a month. He is very pleased. Normally he would never go a day without a shower, let alone a month during which he's had only what he would describe as 'a thorough wash'—uncomfortable, embarrassing.

She has also cut his fingernails and given him a foot massage. She says he is to have a rest today. He does not seem upset. His cardiologist from Gosford calls on him and this is another highlight in his day, even though Dad cannot speak. For the first time I feel a bit of calm and hope. I go back to the baby shop to get some new small pillows to fill in the gaps between the hard hospital pillows.

DAY 25, THURSDAY 29 JUNE 2000

I send an apology for today's meeting of the Women's Reconciliation Network. It's Caillin's birthday, Louisa and Richard's eldest boy. I'm a sort of godmother to their family. I have sent him a card. I cancel a meeting with colleagues planning a corporate seminar on listening. I can't concentrate on anything else just now. I do some phoning to let various people know how Dad is going.

I will not present *Australian Story* this week because the British prime minister has agreed to do it. Our story subject is Peter Thomson, described by PM Tony Blair as 'spellbinding ... the person who most influenced me'. Thomson contradicts any easy stereotype of the pious priest. He smokes, drinks, swears and has a raucous sense of humour. His radical notions were too much for the Australian Anglican Church establishment in the 1960s. They sacked him. But Thomson's ideas were subsequently put into action by Tony Blair in the famous 'Third Way' of new Labour.

Now Peter Thomson has returned home to rural Victoria, to establish an Australian version of his Community Action Network, promoting and connecting groups involved in so-called social entrepreneurialism with the business and social sectors working together. Brigid Donovan has produced a strong story with a good current affairs edge.

Dad has had a bad night but today he is using the alphabet board well and seems to like the new pillows.

DAY 26, FRIDAY 30 JUNE 2000

End of the financial year and normally Dad would be busy getting his banking and other jobs done, at home. But today he is not interested in the outside world. He is fed up but trying to do exercises. He can stand very precariously, with two strong helpers, and has even taken a step forward with nursing support.

The care is wonderful and I feel very grateful but the daily X-ray shows that Dad probably has pneumonia. He is still unable to speak or to eat, being fed through the naso-gastric tube but he writes me a rough note at 1.30, 'U go for lunch', which I do, in the staff canteen, with Maria from Angiography. She has nursed in ICU and I can ask her about it.

In the evening, with friends to a Sydney Symphony Orchestra concert. Stirring music but I hardly hear it because I am worrying constantly and feeling helpless. I never relax. Beauty has lost its power to call me into joy.

Back home, as I hear the eleven o'clock ferry, I hope Dad is asleep and open his diary to read another chapter.

JOSEPH BENEDICT CHIFLEY
PRIME MINISTER AND TREASURER 1945–49
CROOKWELL, NOVEMBER 1946

History records several memorable events during the month of November. Remember Guy Fawkes and his fireworks on 5 November 1605; the cessation of firepower on 11 November 1918; not forgetting Gough fulminating about 'Kerr's cur' on 11 November 1975. But indelibly etched in my mind is a day in November 1946.

I was in my office in Crookwell, a small town in the Southern Highlands of New South Wales, some thirty miles north of Goulburn. I answered the phone. 'He's here!' It was the excited voice of Stan McCauley. Stan was the proprietor of the Commercial Hotel, where I was then residing. He had told me at breakfast that the prime minister was expected that morning for a brief visit and would be calling at the Commercial Hotel.

Ron Chudleigh, the long-time, sole public accountant in Crookwell had died the previous July. Protracted negotiations with his estate had delayed my acquisition of his practice. I had just then (November) taken over the office and staff to find some hundreds of unfinished, overdue income tax returns requiring my urgent attention. Clients were becoming fearful of penalties for late lodgement and I was equally concerned about defection of clientele and loss of goodwill.

I lost no time in covering the hundred or so yards to the pub. Its only bar was crowded, noisy and blue with tobacco smoke. Stan and his wife Neta were busy serving beers and there, surrounded by several locals, was the unmistakeable Ben Chifley, a glass in one hand and his pipe in the other. Stan spotted me, came around and introduced me to the PM. Ben was then sixty-one years of age, an imposing figure with a steady, confident gaze and a firm grip.

We chatted for a few minutes and, when an opportunity occurred, I drew him aside and explained my problem. He listened carefully and then said, 'Well, my boy (I was thirty-nine), you can have until 31 May next year to lodge your returns without any penalties'. What a relief! I hope I was not too profuse with my thanks. He joined me in a soothing ale and I returned to the office with the good news.

I recall advice from my father years ago: if you have a problem, always ask the top banana to fix it. Well, Dad, I could not have gone any higher on this occasion and am forever grateful for Ben's understanding and quick no-nonsense response.

I am indebted also to Stan McCauley for his vital help. He remained a good friend during our sojourn in Crookwell, often reminding me that 'happiness comes from within': presumably from the heart and the mind.

We beavered away during the next six months, lodged all the returns and did not lose a client. Good old Ben! Our encounter was brief, productive and pleasant and I cherish it.

Joseph Benedict Chifley was born in Bathurst in 1885, the son of a blacksmith. He received little formal education. He said many years later, 'I would rather have Mr Menzies' education than a million pounds'. He was an avid reader and on one occasion when asked what he wanted to be when he grew up, he did not hesitate: 'A member of Parliament'.

At the age of fifteen, he went to work in the Bathurst loco shed. He climbed the ladder and at twenty attained full engine driver's rank. In 1914, in defiance of the papal decree—no mixed marriages—he wed Elizabeth, daughter of George McKenzie, a staunch Presbyterian. The marriage took place in the Presbyterian Church at Glebe, Sydney, probably in an attempt to allay sectarian controversy, rife then and for fifty or more years afterwards.

Ben and Elizabeth continued to attend separately their respective churches. By all accounts their married life was happy; there were no offspring. Ben was overheard to say during his time in parliament, 'The Catholic Church does not consider me as one of its favoured sons'.

Chifley took an active role in Bathurst local affairs, such as the ambulance, the fire brigade, shire business, union matters and, of course, politics. Twice he was an unsuccessful candidate for the federal parliament seat of Macquarie.

Chifley regained Macquarie at the 1940 elections with R.G. Menzies as prime minister and leader of the United Australia Party. But united it was not. Dissension caused Menzies to resign in August 1941, to be succeeded by Fadden, who was defeated in October 1941. Then Curtin became prime minister and our nation's wartime leader, with Chifley as federal treasurer.

By 1945 the war had taken its toll on Curtin. Exhausted, he died that year and Chifley became prime minister and treasurer. He was the natural and obvious choice as successor, having been Curtin's right-hand man and of enormous help in the darkest days of the war.

Chifley proved to be a great leader, honest, direct, visionary and a wise chooser of first-rate men, for example, Dr H.C. 'Nugget' Coombs. Not a great talker but a doer, he inaugurated the Snowy Mountains Hydro

Electric Scheme in 1949. In 1955 Menzies referred to the scheme as 'a living memorial to the courage, enterprise and drive of Mr Chifley'.

Chifley's government was returned at the 1946 general election. However, his attempts over the next couple of years to control the private banks led to the defeat of his government in 1949 and the restoration of Menzies as PM.

On 13 June 1951 the Jubilee of the Commonwealth Parliament was celebrated in Canberra. As Leader of the Opposition Chifley spoke in the House and added his welcome to the distinguished guests. Apparently he was not well enough to attend the state dinner that evening or the ball which followed at Parliament House.

He returned to his room at the Kurrajong Hotel, where he always lived when in Canberra, eschewing the ostentation and comfort of the Lodge. That same evening, at the height of the revelry at Parliament House, the music was silenced and some time between 11 p.m. and midnight prime minister Menzies announced the sudden death of Ben Chifley. He said: 'I suggest that tonight's festivities end and that we leave quietly with sorrow in our minds and hearts for the passing of a fine Australian'.

And so with the death of Joseph Benedict Chifley on 13 June 1951, we lost our only genuine prime minister from Federation to this day. That night the 'light on the hill' flickered and has been dimmed ever since.

I have relied on L.F. Crisp's political biography of Ben Chifley for some details.

DAY 27, SATURDAY 1 JULY 2000

Weekend. Unfamiliar staff.

Dad is cranky today and frustrated by our inability to interpret his sign-language communications. Finally we realise that he would like a haircut and a shave. He has a shower, walks a few weak steps, with much help, and exercises, as well as he can, with the physio. The professor visits and explains to Dad why he still has the tracheostomy and still cannot eat or speak. He seems to accept the explanation, although it is terribly disappointing. I give him a foot massage. He communicates to me, by sign, 'Can't you sit down?'

He is breathing quite a lot without the ventilator and not coughing too much. And his eyesight may be a bit improved.

DAY 28, SUNDAY 2 JULY 2000

I dread Sundays. Another long day with staff we do not know. I have bought a new pair of slippers to try to interest him but he can't fit them on because his feet are still swollen. I will need to change them. Today Dad is breathing fairly well on his own, frequently off the ventilator. He is not in the mood for communication. More likely he lacks the energy for it but manages a note: 'Pls fresh air pleas'.

There are no windows that open. To my surprise, they say that he can go outside even though it's mid-winter. It's very exciting but it takes a lot of preparation. We wrap him in blankets, ease his swollen feet into warm socks, put on his tweed cap and manoeuvre him into a wheelchair. With an oxygen cylinder in tow, on wheels, we set off along the corridors, accompanied by his nurse. I have tied a silk scarf round his neck to hide the tracheostomy tube. When we wheel the chair into the lift to go down, Dad is facing a big mirror. It is the first time he has seen himself for many weeks and his eyes widen in alarm at what he sees. He seems very shocked and just keeps staring at the gaunt face which is himself and yet not himself. I look away to give him privacy.

When sister backs the wheelchair out of the lift, we traverse the wide, pink granite foyer, past the giant floral arrangement. After so little variation in his surroundings for a long time, it is all a bit overwhelming for Dad. When the automatic front doors of the hospital slide open he feels, for the first time in twenty-eight days, the surprise of cool air on his face.

His eyes open wide and he breathes in deeply as though he cannot get enough of this unaccustomed luxury. He is utterly absorbed in breathing. It is very cold. We find a sheltered corner under a bare wisteria trellis. He tilts his head back, motions for his cap to be removed and opens his sore mouth to the warmth and healing of the sun.

I sit beside him but out of his eyeline so he will not see my tears. It is a wonderful and pitiable moment which will stay with me forever because, unconsciously, he is showing me how I should treasure the gift of every breath each day of my life. Being in the open air for that half-hour gives me some slight hope that there may be a future for him beyond hospital. I wonder if he thinks that too, or if he has enough on his hands just surviving, moment to moment, in his severe incapacity. When the oxygen cylinder is almost spent and we have to return reluctantly to the ward, Dad motions us to put his cap on back to front. We get it immediately. He's doing a Lleyton Hewitt.

I am in awe of his capacity to lighten his ordeal, and mine, with humour. Dad has told me before that it's important to enjoy every day of your life. I wonder how it is possible to enjoy some of these days we spend together. But time and again, he and the doctors and nurses who care for him, show me the way. His approach to suffering brings out the goodness in most of them. Of course, some are less gentle, less sensitive, less able to put themselves in a patient's position and save him any pain or discomfort. And I am too vigilant, perhaps, acutely alert to any sign of carelessness, and ready to point it out as diplomatically and quietly as possible, to cover my interior anger.

DAY 29, MONDAY 3 JULY 2000

Thank God it's a weekday again, back to something like normal. And it turns into a good day because the speech therapist enables Dad to make a decent sound for the first time in a month. It's achieved by attaching a different valve to the tracheostomy tube. I think it has the effect of allowing some air to be exhaled over the vocal cords to allow them to work. He doesn't have a lot to say because, I think, he feels so weak and sick, but it's a relief to know that, at last, he can speak. It will give him more control.

I get enormous pleasure out of it because I will not have to second-guess his needs and worry that I may be misinterpreting or missing things altogether. The professor working today as intensivist is very pleased with Dad's new ability to speak.

DAY 30, TUESDAY 4 JULY 2000

My day to introduce *Australian Story*. Putting on television make-up seems trivial when I am keen to get to the hospital. But the professional discipline is good for me and, in normal circumstances, I'm very glad to have this job. It's remarkable to me that I still have on-camera work at my age and I am grateful to the program's executive producer Deb Fleming for her confidence in me. She's very understanding about the family problems of any of her staff. All the more reason not to bother her with them unless it's crucial. I haven't missed a commitment yet and I'm quite certain Dad would hate it if I did, on his behalf.

After filming, I have a quick lunch with a friend who has recently lost her beloved father and can appreciate what I'm going through. We are both only daughters and it's good to be able to speak unguardedly about our experience.

Back at the ICU, Dad is not well. He has pneumonia. They have performed an operation to introduce draining tubes into his lungs again. There are containers of liquid, stained with blood at the end of each drain, standing on either side of the bed. Poor Dad, how much more can he bear?

Yet, later in the day, he is quite upbeat with his talking and asking to see Mary.

DAY 31, WEDNESDAY 5 JULY 2000

Dad is quite ill in the morning but, as the long day wears on, he has a haircut and a moustache trim and improves a bit. I am glad to tell him that Mary will be down tomorrow. He requests the speaking valve and tells me that he'll be glad to see her although the visit 'won't be a success'. I guess he is thinking of his weak voice and Mary's deafness and that it will be a strain. He also issues me some instructions to do with the body corporate where they live. I take it as a good sign that he is able to be bothered with such things. He seems a bit better in the afternoon especially as Madeleine, one of his favourite nurses, is looking after him today and they understand each other well.

I need a facial treatment and I am looking forward to it in a way. But when the beautician starts to massage my face, her touch is so kind that I start crying and cannot stop. She has been through a lot of personal difficulties and she understands and is patient.

DAY 32, THURSDAY 6 JULY 2000

Madeleine on duty with Dad again today. She will help to make Mary's visit work well. Dad has had a good sleep on a hefty dose of sleeping pills but is cranky. Is it because the more conscious he becomes the more he understands his plight and feels his pain and dependence?

Her kind neighbour puts Mary on the bus near home and I meet her off the bus at St Leonards and drive her up to the hospital. She seems very small and frail. I have been told to warn her about Dad's condition and appearance and all the tubes, monitors, lines and so on. But she doesn't really listen and doesn't show too much alarm when presented with the sight of Dad. I go away for a while to give them private time together, in so far as that is possible with all that's going on in an Intensive Care Unit.

Mid-afternoon, I put her on the bus for home where she will be met. Dad is absolutely exhausted. In the course of the day he has talked, had a few sips of beer, walked a few steps, laughed, inasmuch as he can make that sound, and now he is at the end of his tether and working hard to breathe.

I feel relieved that he has seen Mary and knows that she is managing alright at home on her own. I ring in the evening, as usual, to check on her and give her any news. She handled the big day well.

DAY 33, FRIDAY 7 JULY 2000

Dad is so tired. He is mostly off the ventilator, using an oxygen mask over the tracheostomy. It is pretty noisy. Occasionally they judge that he needs to go back on the ventilator and, once it is attached, he seems to strive less with his breathing and sometimes goes off to sleep right away. It is a huge relief to see him having a natural sleep, if only for a short time. He seems to have the weariness of years on him, from relentless insomnia, let alone his current ordeal.

As I sit with him, I am darning some of his socks. It's a calming exercise. His pressure stockings are open at the toes which sometimes feel very cold. Dad is too cold and then too hot.

Wimbledon's on the small TV screen above his head. Rafter beats Agassi in a magnificent contest. Normally Dad would enjoy this but he just isn't up to it.

DAY 34, SATURDAY 8 JULY 2000

Agency staff again. One of them has misinterpreted a note to 'remove catheters', taking out the urinary catheter instead of the lung drains. Which means Dad has to suffer the pain of a new urinary catheter being introduced. One careless mistake increases my father's suffering. It makes me feel murderous. Dad needs a rest today and is kept on the ventilator much of the day. Sometimes he sleeps.

For some reason I remember him giving a speech at his eightieth birthday—the shock of hearing him refer to me only once, and as his 'progeny', in the course of a long speech. His generation believes that you do not praise your own offspring lest they become conceited. He would often stand back, appraising me, and find something to criticise. It was his way of showing affection. In recent years he's tried hard to respond when I said I needed him to express his approval and love more openly.

At family gatherings Dad is always the centre of approval, adored and warmly encouraged by two beautiful younger sisters.

I think of all the things he has taught me, both consciously and by example … Dad diving through a wave like a dolphin (we called them porpoises when I was young), giving me courage to follow, to put my head down in the water, swim hard and catch a wave back to the beach. Dad pouring a beer, perfectly. Dad advising 'nil bastardi carborundum'—'Don't let the bastards get you down'. Dad disapproving, going quiet in the presence of a boy or a man I liked, withdrawing into cold reserve, devastating. Dad's love of the bush, plants, birds and the landscape. Like many country people, he loves the land and cares about what is now termed the environment. He was passionate in defence of preservation of a local wilderness area nominated for building development. It must be appalling for him to be imprisoned indoors for so long and never to see a tree.

'DEVELOPMENT'

The council boys moved in with saws, mulchers and plenty of noise and demolished the big tree out the front. Sad to see it razed after nearly fifty years association with it.

Dad gives me a warm smile today.

The 'Woodies' win the doubles brilliantly. Venus Williams beats Lindsay Davenport. Uncharacteristically, Dad doesn't care.

DAY 35, SUNDAY 9 JULY 2000

Another good outing in the sun, accompanied by oxygen. Dad makes the very best of it. Sometimes he manages a weak smile and does not seem agitated. But when his surgeon calls to see him, he finds the energy to use the speaking valve to say: 'I wish that I had never let you anywhere near me!' There's no mistaking his anger. The surgeon's expression is noncommittal.

Later, short of breath, Dad goes back on the ventilator. He rests immediately. He falls asleep for a little while until the joint disconnects and wakes him. I wish the doctors would try it themselves. If they had to put up with even two hours as a patient, I'm sure a solution would be found very quickly.

Day 36, Monday 10 July 2000

The speech therapist comes and Dad does some speaking but finds it hard to concentrate and doesn't seem too impressed with his progress. Breathing alright but he is very, very weak.

Di, one of the porters, speaks to me on my way out along the corridors. She has got to know Dad and speaks warmly about him. She is very sympathetic for what he is going through. I think that he has quite a few admirers for his dignity and courage to put up such a brave fight.

Day 37, Tuesday 11 July 2000

When I arrive Dad looks different. He has decided to have his moustache shaved off. I have never seen him without a moustache before. His upper lip looks red and has some cuts above it. I curse myself for not buying him a better razor. I have been getting disposable ones, through ignorance, believing the staff were using his electric razor. It must have been painful having such strong hair cut with an inadequate razor and I feel ashamed. Unnerved too. I wonder what this shriving means but I don't ask.

A close friend calls to receive some instructions from Dad about his affairs. What does it mean? He is not in very good form today and has to stay in bed. He is breathless. Does he feel that he may die soon? I can't ask him that.

Day 38, Wednesday 12 July 2000

Mary comes down on the bus again. Dad is not up to much communication but I hope it's good for them just to be together, even with no privacy or normality.

A ROYAL VISIT

The 31st day of January 1988 was a gala occasion for Gosford and a memorable day for the James household.

Brisbane Water was sparkling in the warm sun and alive with aquatic activity as Prince Charles and Princess Diana approached by launch from Pittwater. Following a civic reception, the royal cavalcade drove to Terrigal where they were to be entertained by a surf carnival.

Every point along the way was lined with people. Mary says Charlie waved to her as they went by Number 3, York Street. I don't know about that, but bravo anyway.

Some hours later the royal procession returned down our street and categorically—as the politicians say when in doubt, there was no question—Diana smiled and waved to me as she passed by!

About four o'clock, when the euphoria had subsided, we sat down with our Royal Doulton and had a nice cup of tea—Earl Grey, of course.

DAY 39, THURSDAY 13 JULY 2000

Dad has had a sleepless night, woken by the constant disconnection of the ventilator tube. Nevertheless, he seems in pretty good spirits today and submits to his tedious routine with a good grace, although very tired and often short of breath.

DAY 40, FRIDAY 14 JULY 2000

Last night *Australian Story*, produced by Caitlin Shea, featured Nene King. Loud, controversial, generous, she dominated the women's magazine market for a decade as editor of *Woman's Day* and *The Women's Weekly*. The best quote from the story was one of her own: 'Look, you either loved me or hated me. I had staff that would die for me and staff that would want to kill me. I became the dragon lady of the nineties.' Her own life has been almost as eventful as those she documented in her magazines.

———

This morning Dad is very restless. His bed is in turmoil and looks a bit like a rat's nest, except everything is clean. The sister on duty does not have the gift of creating order and peace but she is probably a good nurse.

Dad likes his privacy and not too much talk. I can imagine this constant exposure to a procession of people doing intimate and often painful things to him is hard to take and must require strong self-discipline. He is remarkably gracious. When he is able to speak he always says 'Thank you'. When he can't, he manages to raise a frail hand in acknowledgement.

Late in the day he asks me to arrange for his solicitor to visit him to arrange power of attorney. Is this another intimation of death or just a prudent precaution or both? He has also asked me to be certain that the reason for death recorded on his death certificate is heart disease. Apparently this is recognised by the Department of Veterans' Affairs and will ensure that Mary is entitled to a war widow's pension.

'It's very important,' he says. I promise.

DAY 41, SATURDAY 15 JULY 2000

The dreaded weekend again. The day gets off to a bad start when Dad's naso-gastric feeding tube falls out while he's having a shower. In my mind I blame yet another strange nurse who doesn't know Dad.

It will be painful to have a new feeding tube pushed up his nose and down his throat into his stomach but they decide not to do it and he is encouraged to eat by mouth. With a tracheostomy in the throat, this is an art to be learned. It means keeping your chin tucked in, so you can swallow past the breathing tube. He has a good try at it, tackling some soup, custard, jelly and yoghurt.

In the afternoon he is pleased to have a long-overdue visit from a podiatrist, Joyce. His toes are becoming black and need careful attention.

It turns out to be not such a bad day, as Saturdays go.

This evening's sister on night duty makes a long journey to work by train several times a week from the country. She creates order out of chaos but for some reason Dad groans when he sees her.

She just smiles. Only they know what it's about. Two strong personalities testing each other perhaps? Physically he is forced into dependence and it must take a lot of will to assert himself in such a weakened state. This is a constant challenge for old people. I see it all the time when I am with Dad and Mary—in the shops or when they're driving or in restaurants. One day when we were eating out together, the waitress, standing in a long-suffering pose, pen poised over her order book, asked me, 'Have they made up their minds yet?'

Sitting with Dad today, for some reason I remembered the gut-wrenching occasions when he had to be retested for his driving licence. After the age of eighty-five, this happens each year. The first couple of years he breezed through, so on the third occasion he thought it would be the same, but after a rigorous half-hour test the female examiner failed him. He was devastated. After seventy years of careful driving with an unblemished record and a gold licence, he was issued with L plates, told to have some lessons and come back in a week. The next seven days were full of anxiety but when he was tested again he got 97 per cent and had his licence restored.

I am fascinated to see, in his diary, that after his own account of this harrowing experience, he has written another entry—from the point of view of the testing officer:

THE DRIVING LICENCE

Thursday 8 December 1994

Just another day on the job, mostly on the road, which I prefer. Tested six, failed three. Doing my bit to smarten up sloppy driving. Felt rather sorry for one old chap. His medical said his angina and arthritis under control; no other problem except may need glasses. This Brian, dignified and sprightly enough for his eighty-eight years, was nervous but trying not to be. He drove slowly over our exit stop sign, a quick minus. I put him through all the hoops. He tried some small talk. I did not encourage him. He made three more errors, not alert enough.

When I told him, back at the office, that I'd failed him, he was dumbfounded for a moment or two; most of them are. He protested. I gave him a learner's permit and some L plates. I told him he could try again next week. He walked away, obviously shaken. A week's suspension will do the old boy good.

Thursday 15 December 1994

Old Brian again. Very uptight, very formal. We did the same course. He performed it perfectly. The computer gave him 97 per cent. His relief was palpable; they are never too old to learn. I restored his licence and said 'See you again this time next year'.

I have the impression he is not looking forward to it.

DAY 42, SUNDAY 16 JULY 2000

I cannot help thinking of 'Forty days and forty nights, thou wast fasting in the wild ...', the words of a traditional hymn I half-remember.

Dad's ordeal seems interminable yet there are infinitesimal signs of improvement some days, like today. He has done a sketch to show that Sam helped him to have a shower this morning which I know he enjoys very much. The rare pleasures in this difficult situation must shine like beacons and be a profound relief from pain, discomfort, weakness and dependence, which are hard for anyone, let alone a self-contained, capable man like Dad. I wonder if he feels that his dignity is being diminished. He is tolerant of all the hardships. He smiles when he can. He is eating something occasionally. Samantha is a very experienced and reassuring ICU sister. I think she is the most senior.

I have been to see a film with Val at Roseville cinema but I can't remember what it was. My mind was back at the hospital and so was I, around teatime.

DAY 43, MONDAY 17 JULY 2000

I am amazed to see that they have taken the tracheostomy out of Dad's throat and covered the hole with a dressing. I am thrilled, thinking it is a great sign of progress but Dad is noncommittal. I have to stop myself from asking him how he feels about every change because it is exhausting to have to explain everything. I try to pace myself to him and take my cues from him. I feel that he is not quite the same person as he was before the open-heart surgery.

I have heard about this phenomenon and, if it is true, then it is not surprising. The miracle is that anyone survives such an onslaught at all. It must be the most dislocating shock, not only to the body but to the psyche, the emotions and the mind. Also Dad is taking many medications and some of them will be permanent from now on. This must affect a patient's ability to function physically, to think clearly. And Dad has told me, on previous occasions, that he has not felt well for some time after blood transfusions. He has received so many in the past six weeks and that would be having an effect as well.

While Dad is very good in social situations and excellent in the give-and-take of conversation I think that, like me, he is predominantly introvert and deals with things internally, keeping his own counsel, rather than needing constantly to discuss everything. He observes, he is a shrewd judge of character, he does not rush into acquaintance or friendship. He is strong-minded and there is an authority in his presence that you would not trifle with—even in this depleted state.

The removal of the 'tracky', as everyone calls it, is apparently the prelude to going to the ward tomorrow. This is a significant turning point, one I thought we would not achieve. I am very pleased about it but Dad is reserving judgement.

DAY 44, TUESDAY 18 JULY 2000

The last thing I wanted to do this morning was shoot the *Australian Story* introduction because I needed to get to the hospital, but I do want to keep all my work commitments going. I know that Dad would be upset if I did not. ('Get on with your own life!') He's never demanding.

Helen Grasswill produced the story of Helen Barnacle. It's a dramatic one: twenty years ago, she received the longest drug-related prison term ever imposed on a woman in Victoria. Before her case was heard, she discovered that she was pregnant. When her daughter reached the age of one, the rule was that the child could no longer be kept in jail with her mother. Helen Barnacle won a landmark decision to overturn this and kept the little girl with her.

Sixteen years later, the story has a happy ending. Helen Barnacle is a successful musician and psychologist and has a close and loving relationship with her daughter.

It is late morning when I finally get to the hospital. I have already made a list of what needs to be gathered up to make the move to the ward, in case it all happened before I got there, but it did not:

overnight bag packed with clothes, pyjamas etc.
2 pr glasses in their cases
1 mohair checked rug
1 sheepskin underblanket
1 green pillow, 2 pink pillows
1 pale grey radio
1 jar brown sugar (for porridge)
1 upper dental plate
notebook and pencils/pens
toilet bag
electric shaver in black case.

Dad is sitting in a wheelchair with all his belongings piled onto a second chair, ready to roll. But his bed in the Cardio-Thoracic Ward is not yet ready so we wait quite a long while. It is awkward waiting and unexpectedly emotional when the time comes. We are leaving people on whom his life has depended, quite literally, for the past six weeks. That's a very long time to be in Intensive Care. They have saved Dad and cared for him in extremis and come to know him very well. I think most of them like him and admire him and are surprised by their achievement, and his, in making it this far. You say 'Thank you' but it's so inadequate for what they have done.

Although it has also been a chamber of horrors for Dad, it is an environment which has become familiar to him and the move has psychological difficulties that I had not foreseen. He just manages to hold himself together as we set off in the two wheelchairs but there are tears in his eyes and some of theirs too.

In the ward he is wheeled into a private single room, 102, with its own shower and toilet, wardrobe, refrigerator, pictures on the walls, a chest of drawers and a view of another hospital wing and a slice of sky. The biggest change will be a loss of security. For six weeks he has had one-to-one, round-the-clock nursing. Now that is finished and he has to share the available staff with everyone else on the ward. It's very different. A little more privacy perhaps, but less personal support. It's not going to be easy. We unpack and find a place for things. He sits out of bed in a chair and we start to get to know a new set of people. But they spend less time with us and they are always in a hurry.

Dad is weak and quiet. He is offered a drink with dinner and has a beer without much enthusiasm. Sister is trying to create a more normal atmosphere than the ICU and brings in some small bottles of brandy and whisky to offer. Very kind.

Dad has been fitted with a smaller tracheostomy tube, perhaps to keep the passage open in case it may be needed again. We watch a bit of the evening news on television but he is not very interested, even though we are moving towards the Olympic Games in only two months time. Normally he would have plenty of opinions about the preparations, who was big-noting themselves and so on.

The intensivist doctor calls in on his way home from a long day in ICU to say hello, and Dad is more than usually pleased to see him—a familiar face.

I stay a bit later than usual, until he has made sure he is written up for a sleeping pill. This takes quite a long while because we have to wait our turn here among all the other patients' needs.

We read Psalm 121 as usual and I make sure the buzzer is within his reach and hope that someone will come, without too much waiting, when he calls during the night. I go reluctantly out into the cold of a bitter night and I can't sleep wondering if he's alright.

THE BLUE MOUNTAINS

When we had to leave Grattai, it was a wrench for all of us but it must have been most difficult for my parents. We went to live at Lawson on the Blue Mountains. I remember the day train trip. It was December 1918 and hot. We had to wear masks when travelling because of the bubonic plague.

Although not in disarray, family finances seemed to be tight. Instead of sleepy Grattai Creek meandering through well-grassed paddocks feeding sheep and cattle, we had deep gorges and rugged escarpments and not a sheep or rabbit in sight. So what to do? Well, we kids, in our wanderings, discovered boronia, waratahs and flannel flowers. They were not plentiful and when sighted were growing on some barely accessible cliff side. The wonder was that we didn't break a limb or suffer a snake bite on those inhospitable ridges and deep ravines as we clambered and slithered to collect the blooms.

Anyhow, we hauled the flowers to the Great Western Highway and offered them to the passing motorists, not many in those days, even at weekends. Business was poor and the revenue meagre. The actual peddling of the blooms was really difficult and distasteful for us, diffident and shy country-born kids. But I suppose we were boosting the family coffers, however modestly.

At Lawson another chore came my way. The stationmaster was some kind of family connection. He would arrange for large lumps of coal to fall off the backs of the train engines. Fortuitously these mishaps occurred opposite his home and ours, which were not far apart, in the same street, running parallel to the railway line. Winters were cold on the mountains and it was really a tough but necessary job gathering the coal for our grates and stoves.

DAY 45, WEDNESDAY 19 JULY 2000

Dad's solicitor comes to arrange a power of attorney for him. Bill is wearing a well-cut black overcoat and represents the normality of an outside world which is now quite out of reach for Dad. Bill is shocked by Dad's appearance but tells Dad he's looking good, which neither of them believe, but men keep up appearances with each other. At least they have privacy to discuss things that may now seem urgent to Dad.

Later in the morning I meet Mary off the Airbus. She is confident now about her regular trips. The visit is a success, although Dad is very weak. In the evening he sips a beer, plays with his dinner which is well prepared, gives most of it to me, watches the news headlines and, exhausted from the exertions of the day, looks forward to a sleeping pill and hopes for a decent sleep.

His life has been drawn in now to the confinement of his sickbed in this small room with windows that do not open. I hope

Petrea was right when she said that his strong spirit can soar above the imprisonment of his diminishing body. If the kindness of sleep comes, I hope that he can roam freely in his dreams.

LEAVING HOME

We were at Lawson for four years, 1918–22, during which the balance—some 2500 acres—of Grattai was sold. At the close of 1922 I had completed three years at Parramatta High School gaining what was then called the Intermediate Certificate. I had an undistinguished career at Parramatta except in sport, where I gained some notoriety. I was elected captain of the Fifth Grade Rugby team. We played in the Metropolitan High Schools competition. The one match I'd rather forget was against Hurlstone Park Agricultural College. I played 'breakaway' and early in the game at Pratten Park, my opposite number, a heavy Fijian youth, came around a scrum and we met head on. I was concussed and saw out the match vaguely and mistily from the sideline. We were thrashed 66 to 0!

My recollections of high school are not happy. Long days, sooty train travel on the long daily journeys to and from the Blue Mountains, knickerbockers, scared of teachers, short of pocket money et al. I have a photo of my class of 1922 at Parramatta High. It is a reflection of another time. Life then was lived earnestly and seriously. Frivolity was frowned upon. The photo shows the unsmiling faces of some thirty students and our form teacher, all of us looking solemnly, almost fearfully, at the camera. Of course then we were disciplined at home and at school; no overt smoking, no covert drugs and plenty of homework. We were taught writing and spelling. We added and divided and multiplied mentally, no calculators then. There was no time or place for bodgie subjects. School holidays were heaven-sent.

But were we happy? I think so. The world was less crowded and much safer. Our parents were dedicated to their families and less inclined to indulge themselves or their offspring. If this sounds like a plug for 'the good old days', so be it.

When Dad announced that he had bought a dairy farm in the Hunter Valley he asked if I would prefer to continue school or join him on the farm. I hesitated but not for long. At the age of sixteen, in 1923, I began a career as a more or less unpaid cowhand and farm labourer.

In December 1922, before finishing high school, I had put my name on a list for recruitment to the state public service. After about twelve months on the dairy farm I had resigned myself to a life of milking cows twice a day, seven days a week. It was a steady job alright. Out of the blue came advice to report to the Land Board Office at East Maitland to be employed as a junior clerk, the first rung on the ladder in the public service.

This put the family and me into a flap. But it was decided that I should go. I was seventeen years old, a diffident yokel, ill-clothed, downy-faced and self-conscious about acne. It was a wrench leaving home and my happy family for the first time. I felt bad deserting Dad and his farm. In fact, I never returned permanently. That parting was the first step on my way to becoming a reluctant bean-counter.

DAY 46, THURSDAY 20 JULY 2000

Dad is very weak today. He is sitting out of bed in a big chair in which they have made him comfortable. For a while, a bit of sun comes in onto him. He has no appetite.

'I'm buggered,' he says and I can barely hear him. 'I'm not sure I can go on much longer.'

In a bid for normality, I put on a tape of piano music in the evening and pour a whisky for him, and one for myself.

I was supposed to be at the Police Academy at Goulburn today and tomorrow, teaching listening skills at a leadership course but I have cancelled it. I cannot bear to leave Dad. I hate to let my colleagues down but I am not crucial to the occasion.

Several of Dad's men friends are asking to visit him but he says 'No'. I think he does not want them to see him in this state, or maybe he doesn't have the energy to sustain conversation. They are disappointed and so am I, but he knows what he can manage.

DAY 47, FRIDAY 21 JULY 2000

In the morning a long drive to attend Letty's funeral at St Joseph's, Rockdale. She was a much-loved colleague from the *Search for Meaning* days at the ABC. I wrote about her in *An Authentic Life*, in a chapter on grace. The page is marked, in my copy of the book, with a postcard Letty sent me from Poland where she was on a long-anticipated journey with two of her beloved sisters. The card shows the magnificent, ornate chapel of the famous Black Madonna.

Letty has written to me: 'Dear Caroline, This is the altar of the chapel of Our Lady of Czestochowa, Queen of Poland. We were blessed, my sisters Elena and Aurora, in having attended Mass and staying for a whole day's pilgrimage in this Holy place. Love, Letty.'

I know what joy she would have had on that journey and in the company of her sisters. As I wrote of her originally:

She was the least paid in the section and, in spite of her maturity, the most junior in professional status. Yet her presence brought to a tense workplace an air of courtesy, gentleness and humanity, from which everyone benefited.

She had brought up a large family and nursed a beloved husband until his death. She had a listening ear; she gave everyone the benefit of the doubt; she could do seven things at once with quiet competence and she remembered all our birthdays.

She was a woman of devout faith who lived out all the human virtues, without ever preaching them, in ordinary daily life. Each afternoon, when she left to catch the crowded suburban train home, she took with her an element of serenity that would be missed until her return next day. No doubt her gentleness was equally treasured in her own home.

Like most gracious people, she seemed quite unconscious of her effect. Perhaps that is part of the gift. [5]

The Requiem Mass was poignant but made beautiful by the singing of the choir with whom Letty had sung for many years, and the reassuring conviction of the familiar liturgy:

Priest: Trusting in God, we have prayed together for Letty and now we come to the last farewell. There is sadness in parting but we take comfort in the hope that one day we shall see Letty again and enjoy her friendship. Although this congregation will disperse in sorrow, the mercy of God will gather us together in the faith of Christ.

Come to her aid, O saints of God
Come, meet her, angels of the Lord.

Response: Receive her soul and present her to God, the most high.
Priest: Give Letty eternal rest, O Lord, and let perpetual light shine upon her.

Response: Receive her soul and present her to God, the most high.
Priest: Into your hands, Father of mercies, we commend Letty. We are

confident that, with all who have died in Christ she will be raised to life on the last day and live with Christ forever. We thank you for all the blessings you gave her in this life to show your fatherly care for all of us and the fellowship which is ours with the saints in Jesus Christ. Lord, hear our prayer; welcome Letty to Paradise and help us to comfort each other with the assurance of our faith until we all meet in Christ to be with you forever … Letty, may the angels lead you into Paradise.

Who would not long to believe such a glorious promise? And, after seven weeks of forgetting God, in the consolation of the Requiem Mass, I can pray with heartfelt faith, for both Letty and my father.

ABC friends gather outside the church in the bleak wind, dressed in our unusually formal clothes. Black flatters only Chrisula, in a soft, velvet hat.

～

Back at the hospital I do not mention the funeral to Dad. He has had a wonderful time outdoors in the sun, wrapped up against the wind, with his favourite physiotherapist, Nea. He does not mind the wind. It's the fresh air he pines for. I see them together as I approach from the carpark. She is standing behind him to secure the wheelchair and they are laughing, with their heads back. It's a joyful sight that gives me hope. I go immediately to join them, to share the moment. Only later I wish that I had not because he has me all the time, and they looked so carefree in each other's company. She has been a principal encourager for him in his journey from being mortally wounded to this precarious new chance of life. She is lovely, tall, slim, straight and full of vitality and good humour. She has pushed and cajoled him to attempt exercise and he has resisted and wept and striven to respond. It has been a huge effort of will from both of them, a triumph of spirit over a broken, worn-out body.

Now there is a wretched, new problem, an awful nausea. He thinks it's from the mixture of too many medicines but, in their efforts at a cure, they only give him another injection which makes things worse. By comparison with what he has endured this is minor but it is demoralising; there is no respite from the feeling of being constantly on the verge of vomiting. It is curious that they are so ready to tackle huge problems, like repairing a person's heart, but often quite inept at relieving nausea which makes life miserable for the patient and can seem like the last straw.

DAY 48, SATURDAY 22 JULY 2000

We spend some time outdoors but Dad is still nauseated. I feel angry.

DAY 49, SUNDAY 23 JULY 2000

Last night when Dad was given his many medications to swallow, he just brought them up again. Poor man. He doesn't complain. Today they have revised his treatment and there will be fewer pills and syrups to take. He feels sick all the time. He picks at the meals but cannot eat. We go outside for a while, offering a distant glimpse of return to normal life some day, somehow …

DAY 50, MONDAY 24 JULY 2000

A good outing in the wheelchair to our usual spot under the leafless wisteria. Dad still miserable with nausea. No one has an answer. We learn that Nea will leave next week for a holiday back to England. Bad news for Dad. I think she is important to his recovery. They seem to be kindred spirits and I think he will miss her very much.

DAY 51, TUESDAY 25 JULY 2000

When I tell my friend Jenny about Dad's plight she suggests ginger tea and slippery elm. We try it and, for the first time in days, Dad gets some relief. Why don't the hospital staff know this remedy?

Jenny and I have been invited to Mudgee this coming weekend to give a day of reflection and a dinner talk. It's a long-standing invitation. I am quite uncertain whether or not to go. I don't want to leave Dad. During the afternoon he feels that his room is very stuffy and asks for a fan. A large one is provided and while I am helping one of the nurses to place it in the confined space we let it over-balance. It is big and heavy and it falls onto Dad's hand, lying in his lap, as he sits in his chair. It's a shocking moment.

He does not complain, although the paper-thin skin of his hand is broken and bleeding and there are probably broken bones. We seem to wait a long time for a doctor to come. Dad seems detached. I suppose it is just one more in a procession of torments which have come to seem inevitable. I feel as though I am suffocating.

Eventually the doctor comes, pronounces nothing broken, and uses a skin glue to patch the broken flesh and skin. Dad is impatient after the long wait to get outside in the wheelchair to get some fresh air.

He is able to take a step or two now, with a lot of support. He doesn't talk much but it is a great relief to know that he can communicate when he wants to, after those dreadful weeks of being silenced by the ventilator.

One day when two strong young male nurses had rearranged him into a new position, I overheard him say to them, 'I've never met so many kind people. Is it part of your training or how you were brought up?' One replied that it came from his home in childhood.

Jacinta, the sister-in-charge of this Cardio-Thoracic Ward,

produces a brandy before dinner. I wonder if Dad seems a little brighter. I put on a tape of piano 'dinner music' which he seems to enjoy. I still suspect that he is making the effort to please us because we all so much want him to get better. I hope that he will get some sleep.

SCHNAPPS AND PEPPERMINT

'There's a man to see you, a Mr Joe Simms.' I sensed from her tone on the intercom that Elizabeth's rating of our visitor was pretty low on the client scale.

'Did he state his business?'

'He said it was personal'.

'Alright, I'll see him, about five minutes.'

The agility and flexibility of the human mind is magic. Instantly it can switch from now to then, from here to there. In seconds it can encompass and envisage scenes and events of long ago. I looked at my report and the balance sheet before me but I could not focus on them. My mind leapt back to another time, another place; back fifty years to a small town on the Murray and to a young man named Joe Simms.

Then, circa 1930, we were an average group of young fellows living at Miss Sefton's boarding house. We were office workers in banks and articled clerks from accountants' and lawyers' offices. Joe Simms was head teller in one of the banks presided over by Mr Reynolds, an old (we thought), crusty manager, a stickler for the proprieties and typical of those times when banks enjoyed more public respect.

Simms was about twenty-one, tall, fair and good-looking. His manners were commendable and he dressed appropriately for a bank manager in the making. Joe was a top tennis player and modest about it. He was popular, especially with the girls, envied sometimes by the rest of us. However, those were our salad days, plenty of fish in the sea, no worries, no attachments, except to our jobs which were worth looking after then.

Recreation during the hot summer months was limited to tennis on the hard courts and swimming in the sluggish river. For the less energetic there was relaxation enough in savouring the Melbourne brew, but inhibited to a degree by a chronic and depressing shortage of funds. As Miss Sefton had first call on our meagre salaries, paid fortnightly, there were frequent intra-boarder borrowings of a few bob until the next pay day. Nevertheless, we enjoyed a few beers at weekends which began at noon on Saturday, and sometimes after work during the week.

Except Joe Simms, whose favourite fluid was schnapps with peppermint, tossed down as though he sought the effect rather than the flavour. We all liked Joe, who enjoyed a certain deference because of his seniority and position. However, some of us were concerned at his addiction to the 'Dutch drink' as we called it and the likely consequences. They were not far off.

One night there were four of us in Joe's room at Miss Sefton's, fairly bright after a session at the pub. We all smoked cigarettes. I saw Joe laughing as he lurched across the room to ash his cigarette through the window. There was a crash of breaking glass. He reeled back; blood spurted from the severed artery of his right arm. We managed to staunch the flow with his towel. Miss Sefton arrived, solicitous but not amused. We got him to the hospital not far away for some stitches and a bed for the night.

No work for Simms next day. News travels fast in small towns and when it reached the bank, Mr Reynolds' suspicions were confirmed; he had a teller with a problem. A few days later Simms was on the train to Sydney. We missed his cheery company and we were sorry to hear afterwards of his severance from the bank.

Suddenly I was keen to see him again; to revisit those carefree days we'd spent together in our youth and to find out what had happened since we parted half a century ago. I pressed the bell.

'Show Mr Simms in.'

'He's gone,' said Elizabeth. 'He left a letter for you.' She came in.

I hesitated before opening it.

'How did he look?' I asked.

'Seedy, down and out. He smelt of drink,' said the forthright Liz.

I opened the envelope.

'No doubt you've forgotten but here is the ten bob you lent me at Corowa in 1931, plus some interest. I doubted whether I could face up to a rerun of those Riverina days so I wrote this before coming in. I'm living up the country now. Regards, Joe.'

With his note was a five-dollar bill.

DAY 52, WEDNESDAY 26 JULY 2000

I meet Mary off the Airport bus.

The physios decide Dad can walk along the corridor to a sitting room where he can have lunch with Mary. Even though they help him, it is far too much for him and he feels crook by the time he gets there. The nausea returns and he is thoroughly wretched. So the visit is not a success and he is quite glad when we leave, I think.

In the evening, he is troubled by palpitations of his heart. He tells me that he doesn't think he can go on much longer.

DAY 53, THURSDAY 27 JULY 2000

With Dad's encouragement I have decided to keep my commitment in Mudgee for the weekend, leaving tomorrow.

'You can't let them down,' he says. He is partisan because Mudgee is his beloved home town. It's only a few months since the last of his many nostalgic visits and he instructs me on landmarks and people to look out for. When I tell him that the dinner talk will be at the bowling club, he immediately knows who will be doing the catering there.

'Watch out for Marge Large—she's a wonderful cook.'

He seems enthusiastic that I am going, almost as though he is coming with me. But I am reluctant to leave him for the weekend especially with strange staff on duty. I am concerned that if he does not keep up the ginger tea and slippery elm, the nausea will return. So I have written a notice in big letters explaining this and put it up behind his bed. I only hope that they will take the trouble.

Before I leave he tells me: 'I couldn't have got through this without you'.

I manage to reply: 'Me too'.

DAY 54, FRIDAY 28 JULY 2000
I have packed my gear for the trip and leave it ready while I go to spend the morning with Dad. More than ever, I am reluctant to leave him. He's very frail today. It will be the first time I have left him for a day, let alone two days. He asks what time I will be coming back on Sunday and I tell him lunchtime. He has a friend coming today, to help him arrange some of his tax affairs, I think.

'Have a good time,' he says.

'I'll miss you while I'm away.'

'Me too.'

I link up with Jenny at Sydney Airport and we catch an afternoon flight to Mudgee on a small Hazelton aircraft. It's a dramatic flight over the Blue Mountains, with the western sun glowing warmly on the great ramparts of the range and clouds piling into tall, smoky castles ahead of us.

Jenny works with Petrea King at the Quest for Life Foundation and is used to being with people in fragile, life-threatening situations, so she is good company for me this weekend. We work well together and she is great fun as well.

There is the usual warm country welcome at the airport. They have booked us into an attractive, self-contained house on the banks of the Cudgegong. I have known the name of this river from childhood, listening to Dad's longing memories of the Mudgee district. We want to get to the bowling club early to set up for the talk. A capacity crowd is expected. It's always rewarding going to the bush. Country people support events in their town and come from long distances.

It seems a peculiar coincidence that I am in Mudgee this weekend. I ask who has catered for our dinner this evening. Yes, of course, it's Marge Large and, yes, the dinner is splendid.

A few minutes before it's time to start my talk I'm shocked by the sudden pounding of my heart, high in my chest. I have had little spells of heart-racing in recent years but this is much stronger. My heart feels as though it is trying to get out. There is a doctor present among the guests who kindly has a look at me without drawing anyone's attention and makes a couple of suggestions. I assure him that it usually only lasts a few minutes.

Unfortunately this one lasts for a difficult hour and a half. Somehow I manage to get through the whole presentation in this acute condition. ('You can't let them down.') I'm surprised that people can't see it but apparently nothing seems wrong from the outside.

Everyone is responsive and I think the evening is a success. Eventually, when I sit down, the violent heartbeat returns to normal, just as abruptly as it began. Is it something to do with my anxiety about Dad? I take a note of people whose names and stories he will know, to tell him when I get back.

It's a very cold, clear night. You can see millions of stars here, very bright in a black velvet sky because there's no interference from the city lights. I feel exhausted but restless in a strange bed, sleeping in fits and starts.

Day 55, Saturday 29 July 2000

It's a beautiful morning in Mudgee. There's a mist on the long lawn, rolling down to the river at the bottom of the garden.

We spend a long and satisfying day with a big crowd, mostly women, who've come to spend a day of reflection on their lives. We share each other's stories and talk about the challenges of life and how we find the spiritual sustenance to keep going and to help each other. There's a wonderful resourcefulness in country people. They are prepared to do a lot for themselves and to make things happen. Women are fortunate because it seems easy for us to talk to each other about things that matter. I don't think it comes as naturally to men, so it's all the more touching when it does occur.

We have invited people to bring something which is sacred to them. It always opens the way into a rich conversation.

Someone brings a casserole dish because, for her, the sharing of a meal and friendship brings spiritual sustenance. Another shows us a little bag of wildflower seeds which she is going to plant with her grandchildren. As she speaks, we understand that this is her pledge to the future. A man holds up a jar of rainwater, the first after months of drought. That's sacred to him.

Someone has a quilt woven by Gran in the old country. She says the scratchy texture of it on her bare legs recalls the magic of story-telling time, faithfully observed every night of her childhood. Gran was always there for her, always had time and patience and love.

One man says he cannot actually hold up his 'something sacred' but here she is beside him—it's his wife.

Many of the sacred symbols are accompanied by stories of loss or suffering—they all seem somehow familiar.

A teenager brings two books which helped her through a depression.

A young mother, tired by the demands of three small children, presents a small teapot. She remembers her own mother getting up alone, early each morning to watch the sunrise, with a cup of tea and a piece of bread and butter. Now, with that same teapot, she has taken up her mother's custom, to find some peace before the onset of another busy day.

I bring a scarf printed with the honey-ant Dreaming, a gift from Aboriginal friends. I try to explain how my spirituality has been enriched by coming to know something of theirs.

As we tell the story of our 'something sacred', we share what is precious in our lives. Listening to each other, we fall into a natural reverence: individuality dissolves into an unexpected companionship. We may have arrived at the hall shy, not knowing anyone, but one story is echo to another and slowly it becomes clear that we know each other very well, in the common experiences of our human life.

In this simple ritual, we have stopped measuring time by the clock. The atmosphere in the hall deepens and shimmers as we make ourselves vulnerable by telling what really matters to us.

Apparently ordinary lives become radiant with meaning and purpose.

Nobility is revealed in the modesty of our daily round where we are striving to live a life of love. We are reminded that, against the odds, we are doing our best, and that there is dignity in that.

God is not always mentioned yet we are proclaiming the sacred in everyday life. We are finding a sense of connection and reassurance that, even in our loneliness, we are not alone—and that makes all the difference. Sharing responsibility for the gathering takes my mind off Dad and that's good for me. Maybe for him too.

This is an uplifting day where connections are made, some acquaintances show signs of developing into friendships and we end the day more buoyant and relaxed than we began it. The extended farewells over afternoon tea are a good sign that valuable seeds may have been sown.

Back at our riverside residence we have time for a short rest. I ring the hospital, talk to a sister I do not know and ask her to give Dad a message about Mudgee. She says he is fine but because I don't know her, I'm not sure what that means.

At an informal dinner with new friends, a woman called Victoria presents me with a touching gift. She was at the dinner talk last night and having heard of Dad's illness and his long association with the district, she has brought for him a lovely red river stone from Meroo Creek. She lives on land quite near Grattai, Dad's childhood home. I can't wait to bring it to him, although I'm not quite sure he will like the idea of it being removed. But I am very moved by Victoria's sensitive thought.

I can sleep better tonight as our work here is done and tomorrow morning those who invited us here will drive me an hour and a half to Dubbo to catch the plane home. Distance is no obstacle to arrangements in the country. I hope our visit has been a success and that Mudgee has enjoyed it as much as we have.

I'm looking forward to telling Dad all the things that will interest him about my visit.

DAY 56, SUNDAY 30 JULY 2000

The telephone rings, like an alarm, at 7.30 a.m. Jenny gets to it first and calls me to come. It's the hospital. Dad has had a cardiac arrest and they are trying to save him. I should come as soon as possible. But I'm in Mudgee, hours away. I won't be back until lunchtime.

I can picture what's happening because I saw what they did to Genevieve's husband in the ICU. Everything pushed back from the bed to give them room to work. It's rough and it can be life-saving but surely it's not what should be done to my dear Dad now, not after all he's been through. I can't bear to be so far away. Why did I come here? What a wrong decision it was, after all. I know they will do everything they can but what is it like for Dad? Is he conscious and struggling, in pain or unconscious?

The phone rings again. It's the intensivist on call this weekend. I think he's asking me whether to take heroic measures, if that is what Dad would want. I feel so sure about the answer. Dad has told me he would love to live longer, but not like this. If they save his life I can picture him once again imprisoned on the respirator, right back to square one, with the whole terrible uphill struggle ahead of him. It's not what he wants. I don't believe he wants any more tough things done to him to make him go on living. He's told us he wants to go, a number of times. Surely this is the time to let that happen, rather than force him to struggle on against all reason.

After the call finishes, I realise I didn't spell it out; I didn't say just keep him company, comfort him, hold his hand and help him to make his escape. I hope they will know to do that. The doctor has known Dad for all the time since his operation. He knows him pretty well; he has fought Dad's fight beside him. We have talked before about the right thing to do for Dad should this moment come.

It is time to leave Mudgee, to start the drive to Dubbo to catch the plane back to Sydney. The people driving me are very kind and understanding but I am overcome with sorrow and a desperate desire to be with Dad, not here. It feels strange and unbearable to be in Mudgee without Dad. It's only a few months since we had our last holiday here together. This is unreal. I am behind a pane of glass. What is happening to him now? It's so terrible that I am not there.

When we get to Dubbo Airport I phone the hospital; they tell me Dad died at 8.56 a.m. That would be just as we were driving out of Mudgee, past the turn-off to Grattai.

PART THREE

Through a Glass Darkly

July 2000 – June 2002

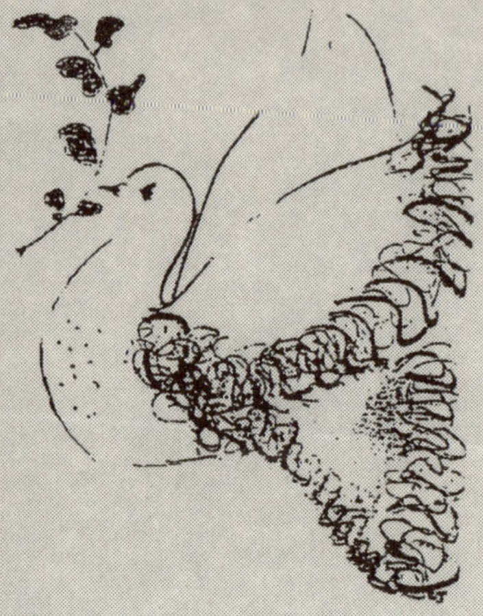

Brian Newman James
5 / 1 / 1907 - 30 / 7 / 2000

"I can see the hills of home…"

*Mary and Caroline
thank you
for being with us today,
to remember Brian with love,
and to give thanks
for his life.*

Psalm 121

A Song of Ascents

I lift up my eyes to the hills -
where does my help come from?
My help comes from the Lord,
the maker of Heaven and Earth.

He will not let your foot slip -
He who watches over you will not slumber;
The Lord watches over you -
The Lord is your shade at your right hand;
The sun will not harm you by day
Nor the moon by night.

The Lord will keep you from all harm.
He will watch over your life;
The Lord will watch over your
coming and going,
both now and for evermore.

An Irish Blessing

May the road rise to meet you.

May the wind be always at your back.

May the sun shine warm

upon your face;

The rain fall soft upon your fields…

And, until we meet again,

May God hold you in

the palm of His hand.

My father's funeral service booklet

On the flight back I feel limp, like a rag doll, but my mind is racing. What, if anything, did my trip to Mudgee have to do with Dad dying? Did my presence in his old home town somehow allow him to escape? Was it easier for him to die when neither Mary nor I were around, holding him back, consciously or otherwise?

Has the hospital let Mary know? I hope not, because she will be alone on a Sunday. I will phone two friends as soon as I get home and ask them to be with her so that when the hospital rings, she will have company. I cannot be in two places …

I will have to go straight to the hospital to make arrangements.

Oh for a brother or a sister now, to give some support and share the decisions.

At the hospital there was that customary weekend semi-deserted atmosphere. The door to Dad's room was closed and a sister I didn't know very well met me at the nurses' station and told me what happened this morning. Dad sat up in bed to have breakfast, but was discovered in cardiac arrest.

She said she was very sorry. She suggested that I could spend some time with Dad now and then make arrangements for his body to be collected by the funeral people. She came into the room with me. It was all packed up and looked uninhabited in the afternoon light. There was a pungent perfume and I saw that she had arranged several beautiful white lilies and irises in a vase. Dad was lying on his bed under the checked mohair rug we used to wrap round him to go outside. Mum and Dad gave me that rug many years ago.

The sister had wound a cloth around Dad's head to keep his mouth closed. That looked strange, like an old-fashioned illustration of a man with toothache. But Dad's face was peaceful, even relaxed, youthful—and he wore the hint of a smile, as though he had caught a glimpse of something pleasing. I wondered if he had seen the hills of home—hills to welcome him back into the landscape of his beloved childhood home at Grattai. The wooden holding cross had been placed on Dad's chest.

I wondered how they knew that he was dead. Certainly he was not breathing, but he seemed very present still. I talked to him, saying I was glad he had made his escape but that I would miss him. I could not believe that, after this, I would never see him again. We had been together all my life.

I had all the news of Mudgee saved up to tell him—that we had stayed on the banks of the Cudgegong, that Marge Large was still catering … I had been looking forward to talking everything over with him when he recovered.

There were no jobs to do. Nothing needed tidying. It was quiet, with the muffled sounds of the hospital coming through the closed door. I sat there with my hand on Dad's arm, under the rug. I had a feeling of victory that he was free at last but also a sense of terrible sorrow for all that he had suffered—and sorrow that I had lost him.

I couldn't think about anything much but had the strongest idea that he was still there … Was it his spirit that I was aware of? It was a real presence, familiar, normal in a way, like every day.

I was still very shocked that he had died. None of us had expected it, or at least no one had told me it was imminent. I stayed for quite a while, just being there with him, reluctant to leave him, as usual. But then I got the feeling that he was telling me to get moving, to drive up to Gosford to be with Mary. I wondered where the energy would come from to do that. I remembered him telling me it was important to enjoy every day of your life but I didn't know how I could do it today. I felt empty. It was the first time I had cried in his presence since the surgery two months ago, for fear of demoralising him. But I didn't think it could do any harm now. Eventually I got up, kissed him on the forehead and said goodbye. It was so hard to leave, knowing that I would never see him again. I couldn't take it in.

I went out to the nurses' station. I thanked them for caring for Dad after his death and the sister asked me if I wanted to take the rug and the cross. I left the rug with him because it was homely and familiar. And I kept the cross which he had held in his hand, to return to his sister, whose gift it was.

I asked to see the doctor on duty to check that Dad's death certificate was filled in as he had wanted. It was the young doctor who used to try to get Dad enthused about the golf on television. He seemed very low-key. They all did. They seemed disappointed that Dad had died. They had put so much effort into his recovery. I thanked everyone and Di, the porter, who knew Dad and was crying, offered to help me down to the car with all his things—the lambswool underblanket, the baby pillows, his clothes, glasses, notebooks, pencils, radio, jar of brown sugar for porridge, warm socks, shaver and toilet bag, books he never read, audiotapes, vases and X-rays. They filled several plastic bags on a trolley. It was sunny but there was a bleak wind in the carpark as we manoeuvred the bags into my car.

As I headed towards the freeway I was exhausted, but calm. I kept saying over and over, out loud: 'He's free at last'. Tomorrow would be the anniversary of my mother's death, thirty-one years ago—an odd coincidence.

THURSDAY, 3 AUGUST 2000

This morning, the morning of my father's funeral, I went out the back into his garden. I remembered one of many mornings we had sat there warming our bones in the sun. Two top-knot pigeons were pecking for grass seeds on the lawn in their restless way, the sun catching an exquisite pink burnish on their sinuous necks, bobbing and weaving, never still for a second.

A little further distant we could hear the murmurous cooing of doves. The sound took me back instantly to Hunters Hill, where I was a small child. But, at the age of ninety-two, Dad said that, for him, the doves had the sound of eternity. He said it, not as a sudden insight, but rather as the fruit of reflection. I wondered if this was one of the things he pondered in the long night hours when he couldn't sleep.

The image has stayed with me. Will we know the cooing of doves in eternity? Or is it that the cooing of doves brought us into eternity as we sat together in the morning sun? Is there just a thin veil between eternity and this everyday time which we call reality and measure anxiously with clocks?

At the Anglican service, in a hillside chapel, Dad's casket was draped with the Australian flag and a mass of wattle, banksia, boronia and Geraldton wax. It was very beautiful. The funeral people had created exactly what we had asked for. A lot of Dad's men friends came and stood around in their suits, talking together on the lawn of the crematorium.

During the service, we prayed Psalm 121. Mary recited the moving passage quoted by King George VI, in his Christmas broadcast, after the outbreak of World War II:

I said to the man who stood at the gate of the year,
'Give me a light that I may tread safely into the unknown.'
And he replied: 'Go out into the darkness and put
your hand into the hand of God. That shall be to
you better than light and safer than a known way'.

Two of Dad's tall, handsome friends escorted Mary, slowly and gently, to and from the lectern.

Mary adored Dad and must have been feeling bereft. But she hasn't put anything into words—not to me, anyway. She is very brave and perhaps does her crying alone. Together we have recalled happy memories of him over the last few days.

Another of Dad's close friends gave a eulogy, and I spoke to tell people that, at the age of ninety-three, after open-heart surgery, my father spent six weeks in Intensive Care, followed by two weeks in the ward; that he had suffered an ordeal during which he had taught me all I would ever need to learn about courage, patience, and surrender to that humility of dependence which most of us dread; that he had maintained his dignity, his graciousness and his sense of humour. None of them would have been surprised to hear any of this.

Helpfully, Dad had left a few succinct instructions about his funeral. He wanted Rev. John Price from Mangrove Mountain to conduct an Anglican service and he wanted to be cremated; we should not hold the funeral on a Wednesday because that would cut across golf appointments for his friends. Above all, he asked us not to be mournful, and we were not.

I was very touched that two of his long-time nurses travelled the eighty kilometres from Sydney to attend the funeral before driving back to start the afternoon shift. Both had tears in their eyes. One of them had been with Dad when he died and told me, with feeling, that his death was beautiful. She repeated that it was beautiful. I felt so relieved by what she said but I didn't get any more details and then they had to leave.

The lawns and gardens at the crematorium are picturesque. After the service we straggled across a little bridge to the tea rooms. Except that most of the men left. I was disappointed because I didn't have the chance to speak to them individually. We sat at tables on the verandah in wintry sunlight and ate sandwiches and hot savouries. Women came round regularly carrying big teapots to fill our cups. I put on a tape of musical favourites from the 1920s and 1930s which Dad liked—'Roses Are Blooming in Picardy', 'If You Were the Only Girl in the World'. But the songs got in the way of conversation, especially for several guests who were hard of hearing, and somebody turned it off. Magpies flew down from the grand old trees to perch on the verandah railings, waiting for scraps of food. Dad would have loved them. Mary shooed them away.

I had a strong sense of Dad's presence. I was composed and felt that he had given me calm guidance for all that had had to be done in the days between his death and his funeral. Is that fanciful or a real possibility? Everything went well. Everyone was helpful, from the funeral people to the tea room. The printer put himself out to get the little booklets for the service ready in time. There was a great deal to be done but there were no difficulties. As I had requested, the funeral manager dismantled the floral canopy on Dad's casket at the end of the service, and sprigs of bush flowers were scattered on the afternoon tea tables for people to take with them.

I was grateful to all the people who came, including people who had cared for Dad and Mary's health professionally, over the years. I appreciated their respect and affection for Dad and their readiness to leave work to be there. My neighbours in Sydney came and friends from work who did not know Dad but came out of kindness to me. And, of course, my dear Val who never lets me down.

It seemed right; we were outdoors, everyone had a place to sit, the surroundings were beautiful and there was something nice to eat. I was tremendously relieved that Dad's suffering was over. I didn't feel like crying and I talked to everyone.

7 AUGUST 2000

I should have known that it wouldn't last. I always have a delayed reaction to crisis. Within a few days, order has given way to a chaos of loss and grief, and anger, which disturbs me. I thought it would dissolve once Dad was at peace.

AUGUST 2000

The days of August have passed in a blur. I divide my time between Gosford and my home in Sydney. I feel disorientated. During the two months with Dad in hospital I had a routine. My long days with him were my top priority. Now I'm having to restore attention to all my other commitments. This return to normal life is probably healthy but I'm struggling to achieve it.

There were two deadlines to meet for my regular article in *Madonna* magazine. One Saturday night friends took me to a concert at Sydney Town Hall. It was a celebration of the history of the Sisters of St Joseph, with popular songs to mark the various decades of their practical, compassionate work in many parts of Australia. It was beautiful but I experienced it as though through a closed window.

One Sunday I made a little shrine of remembrance on top of the piano, with the Australian native flowers from Dad's casket as the centrepiece. Gentle rain was falling that day. My friends John and Jenny called in with a basket of flowers from their garden.

'You look tired,' Jenny said kindly and with understanding, from her own family suffering over the years.

Another night I went to a powerful Sydney Symphony Orchestra performance with Edo de Waart conducting Mahler. I just let it flow through me without concentrating. I've been going to church but I feel somehow detached from the celebration of the Mass. I can't focus on its relevance for my situation. If asked about my faith I would have to say that I don't know. I am still angry that Dad suffered and I don't know where God was in that suffering; that remains a stumbling block for me, even though I know it's a childish reaction.

And I'm not sure where the Church was either. Then I remember Fr Robert, Sr Monica, Rev. Ross Weaver (and Fr Des came one night too, I had forgotten; he was in a hurry) and all the people who were praying for us. They are the Church. They represent God. And I like to be there, at Mass, to hear the prayers, to receive the sacrament of communion, to be part of the community of faith, even if I can't join in wholeheartedly. It's not a very good effort but it's the best I can do at the moment.

I presented a day of reflection for school support staff for the Catholic Education Office, planned months ago. It was thoughtfully organised to be a day of refreshment and affirmation for the people, mostly women, who do much to keep the schools running smoothly and to support students and teachers. It was a good day for me. I felt that I was returning to an engagement with normal life. I hope it will last.

As the month goes on I am still trying to return to my normal routine and to the practicalities of life. During Dad's illness, dozens of letters have banked up on my desk, awaiting reply. They come from people who have heard the *Search for Meaning* programs, or read my books, or from viewers of *Australian Story*. This large correspondence has been part of my life for years. There are letters from many people who want to tell me their story. Now, more than ever, I am touched by the suffering they often contain. I admire the writers' understated bravery and acceptance but, at the moment, in the light of my own recent experience, I mistrust it. I wonder if they may be deluding themselves; if they would not be better off protesting at the injustice and cruelty of life. I answer them as well as I can, but they keep coming and they are overwhelming.

Invitations to speak continue to arrive, as usual. I read them carefully and try to understand what they mean but it's as though I am reading someone else's mail by mistake. They are gracious letters, written with respect and warmth. The ones from the country towns come closest to eliciting a response in me. They remind me of all the happy excursions I've made in the last few years to rural areas, like Mudgee, to gather people from miles around, for a day of reflection; and community dinners where people have shared their stories. I can't feel anything about those occasions now but I know they happened. I can remember I felt I was doing something useful, and gaining a great deal, in the course of all that travelling.

Perhaps one day I will find the heart to do it again. I have no idea. I would have to rediscover in myself hope and inspiration before I could offer it to anyone else. If I stood up to speak in public now I would have little to offer, partly because I am feeling broken but also because I can see now, more than ever, in people's faces, that vulnerability which they strive so valiantly to conceal. I am seeing everything with the eye of pity, which is not quite the same as the eye of compassion. It is, rather, a rage that there should be so much suffering in people's lives. I am like Job, in the Old Testament, shouting at God in protest against his afflictions, or Jacob wrestling with the angel until dawn, except that I have not won the insights each of them gained through their struggles.

If God designed this human life, then what sort of heartless tyrant is God? I am appalled to hear myself asking this question. On the other hand, if He suffers with us in our predicament but cannot alleviate it, then who will protect us? Who will make sure that it doesn't all go too far, beyond endurance?

I used to think that serenity was the condition most to be desired. I have often admired people for their tranquillity, imagining it to be an outward sign of faith and inner peace, most likely hard-won through overcoming adversity. Now I wonder how appropriate serenity is. What reason is there for it when there is so much wrong, so much suffering, so much inequity? Maybe anger is more to the point, righteous anger and protest and constant questioning of the way things are.

I am not yet desolated by the apparent loss of a faith that was so dear to me. I am far too angry. But what will it be like when—if ever—the anger goes? Is this the predictable anger phase of grief I have read about? In a way it feels like someone else's anger and yet I've got it. I'm writing now about what is really happening in my life but it's not what I talk about. I appear to live a normal life. I go to work. I have many commitments. I pretend I'm alright because people don't want you to grieve. It makes them too sad or embarrassed. After the first week or two they expect you to have recovered and, if you don't, it's distressing or tedious for them. I prefer to pretend, for my own sake as well as theirs.

I put the letters aside. They mount up. I simply do not have the energy to answer them all. I am exhausted by the anger which, on some days, turns into apathy. Apparently this is another of the effects of grief. Does it grow out of an increasing suspicion of meaninglessness? It's a feeling of lethargy, a lack of curiosity, a dullness. When I break through it, occasionally, I answer some of the letters. I write that, while I am honoured to be invited, I am in a period of bereavement and do not, at present, have the heart to commit myself to public engagements. Everyone goes through difficult passages in their lives so I can only hope that they will understand. I do not burden them with the fact that I do not seem to have anything to say about the search for meaning.

A tree growing beside the balcony has made unusually swift growth in the last few months and in the cool, southerly change that's just blown up, its leaves brush my arms as I lean on the railings, scanning the night sky. It's a young tree, supple and resilient. Its leaves turn silver in the wind and rustle as though made of foil. During the day it's decorated with vivid, multi-coloured lorikeets. I see them and hear them. For years they have been my delight. But I seem to have lost the capacity to be restored by beauty. Is this how life will be now?

L A T E   A U G U S T   2 0 0 0

I'm not sure what the date is. In the last few weeks one day runs into the next. Every few days I'm on the freeway. I do what has to be done, arrangements to do with Dad's estate. Talk to his solicitor and to the accountant. They each need me to find documents. It's easy enough because Dad was so well organised. I have taken Mary to the Department of Veterans' Affairs to complete the paperwork necessary for her war widow's pension to begin. The man who interviews her is helpful but Mary becomes upset. Deafness is a difficult impediment and can make you look foolish. Because she begs his pardon frequently and does not acknowledge when she has heard him, he starts explaining things to me instead. Quite understandably this is offensive to her. I am sympathetic to her situation but I also become impatient and then ashamed.

Perhaps the impatience is the tip of an underlying anger remaining about Dad's suffering. Is it also possible that I am angry with Dad for leaving me with the responsibility for Mary's welfare? That's an unwelcome thought. Am I in conflict—wanting to do the right thing yet also feeling emotionally exhausted by it and wanting to get back to my own life?

Finally we have thrown out the last of the beautiful flowers people sent when Dad died. There were so many of them that they occupied every table and shelf and even lined the stairs. They became quite demanding as they all needed watering and culling every day. I had some more cards printed to help Mary reply to all the letters of condolence. Sometimes we go out for a drive and lunch to have a day off after so much stress and activity. One day I had to stop driving and just hold onto the wheel because I couldn't stop crying. Mary was embarrassed, I think. She didn't say anything. When I could, I just started driving again.

At home, I've been keeping up my own work and not talking about my grief. People have no time for it, beyond the exchange of a formula:

'I'm sorry to hear that your father died.'

'Thank you.'

'How old was he?'

'He was ninety-three.'

'Oh, well then, he had a very good innings.'

But can life and death be dismissed in terms of a cricket match? It seems too slight a metaphor to cast any useful light on such a profound subject. It makes me cross. I don't show it because people mean well but when someone you love dies, no matter what their age, your world is shaken.

Still, I am surprised by the depth of my grief. In the last few years I felt that Dad's life was stressful because of his increasing frailty, the responsibility of caring for Mary, the pain of angina and the bouts of disabling vertigo caused, apparently, by blockage in the carotid arteries. As he put it, 'Everything's passed its use-by date'.

Once he turned ninety I knew it was only a matter of time until he died. I accepted that; it was the natural order of things. I enjoyed his company and did everything I could to support him. And I imagined that, while I would miss him very much when he died, I would also rejoice that he had at last escaped worry and sickness and that he had gone home. It was a satisfying way to think and it brought me peace. 'Home safe' was the term I had for it. I used often to think of my mother in that way—I missed her painfully but could bear it because she was beyond all her suffering, she was 'home safe'.

But Dad's dying has called into question the very idea of 'home safe' and I find myself wrestling now with unexpected and unwelcome questions. After all, I have no idea where he is. I have just been vaguely subscribing to Christian belief about an afterlife with God without questioning what it might mean or trying to imagine it. And that's easy, when nothing is at stake. But is it like going home? Is it safe? Now I am being confronted by these questions for which I cannot know an answer. I know they're the wrong questions and they'll only lead me into a dead end of my own construction. Yet still they come to me.

As well, I cannot let go my simple longing for my parents to be alive still. I suppose Dad's death has rekindled my grief for my mother. I know this is a childlike longing, not appropriate for an adult. I know that parents die and that is part of the life cycle. I know that acceptance of their death and gratitude to God for their lives is the right response but I just can't make it yet. So I'm not at peace. I suppose it would be different if I had children. Then my attention would be preoccupied with them, their wellbeing and their future.

I worry about Mary living alone but I have no energy yet to solve the problem. She has kind neighbours and two community care visits each week, as well as the cleaning lady, meals delivered and my own frequent appearances. It is difficult to get her to make any decisions. There are plenty to be considered but I am probably expecting far too much of her, at the age of eighty-seven and in frail health, when she has just lost Dad. Even though she does not show it, I need to remember that she is grieving too. Finally she agrees to accept the offer from the Office of Australian War Graves to provide a soldier's memorial plaque at Palmdale Lawn Cemetery.

LATE AUGUST 2000

Australian Story commitments come around regularly and I am doing them on automatic pilot. I hope it doesn't look like that. I try to give the work my full attention while I'm there and that provides a welcome relief from sadness. Some good stories this month. I particularly liked the one, produced by Ben Cheshire and Ian Harley, about the only factory in Australia still making traditional mousetraps. The original machine, built in the 1940s from spare and scrap metal, has churned out about 95 million mousetraps, the design changed only slightly over the years. But now the two sons of the inventor Wes Standfield are closing the doors. I regret such an old craft going out of business.

And I was glad to introduce Brigid Donovan's story about a group of volunteers dedicated to restoring a B-24 Liberator in an aircraft hangar outside Melbourne—a World War II legend reborn. It seems they've retrieved 1.3 million parts from around the world. The unveiling day made a moving climax to the story.

Away from work, my feelings are unpredictable, veering from calm to sadness to irritability to anger to numbness. I'm also very tired. Maybe the eight weeks with Dad in hospital are taking their toll now. There's so much to do. Yet the practical tasks seem worthwhile, to keep faith with Dad.

Mary and I visited a retirement village which was quite glamorous but she didn't like it much. There are many contacts to make to ensure that she is registered as a war widow with her various service providers, and that she has adequate support in her home, as well as the meals which are delivered regularly. Not Meals on Wheels but a small private company run by a couple with whom we have become friends. Dad was concerned about these things and I want to do it all to the last detail.

I thought Mary would accept this as a series of practical matters we would work on together. But I find that I have to tread delicately so that it is not seen as interference. This makes every step more difficult and time-consuming than it needs to be and creates unnecessary, tiring tension. I have to put myself in her shoes and try to see it from her point of view. Sometimes I manage it. I dislike being so much on the freeway. I have travelled this busy road so many hundreds of times and think I must have used up my nine lives long ago.

Although we've spent many years together, Mary is a reserved person and I feel my knowledge of her is limited. Her memory of the past is more acute than her recall of recent events. She tells stories of some adventurous forebears. Her great-grandparents on her mother's side, the Nathans, came to Australia from England on the vessel *Earl of Charlmont* which was wrecked in 1852, off Barwon Heads, near Geelong in Victoria, the location for the filming of ABC TV's *SeaChange*. They lost everything yet they made a successful life in the young colony and I believe Mary's grandfather, Henry Nathan, established one of the first furniture firms in Melbourne. Mary's father, James Cowan, died of typhoid fever in 1915, while working for BHP in Broken Hill. She was not yet two years old and his second child, Winifred, was born after he died. So the two little girls were brought up by their mother, Julia.

I'm asking Mary about her life and writing her story down so that it doesn't slip away from her. When I gave her a first draft to read, and add to, she handed it back with no comment on the facts, but with all my grammar corrected. I was dismayed and irritated, but realised that if I showed that reaction, it would only encourage more of the same. I must try to remember this. Sometimes I pretend she is Jesus Christ or Buddha, and that helps a lot. But then I forget.

Mary's first job was as a model for a wholesale garment firm in Melbourne. One day she noticed, just over the road from the warehouse, the registered teachers training institute and decided that was where she wanted to be. Completing training in 1935, Mary's first appointment was at a dame school in Malvern where the students included members of the Myer family and the young Rupert Murdoch. We used to tease her about her early influence on one of the most powerful men in the world but she never rose to the bait.

In July 1942 she enlisted in the Women's Auxiliary Australian Air Force, the WAAAF, as an aircraftwoman. She trained to serve as a radar operator. In 1943 she was appointed officer-in-command of the first radar station, with the rank of acting flight officer, after which she was addressed by lower ranks as 'Madam'. It's easy to imagine. She made many good friends in the WAAAF and has stayed in touch with a number of them over the years, sometimes renewing their happy times at reunions.

After the war Mary resumed her teaching career and began what was to be a creative period of some twenty-five years teaching at Korowa Anglican Girls' School in Melbourne. During this time she established a library for the Junior School, introduced an innovative system for teaching mathematics and took a special interest in remedial teaching, helping students who were having difficulty. Mary's interest in education and her affection for children have been lifelong. She did not have children of her own.

Mary first met my father during the war when he was a captain in the AIF (Australian Imperial Force) and she a WAAAF officer. It was a brief encounter but must have been a memorable one because some time after my mother died in 1969 Dad got in touch with Mary again and they were married in Gosford in 1973. It was the first marriage for Mary, at the age of fifty-nine, after she had been teaching and caring for her mother in their family home for many years.

Mary has an enquiring mind and an analytical intelligence. She is interested in many things: local district affairs, especially over-development; the need for care of the environment; the beauties of the natural world. She appreciates art and we make many visits to see the changing exhibitions at Gosford Regional Art Gallery. She has an eye for detail and a much longer attention span than my own. She is concerned about the running of the country and disapproves very strongly of prime minister Howard.

Mary and I have a testing time in each other's company because we are different personalities and have had to make constant adjustments to each other. It's been one of the most difficult situations of my life but it's been a worthwhile achievement for me to stay in a challenging relationship and find the goodness in it, when my instinct is to bolt.

I don't know what Mary's religious beliefs are and feel it may seem an intrusion to her if I ask. So we keep to less personal, more objective topics.

SEPTEMBER 2000

Last night, when I made a cup of tea before going to bed, there was a moth, like a little silver brooch, on the traycloth, its wings fanned, still, perfect. I thought it was at rest. This morning I saw that the moth was damaged. It had tried to fly but had succeeded only in dragging itself a small distance, leaving a trail the same colour as its own body. Its wings were twitching. It was upside down. It was mortally wounded but not yet dead. Seeing its plight, I was paralysed. I put my finger gently against its upturned legs to see if it might grip, but it could not.

There is a scent of jasmine in the air. I usually feel the elation of spring when I first smell that heady scent but this year I resent it because Dad is not here. I know that's wrong thinking, certainly not what my parents would want, but that's how I feel. I wonder if grief sends you a bit mad?

S EPTEMBER 2000, G OSFORD

As we often do, Mary and I go shopping and then stop for lunch at a little cafe which looks across a park to the library. There are some big trees tinged with the first pale hint of spring green. I draw Mary's attention to them.

'I can't hear you unless you speak up and look directly at me.'

'I was just noticing the green on those trees. Maybe spring is coming.'

'I'm sorry but I just can't hear a word you're saying.'

'Spring, maybe it's coming!'

'It certainly doesn't feel anything like spring.'

I feel aggravated because I think she is manipulating me with her determined contrariness. Our conversations often go this way and I know the only way to avoid an ulcer is through not reacting. I've tried to learn this detachment over the years but sometimes it slips.

After a lengthy examination of the menu, we order. When the waitress has turned away, Mary remarks loudly that the coffee cups here are rather small.

'You'll see.'

She turns her attention to the passing parade.

'I just can't believe how many women you see smoking now. I think it looks terrible!'

I am surprised that she has the energy for such vehemence. I don't seem to have any at all but I make an attempt.

'Oh, well, I remember when we used to smoke, although it seems a long while ago now. The trouble was that we enjoyed it. It's not so easy to give it up.'

'I certainly never smoked very much.'

I remember happy evenings at their home, featuring Scrabble, solo or cribbage, whisky and cigarettes, but it seems disrespectful to argue, so I change tack.

'Your fingernails look very nice.'

She looks at her hands in disapproval.

'The girl didn't do a good job. They're the wrong shape and she hasn't even put any polish on. Which reminds me that, where you put all that stuff on the floor of our shower, whatever it was, the tiles seem to be corroding. I'll show you when we get home. I hope I also remember to show you that those pants you bought me are wrong. I'll have to give them away. I don't think it's worth having them altered.'

I notice that she is becoming more animated as she develops this theme of my shortcomings. Perhaps, without Dad here to give us a reason to get along, she feels emboldened to say what she really thinks. We have both made a supreme effort, over the years, to overcome a natural incompatibility. Expressing antipathy may be liberating for her. I also need to remember that her critical words may have little to do with me but may be a reaction to some struggle in her own life. It's just that I happen to be the closest person at the time. I find this quite difficult but I read it somewhere and it sounds right.

When our meals are served she looks at her plate in dismay, as she always does. 'Far too much. Unbelievable! I can't possibly eat all that!' Then the coffee arrives and she turns to me in triumph: 'What did I tell you about the size of the cups!' It's not a question.

I am sometimes amazed now by the triviality of people's conversation when life can descend so suddenly into tragedy and chaos. But maybe they are on the right track and this concern with the mundane keeps them anchored in the concrete reality of living. Whereas often I exist more in a spiritual than a physical mode, always half-listening for something, yearning, attending to the practicalities of life in an automatic way without giving them much attention. It's not comfortable. I don't feel earthed.

SEPTEMBER 2000

At a friend's home, I watched the opening ceremony of the Olympic Games on television, with five others. We thought it was a great success from the first moment when the stadium filled with galloping riders in driza-bones and felt hats, flags streaming. Thrilling and very emotional, to have it happening here in our city. Interesting to feel enjoyment again, although I feel a bit guilty about it. However, I loved the whole evening and have been following the events since then. Sydney is alive and exciting, full of happy international visitors. Last night, when I went with friends to a waterfront restaurant at Circular Quay, we were surrounded by the Swiss Olympic team. Apparently it is their social headquarters. The food was very good. It was the first time since Dad died that I tasted a meal with pleasure. Perhaps I'm returning to more involvement in normal life. On the walk around to the Opera

House, it was moving to hear many languages and to mingle with a united nations of smiling people. None of them will want to leave—day after day of sunshine and these perfect, balmy Sydney evenings, with giant screens placed around the city so that everyone can watch the Games. The hundreds of volunteers in their casual, colourful uniforms are an attractive innovation and have become a proud highlight of 'the best games ever held', as they are being described immodestly in the press.

I've been watching Roy and HG on their vulgar and very funny nightly review of each day's events. It's good to hear myself laugh out loud, but strange too. I hope the international visitors are not seeing these shows. What's so hilarious to Australians could easily be offensive to anyone who's not used to us. You could never explain it. Dad would have loved it. Mary thinks they are unnecessary.

When I'm not in Gosford I speak to Mary often on the phone. It is easier for her to hear on the phone as Dad had a volume control fitted.

'I'm just ringing to say hullo. Is this a good time?'

'Not really, I'm so busy.'

'How are you?'

'I couldn't really say. I haven't had time to think about it. There's so much to do.'

'Did you watch the opening ceremony?'

'Yes.'

'Are you watching the Games?'

'I haven't got time to sit around watching television.'

'I'll be up the day after tomorrow.'

'Well, I'm sorry but I can't stand here talking any longer. I must go. The weight-lifting is just starting. You should see the size of these chaps. It's unbelievable!'

SEPTEMBER 2000

I met Wendy and Michael to see a marvellous production of *Darlinghurst Nights* in the Studio at the Opera House. I found it poignant. My mother and father were married in 1933 at St John's, Darlinghurst. These were their times. This was their world. These were their songs, the songs we used to sing together around the piano, with my mother playing.

It's good to talk with Wendy. She understands the mixture of compassion, duty, exasperation and fatigue involved in providing the best care for an elderly, frail parent. When we part, she's off to the nursing home where she sleeps on a cot beside her mother's bed, followed by another concentrated day at work.

Why does life have to be so hard for our parents when they are at their most vulnerable? People can cope with a lot when they're young, but they seem to get everything wrong with them when they've run out of strength.

My state of mind is still unreliable. Sometimes I seem almost back to normal. At other times I'm in emotional limbo, or angry. Driving home over the bridge tonight I felt a deep sorrow. I wasn't prepared for this intense, longing sadness that overtakes me at any time and over which I have no control. I should have been prepared because this is what happened when my mother died. I don't resent being sad a lot of the time. Isn't it only natural to miss the presence of my mother and my father with whom I had so much shared history?

But probably it is not normal to retreat, as I have done, into my imagination, with my mother and father, the two beloved, familiar people who gave me life. They seem more important to me than anything else but they are not here. I would like to be with them, wherever they are. I am not suicidal, more homesick. It's the sensation I had when I was left at boarding school, aged twelve. I feel the same vertigo now that I did then, on the edge of an abyss of chaos, standing on the school steps, watching my parents disappear slowly down the driveway in their little car and knowing the dry taste of abandonment. In both hands I held their parting gift, a brown paper bag containing a perfectly ripe peach which I could never eat. Did that experience get buried, lying in wait to be revived by any subsequent goodbyes?

At a more conscious level, I am grieving that I didn't get the chance to tell Dad about what happened to him following his heart surgery and to find out what it was like for him. I had written it down so carefully. Maybe I wanted his reassurance that I couldn't have done any better. Maybe I wanted his forgiveness for not doing enough. Or did I receive that when he told me, before I left for Mudgee, 'I couldn't have got through this without you'? This is what I often think about now. It's a preoccupation that is relieved only when I can stop thinking and savour the present moment, noticing what is around me and what I am doing, with full attention.

Tonight I noticed there were hundreds of seagulls drifting and wheeling in the artificial light of the great arch of the bridge. And my sadness made way for them.

My greatest comfort is the presence of magpies. I see them from my study, stalking slowly on stiff legs through patches of sunlight on the pale green sward of the park. They materialise all over the place, like messengers. I've always associated them with Dad because he loved them and fed them and called to them, and they seemed to reply.

Today, as I was staring, unfocussed, out the window into the tree, I became aware that one of the shadows in its thicket was a magpie, alone, head tucked into its shoulders in sleep. It stayed for an hour. All day long, they warble and carol as they glide through the canopy of the trees, coming at morning and evening to drink a few dainty sips of water from the bowl on the balcony. Pausing, between sips, to gaze at me. This afternoon, one flew from the bowl up onto the balcony railing and stayed a long time.

In the top of one of the old pine trees, there's a nest which they use each year. There's always an adult coming and going; they take it in turns to keep the eggs warm. One day soon there'll be consternation as the eggs hatch and the parents must find a constant food supply to satisfy the shrill nestlings. The instinct to duty is demanding and not to be ignored.

We'll miss the Olympics. All the excitement has come and gone too swiftly but now there are the Paralympic Games to look forward to and I'll definitely go out to Homebush to see them.

A welcome letter from Daoud in Bethlehem today, in response to my phone call about Dad's death. Letters between us take many weeks to arrive. The airmail envelope carries a stamp issued by the Palestinian Authority, depicting two shepherds tending their flock of gentle-faced, black-eared sheep, on a hillside. There are palm trees silhouetted against a navy blue evening sky, in which golden stars are beginning to appear.

'We were so sad about your father's death. We wish for him to be in Heaven. It is difficult for you now without your lovely parents. Me and my wife have our parents still alive. They are everything in our life, better than money and anything else.'

Daoud always puts things into perspective. I met him in this month, September, in 1989, in the course of an unforgettable pilgrimage to the Holy Land. In Bethlehem, after visiting the Church of the Nativity, we went to one of the Christian souvenir stores to buy little figures for the Christmas crib, hand-carved in olive wood. Daoud was behind the counter, noticeable because he walked with a lurching effort, dragging a crippled foot. He spoke very good English with a strong Arabic accent. We had a few minutes of conversation as he wrapped our purchases in thin brown paper. I sent a card at Christmas. In February he replied: 'God with you, protect you and your family. Next time I invite you to visit us, my wife Ibtisam, my son Fadi and my daughter Lina.' We've been writing ever since.

The Gulf War created the first serious drought of tourists in 1991. Daoud wrote: 'Every morning I am going to search for a job but no place to work in because the War damaged everything. In God we trust and praying for a peace to have a better life.' Eventually, the pilgrims and tourists began to come again and during the 1990s his letters were more optimistic. I learned about their family life and that they go to Mass at the Church of the Nativity in Manger Square, only a few minutes from their home. The Arab Christian community in the West Bank is steadily diminishing, as life becomes more difficult for them. It's been a gift for me to have this deepening communication over the years and Daoud's constant faith, in the face of the struggle of his life, has been a great example to me, and puts my own doubts to shame.

Daoud's are not the only letters I receive from Israel. I also correspond with Esther and Gideon, old journalist friends in Jerusalem. I have sometimes thought of putting them in touch with each other—my Jewish friends and my Arab Christian friends. They live so near each other and they all yearn for a peaceful land in which to raise their children. But I know that, from this distance, I cannot appreciate the complexities of their long and painful conflict. I have asked them what I can do to help and they both say just remember us and pray for us and pray for peace.

I have some treasured friends who endured and survived the Holocaust, when they were children.[1] They also give me an inspiring example of courage and faith in life. They were trusting and dependent little children when their homes were stolen and their families ravaged. They had their parents for only a few precious years and came close to death themselves. They are now mature people. Their answer to horror has been to have children and grandchildren and to invest their lives in the future of Australia. They survived fearful events that no child should witness, yet they possess an essence of spiritual strength (not necessarily religious), forged through suffering and refined by the enduring grief of their losses, a grief held in dignified reserve.

All these privileged friendships enrich my life profoundly.

26 OCTOBER 2000

This afternoon I ran into my friend Maria and we stood together on the footpath, outside the shops. She lost her father at almost the same time and in the same hospital. This means we can understand each other and say how we feel without reservation or fear of trying each other's patience. She is very shocked and sad about her father's death.

All around us the children were relaxing after school, as they do every day, pausing with one foot on their scooters to suck an iceblock, drips running down to their elbows. They are top-heavy with crash helmets, the big heads on their little bodies out of proportion, grotesque. It is as though a cohort of happy aliens has landed.

Maria used to be the postmistress in the days when our little local post office was run by the Postmaster General's Department. She knows everyone. I have known her for thirty years, have watched her children grow up, marry and have their own children. Of course I knew her father too. He owned the general store and his fruit and vegetable display was impeccable. I remember him polishing the apples and indulging my scant knowledge of Italian with patience and great courtesy. He would greet me and inquire after my health slowly enough for me to understand him and to reply. He would then revert tactfully to conversing in English before my childish attempts at his language could embarrass me.

He dressed rather formally, wearing a jacket and tie. He commanded respect from his staff. He was of the old school. When he retired, his son-in-law and grandson took over but he would still come into the shop and rearrange the display. They tolerated this but he had relinquished his former omnipotence and I think he felt the loss. He lived in the house next door to the shop, with the old-fashioned pink climbing rose he had planted cascading over the wall onto the footpath. Maria lives there now.

She was gulping air as she told me what had happened. Her father shouldn't have died. He went in for routine surgery. It wasn't expected to be life-threatening. The evening before, he was going round cheering up the other patients in the ward. The next morning, after the operation, he died. It was such a shock. It was unbelievable. It should never have happened. Something went wrong. No chance to say goodbye.

Maria looked like a bewildered, very sad child. I told her that I would write her father's name in the book of prayers in Mary MacKillop's chapel, the book which goes onto the altar at every Mass. She seemed pleased, and perhaps a little comforted.

When we parted I went in to do my shopping. The shop is run by a Cambodian couple now, Joe and Paula. A few minutes later, in the aisle between the soap powder and the birdseed bells, Maria was at my side again. She had cut several long fronds of the rambling rose—they were spilling generously out of a white plastic bag—for me to take home. They have filled the room with the perfume of old roses. I treasure Maria's beautiful gesture. I am moved by her loss and she is touched by mine. It reminds me that grief is a universal human experience and that we cry together, not in isolation. As well, I am buoyed by the evidence of Maria's faith in prayer. Such small glimpses of the sacred in the everyday are as close as I come now to recapturing the fullness of my own faith.

Helen Grasswill produced tonight's *Australian Story*, on three Newcastle University law teachers who, with their students, have been re-investigating some of Australia's biggest criminal and civil cases, uncovering evidence which challenges both legal and police practice. Newcastle is the only law school in Australia where a degree can be achieved on the basis of practical public-interest advocacy. This is expected to promote a pro bono legal culture among students. These are some of the best programs we do, where the personal story illuminates an important social issue.

The midnight ferry is just leaving Valentia Street wharf. I hear the familiar acceleration of its engine, a sound I have known for thirty years, and see its red port light gliding through the trees. I don't look forward to going to bed. I don't sleep well anymore and last night I had a vivid flashback to one of the worst moments in Intensive Care. I saw Dad gagged and restrained and felt again my despair and helpless anger. It was distressing and made my heart race uncomfortably. I tried to get rid of it by turning on the bedside wireless as I do now when I cannot sleep. I have discovered some excellent programs coming from overseas, via ABC News Radio and Radio National, in the early hours. Dad used to find the wireless a good companion on his sleepless nights. I wonder if the flashback is normal and if it will come again.

27 OCTOBER 2000

Louisa rang today and left a heartwarming message, thanking me for being her friend. I remembered suddenly that it was her birthday on 8 October and that, for the first time, I have forgotten it. I'm amazed. It's a measure of my disorientation. But there was no reproach. She appreciates, I suppose, that my concentration is in chaos. But I feel sorry because she is so thoughtful about anything to do with my life. No doubt, with three children of her own, her focus is more on their celebrations than on her own.

On the day of her little girl's baptism last year there was a storm. As godmother I carried her into the church under a big umbrella. There were to be several baptisms after Mass. The tribe of small children accompanying their families had caught the caprice of the wind; they were running and writhing out of their parents' grasp, showing the whites of their eyes like wild ponies.

But the priest remained patient and prayerful as he welcomed our little girl into the community of the Church. In the best photo of her baptism party, my goddaughter, held in her parents' arms above the cake, is kicking bare toes dipped in chocolate icing and smiling beatifically. Since that day her smile has seldom been absent. I love to hold her in my arms beside a wind chime and see her enchantment at the sound she can cause with the gentlest touch of delicate fingers waving like sea anemones in the current. She is perfectly attentive to the moment.

The first time I met her I put my face too close to her too quickly and she screamed. But she knows me now. She is easily delighted and happy to explore her world with wonder. Laughter is second nature to her and if I sing to her she sings. Being with her is a direct invitation into contemplation. She calls me out of preoccupation into a sudden, vivid glimpse of reality. Has she come so recently from heaven and brought it with her to remind us? I would love to believe it.

11 NOVEMBER 2000

The *Australian Story* this week, produced by Wendy Page, could have been Dad and Mary's story: a chance meeting between two young people in the armed services in wartime. An innocent romance. The two go in different directions but the memory of their brief encounter remains. Forty years later they meet again and fall in love again. Very romantic and in the space of a half-hour program we need only hint at the complications involved and leave it to the audience to wonder and hope and perhaps reflect on what might have been in their own lives. The theme music, 'We'll Meet Again', was perfect. Again, a strong audience response, mostly positive, and good ratings. Let's hope we can keep it up next year. It will be good to have a break now.

There's been a stormy sky for days but rain has fallen only occasionally and at night. The pattern of clouds is constantly changing. Sometimes great grey and white thunderheads boil up slowly on the western horizon. They matched my mood yesterday, as a dull anger resurfaced, with memories of Dad in hospital. I had to suppress it back then, five months ago. When it returns, I don't know what to do with it, but the stormy clouds gave expression to it. And then, later in the day, it passed.

Today the water in the river below is a wonderful slate green. Red coral trees and the saturated mauve of jacaranda are startlingly vivid against the green and, surprisingly, I am alive to their beauty. So different from yesterday. My emotional state is still inconsistent, not to be trusted. Dull days suit me when I am feeling low; they do not demand response and action, as sunny days do. The greyness is restful. It allows me to be quiet, if not entirely peaceful.

I can sit and gaze at the riot of petunias, white and purple and pink, spilling over the rims of the pots on the balcony. I planted them only three weeks ago and they have grown and massed and bloomed quickly. Dad always planted his petunias earlier than I did and got spectacular results, weeks ahead of me. This year there's no competition but I feel some poignant pleasure remembering it.

I'm noticing that there is solace in a moment like this when I can savour beauty once again. It lifts a load, calling me into present time, away from regret and anxiety. I must remember this and try to do it more consciously.

Soft, grey weather seems compatible with this Armistice Day. At the eleventh hour of the eleventh day of the eleventh month, we remember all our fallen. I wear the red crepe-paper poppy I have kept for years. I wait for the consolation of familiar phrases like 'our countrymen and women who made the supreme sacrifice'. People gather at the Cenotaph in Martin Place. Families, little children and some veterans. Wreaths are laid. 'At the going down of the sun and in the morning, we will remember them.' The last post is sounded. And I am reassured that this is my Australia in which I grew up and where I am at home, as my father felt at home and his father and grandfather before him. 'Lest we forget.'

At the shop I asked Paula for some goat's cheese and she looked puzzled. 'Maybe in refrigerator?' She explained that in Cambodia they do not eat dairy food, so she doesn't know much about cheese.

I admire Paula and Joe very much and, for some reason, I feel protective of them. They both work long hours; they are saving to educate their daughters and so that, one day, they can go back to see family left behind. Paula is small, strong, very beautiful, and her eyes fill with tears as she tells me about her family so far away. But she has to keep passing items across the electronic machine that reads the bar codes, as she speaks, because there are customers waiting behind me. She is very tired and my questions about her family have made her sad. I should have chosen a better time to ask. I only told her my name once and she remembers it every time.

When I think of the anguish of Joe and Paula's families under the murderous regime of the Pol Pot government, I marvel that, despite all their trials, they have kept their faith. There is a small Buddhist shrine on one of the shelves near the checkout, above the potato chips and packets of sweets. I enjoy going to the shop as I have done for thirty years. It's part of my routine—familiar, reassuring. There is always a smiling welcome. They run the business well and contribute generously to community causes. Tony, one of the original Italian staff, is still there, in charge of the magnificent array of fruit and vegetables. It wouldn't be the same without him.

A letter from Daoud in Bethlehem. He writes that they are having 'hard and unsettled days' and that things have degenerated, that the streets are dangerous. 'I staying at home now and pray to my God one day to have our normal life and job as before.' Ibtisam has not been well. She works very hard at cleaning jobs to bring in some money. No tourists are coming on pilgrimage and that means no work for Daoud. But everything goes towards the children's education and they are doing well at school. Fadi is fourteen now and Lina twelve. As always, the letter finishes with a promise of prayers for me at the Church of the Nativity and the words 'Thanks God for all our gifts'. He encloses some hand-made cards of Jesus in the manger, decorated with colourful, dried petals of flowers from the Holy Land.

Early January 2001

First Christmas without Dad. My birthday on 1 January, Dad's on 5 January. I suppose at times of celebration and family gathering you miss especially those no longer here.

Mary is often unwell and spent Christmas in hospital. Suspected tuberculosis. Isolation ward. Visiting her requires gloves and gown. Conversation doubly difficult through masks. It must be lonely for her but she doesn't disclose her feelings to me. The need to speak loudly to someone who's deaf makes it difficult to initiate the sort of personal conversation usually conducted in quiet voices. So we stick to practicalities.

January 2001

Mary's out of isolation now and having a period of rehabilitation at a private hospital. I visit every two days to keep up the washing, to encourage her and to be her advocate. Her deafness puts her at a disadvantage in this situation. Her frequent lack of response to a question or a direction makes her appear slow or lacking in comprehension and she is treated accordingly. It makes me angry to see her humbled. So I explain her deafness to every member of staff I encounter and also put a notice above her bed to say that she hears better in her left ear and needs to see your face when you speak. I am surprised how few people make an extra effort when communicating with the deaf—especially health professionals who should appreciate the problem.

If I'm really honest with myself, I admit that caring for Mary sometimes seems a burden. At the same time, supporting her does alleviate my grief, transferring my attention to someone else's needs instead of my own concerns. I admire Mary's courage and I'm very fond of her, even though she sometimes drives me mad. I'm not sure how she feels about me. I think I aggravate her, at times, unintentionally.

It's a very hot summer. Sometimes, when I get to the hospital, I can't remember the eighty-kilometre drive. I must be on automatic pilot.

18–19 JANUARY 2001

I noticed the crepe myrtles everywhere today as I drove over to St Ignatius', Riverview. They are the best for years, almost luminous in their array of pinks and mauves, and bowed down with the weight of their massed, frilly blossoms. They thrive on the hot, dry summer which has left most of us exhausted. I am going to a summer school on Australian spirituality with David Tacey, because I'm still confused and doubtful about my religious faith and I would like to recover its fullness. Perhaps it was only ever a childish faith, suitable for the good times. Dad's suffering has changed me and I may need to find new ways to think about God and faith and hope because what I've got isn't working any more, and it's a great loss.

My predominant emotion at present is outrage. Even though I know it's probably wrong thinking and self-defeating, I feel outraged by the pattern of life. Since my father's ordeal, I have become aware of all the suffering around me—people dying painfully of cancer or paralysed by a stroke, and an unusual incidence of brain tumours. This is what happens in life, yet I feel stupidly appalled by it—the recurring pattern of struggle, suffering and finally annihilation. What makes us think it's bearable? How do we endure it? Why don't we rage in protest? Why don't more of us go mad as a result of the plight of the human condition?

The answer, in many religious traditions, is that we believe the pattern of life is a journey of setback and overcoming, testing and growing, in small and large ways, over and over throughout life until, when we die, we go into eternal life with God—or, for the Buddhist, into another cycle of learning on the way to nirvana.

But what if these are fairy stories we have invented because, without them, we would sink into despair? I have appreciated David Tacey's books and I hope that his summer school will offer some insights, and suggestions for a more mature spirituality.

I'm planning to write notes in a small, gilt-bound exercise book, on lined paper. This is how we worked when I was a child in school. It's familiar, reassuring. It wasn't only the content that mattered but the look of the completed page. Had you kept a neat margin on the left-hand side? Were the words well spaced? Did the writing flow, sloping slightly forward? Backward-leaning letters were undesirable, a sign of some weakness of character. And it was vital to spell correctly. The reward for good work was a star stamped onto your page. For excellent work, a gold star. An exercise was given a mark out of ten. I would have been disappointed to get less than seven out of ten, for anything. We covered an exercise book for each subject—English, Geography and so on—with brown paper, neatly folded inside the front and back covers with hospital corners. The same as tucking in sheets when making your bed. Coloured pictures were saved from magazines, calendars, seed catalogues or postcards, to paste onto the front cover. The paste was home-made from flour and water. Covering the books gave a sense of anticipation of what you would learn in the year ahead.

I'm still excited by the sight of an empty page. I smooth it diagonally upwards, from left to right, with the heel of my right hand, before I start to write, to enjoy the feel of the paper. This paper is slightly glossy. A matte texture would be even more pleasing but this is quite alright. It is empty, waiting, inviting. I'm glad that I'm noticing and taking sensuous pleasure in such things again, but my underlying anger is disconcerting, out of character, in need of healing.

When I arrived, early, for the second day, I cut some long fronds of blue plumbago from the garden outside Ramsey Hall and draped them across the lectern and the speaker's table. They relieved the starkness of the black velvet stage curtains which I found depressing on the first day.

Already David has offered many useful reflections. He suggests that spirituality constitutes the largest part of the psyche, that if we deny our spirit, we cut ourselves off from our root system; we lose orientation. When Australia's Indigenous peoples were colonised by the English two hundred years ago, a richly spiritual life was confronted with scientific rationalism—two different aspects of the human psyche came into conflict and are trying still to reconcile with each other.

He suggests, too, that spirituality goes with maturity, as Aboriginal people have always understood. They let their children be carefree and play until, at puberty, they subjected the boys to painful and rigorous initiation to begin the rite of passage to adulthood. The initiation began the process of learning the law, custom, taboo and responsibility to the ancestors. They had to learn tribal and family groupings and obligation to the land, in an intricate, complex cultural understanding of what it is to be human.

They knew that attaining spiritual maturity was no easy task, that you could not just leave it to chance, that it must be ritualised through ceremonies. They knew that their service of the sacred would need to be carried out through songs sung, and stories told and dances danced in ritual ceremonies, to be performed over and over, lifelong.

Through the painful, testing rites of initiation, young men won meaning and purpose, status, self-discipline, responsibility, crucial knowledge and courage. So there was purpose in the suffering. Is that an answer for me—that suffering is a gateway to spiritual growth and, hopefully, maturity?

Having grown up in Alice Springs, with many Aboriginal friends, David tells of a recent visit to an Aboriginal elder. They went together to the Alice Springs Hospital to see youths who were ill and deranged from sniffing petrol. The elder said it was because 'these young fellas have lost ceremony'.

Speaking of the high rate of teenage suicide today in Australia, David wonders if depression might be an indication that something 'down below' is asking for attention. He puts up a slide of a Leunig cartoon. It shows a person kneeling on the ground peering down into a dark hole. As he looks more closely into the darkness there is a glimmer of stars—and even the crescent moon of hope. David places great value on Leunig's insights.

David thinks we are in a time of spiritual crisis and that the twenty-first century may see widespread depression in the West unless we give spirituality a place in our lives and allow it to make its claim upon us—the claim to be of service, to help each other, to care for the earth, to honour God. We are deluged with consumerism and with more information than we can handle, yet what we really need is a formation and nourishment of the spiritual life.

David mentions that his father has died recently and that he is devastated by his grief. In the lunch break he tells me that he often sobs without warning, even on public transport. It's a relief to see his eyes brim with tears. We can speak to each other about this with real sympathy and understanding. We want to hear each other, to know what this grief is like, for each other; to search for words to describe these unfamiliar emotions, surprising in their intensity; to name the gnawing core of sadness that goes to sleep with us each night and wakes with us each morning as an intimate companion. His sorrow validates my own. Others join in. We are at a stage of life where many of us are losing our parents and being shaken by the strength of our grief and shocked by our unexpected bouts of anger. We've had no training for this.

I'm trying to find Les Murray's poem about the death of his father. Les is a good friend of David's. It's consoling to be in the company of another grieving person.

Something about the day stirs a memory from the deep, like an ocean current disturbing submarine fields of kelp. When I was a child, one of the women always brushed my hair at night—my mother, my grandmother or my aunt Brownie. It was like a benediction: their kind, calming, long strokes with the brush through my hair.

David says that a lot of his students at the university have been raised by atheist parents, yet they come to his spirituality course, curious, searching for something they lack. His peers on the teaching faculty are suspicious of him but some of them sneak in too. (Jung had an inscription above his door: 'Called or not called, God is always present'.)

David believes that spirituality is about what we don't know, about listening to the self, to others, to what's happening in the world. He thinks that either you go spiritual or you go mad. I think I've gone a bit mad. Is that from neglecting my spiritual life, or from grief, or both?

By the end of his summer school, I have something of value to think about: that, while life is a magnificent gift, it is also very difficult—that we are all in it together and we must try to see each other through it. At the same time I know that my journey (to God?) must be travelled uniquely and, at an interior level, alone.

And now I have found Les Murray's wonderful poem about his father Cecil, who died on 6 January 1995, the feast of the Epiphany: 'Don't die, Dad—but they die ...'[2]

According to his biographer, Peter Alexander, Les Murray experienced a sense of renewal and healing after the death of his father. At the funeral he delivered a eulogy in the Bunyah church and wrote to a friend two months later: 'I was managing very good aplomb because I hadn't started grieving but rather had largely finished grieving: I'd been helping Dad with his 43-year mourning for Mum all that time and really mourning him as well. And now I could lay the burden down ... Queer to be an adult too.'[3]

Reading this, I thought it was partly true for me too—that I had done a lot of the mourning for Dad while he was still alive. What I am grieving most deeply is the fact that he suffered.

I have always felt a bond with Les Murray. Although we have met several times, once for a *Search for Meaning* interview, I know him mainly through his poetry. We are exactly the same age. He, too, is an only child. We grew up among similar people. What is now termed 'rural and regional', we knew simply as living in the country. In all the controversies he's been involved in, I am inclined to be on his side, even when he's possibly wrong. Loyalty has a higher value for me than logic.

I cannot understand all his poems but I love to read them and to intuit them and to connect with the familiar world they evoke. I never tire of them. I appreciate the sound of them, especially when read, rather too quickly, by Les Murray himself. Alexander claims that Les Murray has no modern peer in the poetry of human grief.

How significant they are, these friends of the spirit. When Wendy was in hospital I used to ring each day and visit less often. One day, on the phone, I asked her if she would like me to visit the next day.

'It doesn't matter, you're here anyway, in my head.'

And I knew what she meant. That's what it's like for me, too, with the kindred spirits—some of them you've never met but you know their poems or have read an article about them, or have seen their paintings and you are instantly in tune with them. It's reassuring to know that, no matter how many people don't know who you really are, there are a few who do, a few who seem to live their lives with a sensibility akin to your own, even if you don't actually know each other in the flesh.

As always, when Mary is in hospital, I soon become used to the rhythm of the three-hour round trip every two days to keep her company and attend to her needs. She's making slow progress. I wonder if her recovery this time is hampered by unspoken grief. After twenty-seven years with a dear companion, she must be feeling bereft but she doesn't speak about it. I hope she has someone to confide in, maybe one of her long-time community carers, Jo or Sue, who have become her friends.

SATURDAY, 20 JANUARY 2001

Last night I went with friends to the Concert Hall at the Opera House to see the Australian Art Orchestra do Paul Grabowsky's version of Bach's *St Matthew Passion*. It was reassuring to feel touched by its exhilaration and power. Afterwards we drifted down the steps of the Opera House where people were waiting for the arrival of the spectacular Rainbow Serpent. We passed it as we wandered under the colonnades. There were still masses of people promenading at eleven o'clock, even though it was nearly the end of the Festival of Sydney. Couples hand in hand, each with a mobile phone pressed to one ear, talking to someone else. Families with babies in high strollers, young travellers trailing suitcases on wheels. Surreal, balmy, beautiful night-time Sydney, with palm trees growing out of the paving stones along Writers' Walk.

We had coffee and dessert in a cafe right on the harbour's edge, watching ferries glide in and out of Circular Quay. There were people leaning on their balcony railings on upper floors of the Toaster, the apartment block that caused such vehement protest but has now become a clumpy, regrettable fixture.

When we parted, I drove home with the car windows open. There were men with luminous strips on their jackets doing night roadwork. I had had a lovely evening, but I started to cry. I could not imagine there would ever again be a time when I am not sad.

I heard the protests of both my parents, as though they were with me in the car. Mum said: 'Get on with your wonderful life. You've got everything, beautiful friends, interesting work'; and Dad was amazed: 'What on earth are you bawling for? Be happy, have fun, get on with it. We've had our turn.'

I knew they were right but how do you do it? While I was waiting at red lights, a police car pulled up beside me. I turned to face a woman constable, no more than a metre away. She looked at the tears on my face, kindly enough but unsurprised, familiar with the tragedy of life on a daily basis. The lights changed.

Round the last corner before home, looking across the harbour at the beauty of the city skyline, red and blue neons, the bridge, calm white clouds in the navy Brett Whiteley sky, a waning moon … it was so ravishing you could forget to breathe. There seemed little to separate this from eternity.

Deep and dissolving verticals of light
Ferry the falls of moonshine down … the Harbour floats
In air, the Cross hangs upside-down in water.[4]

26 JANUARY 2001

I celebrated Australia Day by taking delivery of my new car, made in Japan, which is a bit hard to explain. I'm surprised they were open today. I still felt unaccountably upset at trading in the little white vehicle that has carried me safely through several hard times, over 90,000 kilometres in the past ten years, up and down the F3 to Dad and Mary hundreds of times. But Dad had been encouraging me to get a new car.

'You don't want to be the richest woman in the cemetery, do you?' Generously, Mary has given me Dad's trusty old station wagon to use as a trade-in. I don't like parting with it either, having to take out Dad's maps and all their picnic things, never to be enjoyed together again.

I had asked for the registration plates to be transferred from my old car to the new one. I thought that would give me some continuity. When I arrived, the salesman was ready with tools to make the changeover. I glanced without interest at the plates I was about to discard from the new car. The letters were my own initials. What are the odds against that? I took it as a reminder to trust more readily; that there's no need to intervene; that things will go well without the need for manipulation. In the words of the prophet Isaiah (Isaiah 43:2): 'Do not be afraid, I am with you. I have called you by your name. You are mine.'

I drove the new car carefully to a suburb further west to attend a citizenship ceremony. The doors of the Civic Centre were open and people were finding chairs for their small family groups. There were Chinese, Pacific Islanders, Iranians, Africans, Egyptians, Indians, Serbians and many more, all ready to become Australians today.

I sat with two young Chinese women who could barely contain their excitement. One had become an Australian citizen this time last year. Now it was her friend's turn. A council official came along the rows to say that candidates should sit at the front so we rearranged ourselves obediently.

The official party arrived, led by the mayor, a second-generation Italian Australian, perspiring freely in his fur-trimmed robe and gold chain. Following in the procession were local clergy, councillors, a police sergeant and constable, a member of parliament and an Australia Day ambassador. They sat on chairs at the front, facing us.

Short speeches were made at the lectern, decorated with two Australian flags, crossed, and a potted palm. Then the candidates were asked to stand and take the pledge of loyalty to Australia. They had a choice of two versions, one with God and one without. Then, each name was announced and they were presented, in turn, with their medal and certificate, and an Australian native plant and photographed shaking hands with the mayor and ambassador. It was moving to see how much it meant to people to take this momentous decision, half a world away from their homelands, on a Sydney summer morning. Some people seemed to be on their own. There were also whole families. At morning tea time there were tears and smiles and more photographs. The police sergeant was coerced away from his paper plate of small, triangular sandwiches to be a popular centrepiece in one group picture after another, handsome and self-conscious, surprised by all the attention. In many of the societies the newcomers have left, the police probably don't take morning tea with the citizens.

The mayor, still perspiring, was circulating. He said it was nice to see me there and unaccountably assured me that the fur edging his robes was rabbit, not ermine, just in case I was concerned. He said he enjoyed *Australian Story* and I congratulated him on the ceremony. It was just right, not too long, not too formal, friendly, welcoming and a very significant milestone for these forty or so new citizens. And this scene was repeated all over Australia today. How many wonderful Australian stories there were, waiting to be lived out. I hope they'll all be rewarding ones, to make up for the struggle of the past and to justify the hard decision of leaving the lands of their birth. I couldn't do it. It would break my heart to leave my country and it must feel like that for many of them.

This will be something interesting to tell Mary about when I go up to Gosford. She and her family befriended a Lithuanian couple who came to Australia as refugees after World War II. Both were doctors but, since their qualifications were invalid here, they did menial work in hospitals and elsewhere. Eventually they sat all the examinations again and went to practise medicine in the United States. They have remained lifelong friends with Mary, exchanging letters and cards for over fifty years. The friendship has been precious to Mary. She has often shown me photographs of the growing family and their changing circumstances.

27 JANUARY 2001

It's after eight o'clock, still dusk, yet a butcherbird is calling and there are a few other chirrupings I cannot identify. It must be a relief for them, as for us, to have rain at last after these many hot January days. It came in with a storm about an hour ago, thunder and lightning breaking the tension of humidity. Now it's settled into steady rain, light drops spattering the leaves outside the windows, open onto the balcony. The sound is calming, restful, a relief. The gutters are starting to overflow; little streams are trickling down the hillside, the liquid sounds refreshing.

When I got home this afternoon, after the long, round trip to the hospital, but before the rain, the rooms were oppressively hot. I began to draw the curtains against the westerly sun. On the windowsill, motionless between shells, was a large Blue Triangle butterfly. I've never seen a butterfly come into the house before. I touched it very gently. It was dead, yet still a brilliant blue, and perfect, proclaiming the possibility of beauty after death and a reminder of the several cycles of death and rebirth which a butterfly endures in the four stages of its life cycle.

The discovery gave me a moment of grace, allowing wonder to replace the sadness which has become a frequent companion now, largely displacing anger.

SUNDAY, 28 JANUARY 2001

For the first time, I got right through Mass this morning without crying. I'm not even sure what I'm doing there. I don't want to cry, but there's something about the Mass which opens my heart and makes me vulnerable to what I am really feeling, underneath the protective, everyday mask. It's embarrassing to cry. There are many people here carrying their own suffering without showing a sign of it. I sat beside a woman who has just lost her beloved husband after nursing him through a long illness at home. We were good company for each other, speaking briefly but quite openly about our grief.

She said it's important to maintain an interest in things. I said that I can see it all going on but feel that I am behind a pane of glass—that, often, I cannot register the significance of things. She thinks this is a dangerous path. Glancing up towards the sanctuary, she said: 'I think this is really what keeps me going'.

I could not bring myself to say that, for me, faith also seems to be behind glass. I remember having it but at present I cannot connect with the clarity of it that I used to know.

The second reading was the famous passage, popular at weddings, from St Paul's first letter to the Corinthians, Chapter 13—'Love is always patient and kind …'. But it was one of the later verses that caught my ear today. Disappointed, as usual, by the desiccated modern version, translated with little ear for rhythm or cadence, I transposed it mentally into the familiar words of the King James Bible of my childhood (13:12): 'For now we see through a glass darkly but then face to face: now I know in part; but then shall I know even as also I am known.' It's a call to trust without knowing, yet. A real call to faith. I can only hope that it is true, that, one day we will understand what God and life are all about. At the moment all I can see is the suffering of people. It seems to me that we are like dumb animals grazing in the paddock beside the slaughterhouse, powerless, subject. Even as I think this, I recognise that the image is crude, that it leaves out too much to be legitimate. Grief seems to pick up your psyche and shake it, like a dog worrying a rag doll: what you trusted before you don't believe now; it is as though your framework of meaning is being dismantled. You wonder what will put it together again, and if you will be the same person.

Although my view is so bleak and uneasy, there are certain images which break through, bringing lucidity and calm. I am reading *The Edwardian Lady: The Story of Edith Holden*.[5] Edith kept nature notes, a naturalist's journal of notes, quotations from the poets and exquisite sketches made in the English and Scottish countryside. The reader can see the seasons of a full year through Edith's keen eyes and I am captivated by her sensitive observation and the detailed beauty of her drawings and watercolour paintings. Her *Country Diary*[6] became a bestseller seventy years after it was first written.

It is when she roams in South Devon that I am stirred by a mysterious sense of recognition as though I know that country. Can I have inherited the memory from my forebears who lived in that part of England several generations ago? It's a remembering I have experienced before when seeing paintings or photographs of that landscape—the green wooded hills of farms that run down to the sea—or when reading the novels of R.L. Delderfield, like *A Horseman Riding By*. The country he describes and the people in it are not strangers to me. I've written of this before. It's real for me. I've heard people speak of past lives but I wonder if this impression of deja vu could be fragments of memory inherited in the DNA, like the gene for a heart condition. Or, even more interesting, might it be that shards of recollection are inherited in the spirit which is subject neither to time nor biology?

However it may happen, it is consoling to feel a kinship with people who seem still to be real, although physically inaccessible. It adds a kind of evidence to the intuition of a life after death, or a life beside this material life that we know now, and hints at some hope of longed-for reunion beyond death.

~

This evening at twilight a butcherbird chose its resting place for the night on a branch just outside my study window. We watched each other for a while. Then it raised its throat to give voice to two last strong warbles of its distinctive song, fluffed itself up and settled onto its well-concealed perch. It was unusual to see it there alone … and comforting to see another solitary creature apparently at peace with itself, so unlike me. I recall a priest saying that one of the gifts of his celibacy was that he could be a witness to the single person, the widow or the lonely; that he could live in spiritual solidarity with their state because he knew it himself. It's a compassionate idea that lends meaning to a state of suffering.

Now it's completely dark. The possums are crashing through the trees and further away there is the sudden high-pitched squeal of a small animal caught. Instantly my heart starts thumping wildly against my chest. I can only submit to the alarming pump of muscle pushing blood out into arteries much too fast and wait for its racing beat to subside, as suddenly as it began, half an hour later.

31 JANUARY 2001

Fortunately it's time to get ready for a new year of *Australian Story*: our sixth year. Each year I suggest to our executive producer that it's time we put up a young presenter for the program. I think the last few months have aged me noticeably and I offer the name of a younger person. But she is quite sure that she wants me to continue presenting *Australian Story* this year. She says I suit the demographic. Thank goodness for that and for the forty-odd years of experience which have given me a good memory and a capacity to concentrate completely on work when I need to. I never bring my grief into the professional part of my life, not consciously anyway. No doubt all my colleagues are coping privately with something challenging. Also it is a relief to have to rise to the occasion. My parents always insisted on the value of interesting work for a fulfilling life and they were right. I'm grateful every day for their encouragement and this is a good time to try to live up to it as they would most certainly expect.

'Get on with your life. Make the most of it!' As ever, I can hear their voices quite clearly.

I think Mary will be discharged from hospital soon and then we will resume our quest for a good retirement village. But I wish I had more energy.

Away from the discipline of work and driving up to Mary every few days, this brooding humid weather gives me an excuse for apathy. I don't care about things as I would normally. I read the newspaper and fail to find any item that holds my interest. My eyes slide away from the headlines. I watch *Wildside*, *Heartbeat* and *The Bill* on television, for distraction and escapism.

Why am I handling this loss so badly when I had eight rich years listening to people keeping faith in life through their hard times on the *Search for Meaning* programs and now, *Australian Story*? I should be drawing on their courageous stories for sustenance. Perhaps we do not really learn and understand until we experience something personally. Only pictures of the earthquake victims in India stir

Dad's beloved 'Grattai', his lifelong, spiritual home

Dad, third from right, with his parents, George and Jessie James, and Melvie, Paul and Gwen. 'When we had to leave 'Grattai' it was a wrench for all of us'

Dad and his parents on a picnic in 1930.
'Honourable, industrious, rich in character,
with a fine sense of fun'

At twenty-seven Dad had an eye for
fashion and cars, but no money in the bank.
A would-be young man about town, he was
a reluctant trainee bean counter

A picnic with Nancy Pountney
in the early 1930s. No money
but plenty of style

Carefree, salad days in the
1930s. Dad and Nancy at Rose
Bay, Sydney, and with Laurence
and Ida Henderson. 'Anyone for
boat tennis?'

My mother Nancy and her mother, Granny Pountney, looked suitably stylish in Sydney's George Street, 1936

K. Day drew this lovely charcoal sketch of my mother two years before I was born

Returning home with my mother and new baby to support, as well as a car, Dad had just ninety pounds in the bank

In our sunny Hunters Hill, Sydney, garden in 1938

Sydney in wartime and Mum and Dad step out in style. He enlisted to serve his country, but it meant leaving home and family

'Where's my Dad?', Hunter's Hill, Sydney

With Mum at Hunters Hill, Sydney, 1940, before we went to live with Granny Pountney on Mayne Street, Murrurundi, NSW, for the rest of the war

A seaside holiday at Jervis Bay, NSW, 1943 while Dad was away 'at the war'

Dad, right, 'Somewhere up north', 1943. He wanted to fight overseas, but despite many attempts he was never posted

Awaiting orders, 'Somewhere, 1943'. Dad, in the beret, made the inlaid wooden chess board

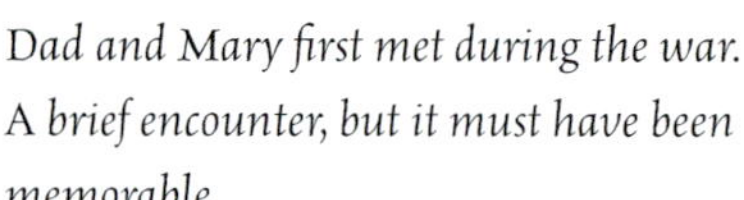

Dad and Mary first met during the war. A brief encounter, but it must have been memorable

With my beloved mother and our cat, Mrs Tiggy Winkle, at Murrurundi, NSW, when basin haircuts were the fashion

As an Acting Flight Officer, Mary, kneeling, was addressed as 'Madam' by lower ranks

As this drawing by G. Patton rather suggests, NX121935 Captain BN James, AIF, was 'a handsome, rather intimidating stranger who sometimes came home on leave'

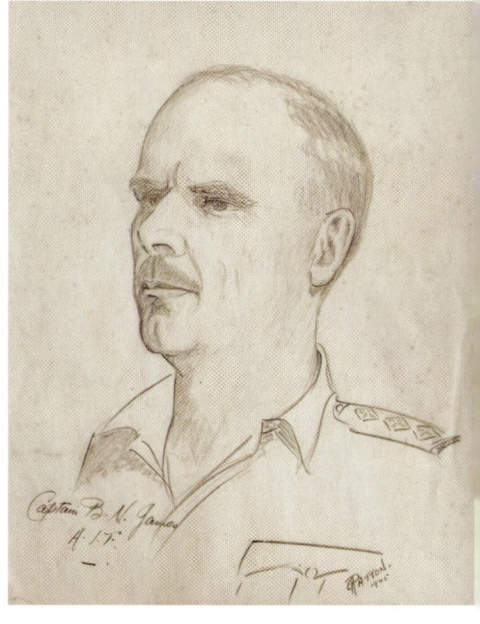

Seven years old and hoping Dad will be 'home by Christmas'

With other country kids, second from right in the middle row, in 5th class at Murrurundi Central School, NSW, 1947

Ten years old with Mum, Dad and cousin Dinah Gray

Aged twelve and 'abandoned' at boarding school, SCEGGS, Moss Vale, NSW

Dad's most prized qualification, the 'Hole Out in One' golf cartoon he was awarded at Gosford Links, NSW, in 1965. He repeated the feat in February 1985

'All that artistic desire buried under the tedium of balancing figures'. Dad's sketch in oils near Gosford, NSW, 1975

Dad and Mary married in 1973 at St Andrews Presbyterian Church, Gosford, NSW

'King James' turned eighty in 1987.
The next year we had a holiday at
O'Reilly's on the Lamington Plateau in
Queensland

With Dad and Mary after receiving the AO, Government House, Sydney, 1988. 'I must remember that I cannot make her happy'

Another family visit safely negotiated. 'We understand each other far too well…'

After Dad's death in 2000 Mary was 'very brave and perhaps does her crying alone'

With Mary and Frank Bock at The Mad Hatter's Tea Party. The beautiful old roses came from Heather and Frank Bock's garden

This moment at Heather and Frank Bock's home produced the rare, unguarded smile of a child from Mary

Mary at Yallambee Lodge, Gosford, NSW, 2001.
'This is a lovely photograph of you.' Her reply, 'I can't stand it!' Always the last word

My Bethlehem friends. From left, Ibtisam, Daoud, Fadi and Lina Abu-Jaber. 'Daoud's constant faith in the face of struggle puts my doubts to shame'

my compassion now and reinforce my present dark understanding of life as a tragedy in which the only redeeming features are the nobility and dignity of the suffering people and those who seek to help them.

I sleep lightly, as though I am on guard, and wake easily at any noise. Once, during the night, a possum comes in. It jumps from the windowsill onto my legs. In a reflex action I kick and it bounces back onto the sill and out into the bushes, coughing. The tenant upstairs comes in after midnight and wakes me again with his heavy tread. He seems unconscious that his floor is my ceiling.

EARLY FEBRUARY 2001

I bring Mary home from her long sojourn in hospital and stay a few days. She is a bit insecure after the routine of hospital and not as competent as usual. She is dismayed when she has an occasional accident but she allows me to help. It must be very humbling for someone who has always been efficient, independent and fastidious. 'Unbelievable,' she protests, in a small voice. 'I can't understand it. Nothing like this has ever happened before.'

I'm glad she doesn't recall the previous occasions. Sometimes she even manages a weak laugh which is a pretty good effort. I concentrate on maintaining her dignity when privacy is no longer possible, to make sure that nothing becomes a drama. I wonder how nurses do this every day. I suppose they develop a professional approach to giving intimate personal care which is not complicated by any past or future personal relationship with the patient. I pretend I'm a nurse.

As usual, when I give my attention to Mary, it is healing for me. That knowledge is so profound that I should not have any further questions to ask. I should just care for her with gratitude for the gift.

But sometimes I forget and seem to have to remember over and over again.

When she's been home for a while, Mary gains more confidence and mishaps are soon forgotten as her short-term memory seems to be quickly erased. She tells me the same thing several times in the course of a day. The Aged Care Assessment Team (ACAT) is arranging some more support for her to stay at home and is also encouraging her own idea that it's time she went to live where there's someone to look after her. I think she will feel much safer in a retirement hostel with round-the-clock care, meals provided, cleaning and washing done, activities, outings and companionship. Then again, she may loathe it. It's certainly a big decision and she needs time to come to it. It will be hard to leave the home where she's lived with Dad for twenty-seven years. I will research some more villages and visit them with her. There's a lot to find out about who owns them, how well they are run; and the financial arrangements need investigating.

15 FEBRUARY 2001

My mother's birthday. The white peaches are in season and I can smell their perfume as soon as I come inside out of the heat. Their velvety skins are rosy and their flesh palest green and fragrant, clinging to the red stone. They are one of the most sensual joys of summer, yet I find consolation does not come so easily now. Sadness runs deeper as I grow to understand that time does not heal it, that it becomes a part of you, either more or less conscious from day to day. At the same time, I try to act on my father's admonition that it is important to enjoy every day of your life, even if the enjoyment is more determined than spontaneous.

This evening the fading pink sky was streaked with long grey clouds, backlit by the setting sun. It reminded me of an evening dress my mother made to wear to a ball in one of the country towns where we lived. It was elegant, waterwave taffeta, the flared skirt full length in shimmering grey, cut on the cross—an unusual choice for evening—and a grey stole lined with cerise. It was original and striking. Behind the events of my everyday life, I'm always watching and listening for a sign of my mother and father. In the uncertainty of dusk, neither day nor yet night, there seems more opportunity to slip through into the infinity where they might be, to catch a glimpse of them, to hear them call my name. I feel incomplete, as though some vital part of my self is missing.

Is this how all bereaved people feel—that the purpose of life has disappeared with the loved ones? It's as though they have gone home without me and my only desire is to catch up to them.

No doubt there is something wrong with this state of mind but that's where I am at the moment, and I'm trying to be honest in what I'm writing.

20 FEBRUARY 2001

We've had a strong response to the kidney transplant story produced by Helen Grasswill. Predictable when you consider the extraordinary generosity of helicopter pilot Nick Ross's gift of a kidney to his employer and friend, Kerry Packer. It was moving to hear the two men speak about it and to see what an ordeal it was for both donor and recipient. A painful and risky procedure which, in this case, has gone successfully. No doubt it will give a boost to the idea of organ donation, especially since two powerful, articulate, high-profile men are not only supporting it but actually showing how it is done. It fascinates me that we can never measure the impact of *Australian Story*. It is a good use of the medium and I'm fortunate to be part of it.

Today I'm sorting through Dad's clothes, to take to Sr Myree Harris at Gethsemane Community at Petersham. Myree is a Sister of St Joseph who has made a home for twenty years for four people with various mental illnesses. They are her household. As well, she is an advocate for the mentally ill people who live in boarding houses in the inner west of Sydney—places to which they migrated as the big psychiatric institutions were shut down. It was a well-meaning attempt to bring the mentally ill out from behind walls into the community but it was only half a plan. Where and how were they to live in a happier situation? Today many are homeless, sleeping rough, or in jail or sometimes finding a bed in the night shelters like Matthew Talbot Hostel for Homeless Men or living in a single room in a boarding house. Some of these places are alright, providing a basic level of accommodation and company. In others, the proprietors take the resident's whole pension and offer only wretched amenities in return.

Myree befriends these disadvantaged residents, responds to their needs and reports any poor standards or infringement of people's rights to the Department of Ageing, Disability and Home Care. As a member of the NSW Boarding House Advisory Group, she is able to influence policy. St Patrick's Church Hill parishioners fund hundreds of Christmas gift parcels which contain toiletries, underwear, socks, sweets and cosmetics for residents of boarding houses, those now in aged care, and other frail, aged people without family support. Many food hampers are provided and each person receives individual Christmas cards. The packing is done by Myree's household at Gethsemane and volunteer students. Supported by St Vincent de Paul, Myree brought Compeer to Australia from the US—a friendship program which matches appropriate community volunteers with people receiving treatment for mental illness.

Myree is an inspiration to me. She seldom takes time off. After early Mass each day she works until all hours. Very occasionally, if she can find someone to take responsibility for a night at Gethsemane, she will go off somewhere quiet, sleep for hours, read and have a meal, before driving back next morning. She enjoys a rare outing for dinner and a good laugh and a glass of red wine, and most Christmases she sings in Handel's *Messiah* at the Sydney Opera House. One year I went to hear her. It was magnificent.

When I'm feeling dispirited, I think of Myree living each day with faithful purpose. She rolls up her sleeves and brings the hands and eyes and the righteous anger of Jesus Christ to a troubled, unfashionable area of society. She is astute and fearless in giving a voice to vulnerable people who have no influence and she is calm and constant with people who are not always easy or pleasant or grateful.

I feel right about taking Dad's clothes to Gethsemane. Most of them are very worn but still wearable. He did his own washing and mending and everything is clean, neatly folded or hung in its place. In the top drawer, white cotton interlock singlets and underpants. In the second, many pairs of ancient socks, darned by himself, rolled together in pairs, and his two wool singlets with sleeves. Some of the pyjamas are too far gone, mended over and over. As he became thinner, he cobbled their waistbands into big looping pleats, so they wouldn't fall down. His woollen jumpers will need a wash. Belts and ties are hanging methodically over two lines he's rigged inside the wardrobe door. Here's the old Imperial Services Club tie he wore to hold up his gardening pants. He had few occasions to wear a tie, in recent years. I'm not sure why that particular one was demoted to humble, backyard appearances but I often sensed an ambivalence in him about his war service.

Everything smells strongly of Dad. I'll keep one of his jumpers and two of his shirts to wear myself, and two silk scarves I brought home for him from India forty years ago which he liked very much and wore until they were threadbare. This woollen beanie, knitted for him by a friend, he wore to bed in winter because he slept beside an open window for fresh air. There's a smart green felt hat, with a guinea fowl feather tucked into the band. Men don't favour hats now except to go to the races. And two white cotton sun hats he used to wear doing jobs outside. I don't think he'd bought a new pair of shoes for many years but there are five pairs of old brogues here, all well polished. Every shirt is clean on its hanger and each pair of trousers hung neatly by the cuffs. A winter dressing gown, an ancient dinner suit, a windjacket. Nothing extravagant. He always looked good in his clothes.

It feels strange to be taking his clothes out of their drawers and off their hangers to carry them out to the boot of the car. It feels wrong, like everything else. It's taken seven months even to contemplate it.

Yesterday, when I suggested to Mary that Sr Myree would be glad of Dad's clothes, she agreed immediately that it was a very good idea. I asked her if she wanted to keep anything but she said, 'What's the point?' I'm putting aside for her a few of his best, soft handkerchiefs. I'm glad she hasn't come into his room to supervise me.

Finally everything is out. The car is filled with black plastic bags and the drawers and the wardrobe are empty. They look desolate. By the time I finish, I feel giddy with the exertion of doing something that I am so unwilling to do and I've got bad hay fever and a racing heart. Upstairs Mary and wonderful Heather and Frank are completing a mammoth session of bookkeeping. Heather and Frank have appeared like angels into our lives to support Mary with her accounts, investments and record-keeping. They were recommended by the solicitor. As another accountant, Frank knew of Dad which makes a nice connection. But whoever heard of accountants making home visits? It's too good to be true. Mary takes their visits as a matter of course. I don't think she has any idea how fortunate she is to have their professional expertise. Frank used to work with one of the top firms in Sydney until illness made him retreat to local work. He's in remission just now.

As I carried out my sorrowful task downstairs, the murmur of their voices has been agreeable. When I go up Mary says: 'Well, have you had a nice rest while we've been working?' And I say that I have.

'Yes,' she goes on, 'your father liked to sit and watch the cricket on television all day. Or golf. Of course, I never had time.'

I rejoice silently that Dad is no longer here to be riled by the provocation of this frequently voiced myth. In recent years, instead of reacting, he had taken to rolling his eyes comically in reply to these barbs. I certainly can't find the energy to defend him to Heather and Frank. My recently acquired practice of detachment is working well at present. I hope it lasts. It's a great improvement on the old reaction, rising in irritation to every bait and then being ashamed of my inappropriate impatience with a frail, bereaved, elderly lady.

I notice that married people seem to like announcing each other's shortcomings in front of others. Such things can be said in public as a sort of joke whereas in private the statement may provoke conflict. Perhaps it's also a means of claiming the status of partnership, and providing a readily accepted way into conversation with another couple. Dad used to do it too. To me it's chilling, like a little betrayal. More likely it's just one symptom of the dense complexity, ambivalence and contradictions of intimate relationship. Was it actor Peter Ustinov who said that love is an act of endless forgiveness?[7]

Frank and Heather stay for afternoon tea which is gracious of them. It's probably the last thing they feel like doing. Maybe they can tell that we are in need of company—or an umpire. Their heads must be spinning from repeating everything loudly three times but they seem to like Mary and admire the way she's tried to keep her books in order, in the last few months, without Dad.

I bring in the teapot and some things to eat and get ready to pour.

'How do you like your tea, Frank?'

'Strong, with a bit of milk, thanks Caroline.'

While I'm pouring it, Mary, who has not heard me, says, 'How do you take your tea, Frank?'

'Strong, with a bit of milk, thanks Mary.'

'Strong or weak?'

'As it comes, thanks Mary. On the strong side.'

'Do you take milk?'

'A bit of milk, thanks Mary.'

'You can pour Frank's tea strong and not too much milk.'

She watches me closely as I'm pouring and says, 'If you'd thought, you could have poured mine first because I have it black and not too strong.'

'Yes, I've poured yours first, Mary. Here it is.'

'I beg your pardon?' Is she putting on airs for the visitors?

'I've poured your tea Mary. Here it is.'

'Put a bit more hot water in it then and fill it up.'

Heather volunteers, 'With milk, not too strong for me, thanks Caroline'.

As I'm pouring it, Mary inquires, 'Now Heather, how do you like your tea?'

'With milk, not too strong for me, thanks Mary.'

'Heather has her tea not too strong. You could have poured hers second so it would have been weaker, like mine.'

'Yes, I've already poured it.'

'What?' (What happened to 'I beg your pardon?')

'I've already poured it. It's not too strong.'

'She doesn't like it too strong.'

Fortunately Heather and Frank seem to find all this quite good fun and when, in tension, I knock over my own cup, full of tea, the hilarity increases. They are very easy to get on with. These days I can relate best to people who've been through their own suffering. They have a more acute sense of what matters and what does not.

'You can pass Frank some of that slice. And ask him if he'd like a second cup of tea.'

Mary has slipped into her WAAAF officer mode, commanding minions.

'Would you like another cup, Frank?'

'What about you, Frank, another cup?'

He declines both offers, saying he's really more of a coffee man. I'll be sure to remember next time. He's a big man but he can't resist three bits of chocolate slice. It's degenerated into something like the Mad Hatter's tea party. Mary says she's got no idea what we're all laughing at, but she is enjoying it too.

When finally they push their chairs back, ready to leave, I think I hear the rustle of wings.

21 FEBRUARY 2001

The streets of Petersham are lined with pretty, two-storey houses of a past and faded grandeur, many with 'sleep-out' additions tacked on, or verandahs closed in to make an extra room to rent. When I got to Gethsemane Myree was pruning a grevillea near the front door. Her beloved, rickety old dog, Paula, was posing in a winsome fashion, head cocked to one side, among the snapdragons.

Myree said she'd call the troops to help me unload the clothes. Agreeably, the residents of Gethsemane turned out onto the footpath. Beverley gathered up Dad's dressing gown and a navy jacket and the good suit he had worn when they made him a Fellow of the Society of Certified Practising Accountants, and the plastic bag containing his hats and the knitted beanie. With her arms full, she stopped suddenly in her tracks when she caught sight of the polish on my toenails.

'Nice colour,' she said and we talked a bit about how it was lovely to have painted toenails but difficult to get at them.

'Nice shirts,' Harold said, as he folded them carefully over his arm. I asked if he thought anyone would be likely to wear the checked wool waistcoat. He considered my question for quite a while, as he stood with me beside the open door of the boot, then he said, 'Someone will take a liking to it when winter comes'.

As we carried out this surreal dismantling of my father's life I began to feel sick but the calm kindness of my companions made it seem almost acceptable to be hanging Dad's clothes in a strange wardrobe far away from his home.

Myree said they'd be great. She had some recipients in mind, all mentally ill people, over fifty-five, who live in a facility run by the Uniting Church. Many of them are on the pension with no money left over for clothes—and there is an important outing coming up soon. An evening occasion. She knew several gentlemen who would enjoy having something good to wear.

At the last moment I couldn't part with Dad's knitted, multi-coloured beanie and stuffed it into my handbag before we went into the parlour for afternoon tea, accompanied by the rugby league match of the day on television. When I left, everyone came out onto the front steps to wave goodbye.

TUESDAY, 27 FEBRUARY 2001

This evening there was a play on television about animal rights activists in Britain. An idealistic young woman was describing the event that first moved her to become involved in public protest. She had been on a guided tour of an abattoir when pigs were being slaughtered. First the animals were stunned and then, unconscious, hung up on hooks to have their throats cut.

But she saw that the stunning was effective on only some of the pigs, while other poor beasts seemed to remain aware during their ordeal. As she watched, appalled, she thought that their eyes met hers, that they were beseeching her help. But there was nothing she could do. She started to cry at the memory of her helplessness to intervene. 'I felt as though I had betrayed them—and I've never lost that feeling.'

The short scene struck a raw nerve and I was overtaken yet again by the fearful impotence of my weeks with Dad in Intensive Care. When that feeling comes, with flashbacks, it brings a flood of vertigo, leaving room for nothing else.

In an instant, the pleasure of the day vanishes—the visit of my friends, the care I had taken arranging the pots of petunias on the balcony, cleaning the windows, setting the table, preparing lunch, making a bowl of punch to quench our thirst on such a humid day, the conversation, the laughter, the welcome deepening of our friendship and ease with each other. I treasured it while they were here. I would have kept them as long as I could.

But now the happy day seems irrelevant, unreal in comparison with my vivid recall of the terrible weeks of Dad's suffering. When

I descend into this futile darkness, at least I retain the insight to know I'm not thinking straight. Dad wouldn't want me to be thinking this way, constantly revisiting the weeks of his illness.

But what if I am reacting so strongly because I did betray him, because I didn't ask enough questions of the doctors, didn't protest more vehemently about his treatment? Why did I not insist that alternatives be found to free him earlier from the ventilator, or to relieve his nausea? I know that everything they did was to preserve his life and give him a chance to recover but much of their treatment was so wretchedly distressing for him.

I'm on a treadmill. I cannot come to peace with this and let it be. Why is that? Is it because I am still suffering the traumatic shock of it eight months later, like people getting flashbacks after a car accident, or an attack—or because I am being prompted to do something? I'm going round in frustrating circles again.

I'm not going to find an answer tonight. All I can do is write it down. And record what I can be grateful for today, in order to restore some rational balance. There's so much to be grateful for. I make a mental list:

After lunch, two young magpies flew in to warble their melodies on the balcony. The fruit punch was a success. Even though it was thirty-two degrees today, Dad's ancient green fan kept us cool enough, its heavy head rotating slowly and silently from side to side in a wide arc. I thought of a small way in which to help my friends—they always do so much for me that I can seldom repay them. And, finally, there was a sliver of new moon hanging in the western sky tonight. You're meant to make a wish on the new moon. I made a wish that my mother and father are safe and peaceful somewhere and that I will see them again some day. Even though that is our faith, as Christians, it seems so far-fetched, so unlikely, that I hold on to the hope of it, in longing, rather than with any certainty. The alternative is unbearable.

I am grateful that some people seem resolved and calm in their faith. They can do my share of believing while I am unable.

In the last two weeks the Liberal/National Party coalition has lost elections badly in Western Australia and Queensland. Dad would be cheering: 'That will give the little bastard something to worry about'.

THURSDAY, 1 MARCH 2001

This morning a card from my friend Barbara carried a quote from Henry Miller: 'The aim of life is to live, and to live means to be aware, joyously, drunkenly, serenely, divinely aware'.

The way I feel at the moment, that sounds very glib. It's the sort of thing you can write with confidence when everything's going well. I probably even agree with it but I cannot feel it. Inside the card, my friend has written: 'Perhaps it is presumptuous on my part but I have a strong feeling that you are really healing. I am sending this card because your awareness struck me a lot—little things like your birds, your petunias, your love of your precious things, your awareness of us seemed to indicate you were returning to your previous joyousness—perhaps not all the time but I am so glad it is taking hold more than before—your sadness has prevailed because of your great loss.'

Is it possible that someone else can sense healing in me before I know it myself? It's reassuring to know what my friend senses. It touches me, first that she noticed, and second that she has told me. It is an act of generous friendship.

People will give you advice or tell you how you should feel or tell you their own concerns but it's unusual to be offered a perceptive, impartial appraisal of yourself. I find it helpful. It's evidence from a trustworthy witness and I need it because I feel now that life is very unpredictable, that anything can happen and that there is no final authority, God, who will take responsibility, who will step in to ensure that things don't get completely out of hand. Or do I need to let that expectation go, to find a new image of God to replace that child's image of the powerful father-in-charge?

The Sisters of Mercy have, as their emblem, a cross which symbolises light coming out of darkness, claiming that, however hopeless a situation might be, God is able to bring something good and worthwhile out of it. This could be something unforeseen, both the event and its timing.

I find it a difficult and demanding belief about God's activity within our world and within us. Yet I suppose if we can believe that God created the world out of the darkness of nothing, to start the process of evolution, then clearly there is nothing God cannot do. It's a struggle for me to believe this, and to believe that it would apply to me personally. But it would be a satisfying image if you came to trust it.

My friend Stephen is nearly fifty. He cared for his elder brother in the final months of a long, wasting illness. In describing the intimacy and the suffering of that time he spoke of a moment when he was supporting his brother to take a few struggling steps from the bed to the wheelchair. It took a huge effort which left his brother bleached and trembling. Suddenly the situation seemed too difficult to manage and the thought came to Stephen, 'When will one of the grown-ups come to help us?'

Then he had to accept, with great reluctance, that there were no grown-ups left to come to their aid. Their beloved parents were long dead and Stephen was now the grown-up. Even though Stephen is a priest and has faith, he said it was his moment of feeling orphaned. Is there part of us that wants to keep something of the innocence and lack of responsibility of childhood forever? But perhaps it was also his moment of growing up. Is our suffering a call to grow up, to grow in maturity of spirit, and in service to each other?

~⌒~

The wind has turned around to the south-east. The freshness of it is lovely after all these humid days. It's the first evening with the rumour of autumn in it. And this weekend, they'll declare the vintage in the Barossa Valley.

FRIDAY, 2 MARCH 2001

There was a mention of Betty Cuthbert on the news. She was a heroine of mine in childhood. She was the personification of speed—lean, muscled, intense in concentration on the track; she was both blithe and modest, even in Olympic victory.

I met her recently. It was a great occasion, to celebrate the naming of Australia's 100 National Living Treasures. Of course she was one of them.

Like many others, I joined the queue to speak to her. But, from a distance, I was dismayed to see that she was in a wheelchair. Virtually immobilised, she seemed robbed of her rightful stature, of all that she symbolised, of her very self. How could this be Betty Cuthbert? I had come to pay homage to a champion but I hardly recognised her.

Nothing prepared me for the experience of standing right beside her. Certainly she had been stripped of all that she was famous for, but her presence was powerful. She was radiant. To be near her was to be both warmed and enlivened. She had that rare quality of giving you her full attention. In her expression, she communicated peace and integrity and the joy of living. I wondered how this was possible, given her disability.

Our conversation was brief because there were so many others waiting but she told me that it is her faith which sustains her and she was convincing. It was a revelation for me to see her for who she is, beyond her athletic achievement. She's still my heroine but for more profound reasons now.

She seems to be a person in whom physical suffering has been transcended, or transformed into spiritual maturity and acceptance. I would be very happy to reach that state of being but maybe it takes a long time or a different temperament.

SUNDAY, 4 MARCH 2001

When I'm in Gosford, I've taken to sleeping in Dad's room. It started when all other beds were taken, at Christmas time, and we didn't like to offer Dad's room to anyone else. I thought it might be upsetting for me but it's not and Mary is happy because I'm just next door to her.

It's companionable to look up at the square of night sky which he must have explored year in and year out, noticing the stars turning in the heavens. Last night there was a half-moon waning and the 'saucepan' was bright in the western sky, tipped on its side. Mary often mentions the diamond necklace of stars she can see in the night sky at certain times of the year, as she lies in bed.

In Dad's window frame, a big fan of frangipani leaves, black in silhouette, juts into the bottom of the picture. He made an ingenious curtain cord on pulleys so that he could draw or open the curtain as he lay in bed. Right beside his pillow, there's an open sliding window with a sawn-off broomstick lying along its runners, to prevent it being pushed open by an intruder. I used to worry about the vulnerability of two frail, old people living alone in their home but there was never a break-in.

The chorus of crickets is a lullaby familiar since childhood. Once it starts it's so constant that, after a while, you don't hear it anymore. It blends into your consciousness and accompanies you into your dreams. You only notice if it stops.

At one o'clock I was wakened by someone calling me: 'Caroline, are you there, Caroline?'

I did not know if it was the remnant of a dream. I got up to check on Mary next door but she was sleeping. She looked very small in her bed.

It must have been another flashback, a memory of the night before Dad was due to go into hospital for the open-heart surgery. That night, nine months ago, I was wakened by the plaintive ringing of the little bell kept on his bedside shelves to summon help. That night, too, it had taken me some moments to disengage from sleep and register that he was ringing and ringing and calling.

When I got to his room, he was struggling to endure severe pains in his chest. He was red in the face, gasping and in distress. He explained that he had used the nitrolingual spray but that it was not giving him any relief. He said he might wait a bit longer but he thought I might need to call the ambulance.

Unusually, we waited quite a while before they came. Through some mix-up, two crews came and four big strong-looking young men and women in uniform crowded into Dad's little room, with their radios crackling messages to tell them where else they were needed. One of the paramedics propped Dad up on his pillows, not pleased to see 'a heart case' lying flat. I felt sorry that I hadn't known what to do. He asked Dad questions while they got him ready to leave. Their presence reassured him. He'd been through this so many times before. He knew the drill. I wonder if he knew that he would never sleep in his own bed, nor return to his own home again.

Mary did not wake and I decided to spare her the distressing experience, for once. They took Dad out into the cold night. I packed an overnight bag with what he would need, left Mary a note and headed off to the hospital. At that early hour there wasn't another car on the road.

In Emergency it was just like any busy daytime. By some happy circumstance my beautiful young cousin Monique was one of the sisters on duty. It was comforting to hear her call Dad 'Uncle Brian' as she helped him. As they strove to relieve his pain and stabilise his condition, one of the injections gave him a sudden violent diarrhoea. He was embarrassed and white with exhaustion and did not get any sleep for the rest of the night.

It was appalling to think of the weak state in which he would be transported by ambulance, later that same day, to the city hospital for open-heart surgery. It was all wrong. Not a fair fight.

It all happened nine months ago yet I have such a clear recollection of it. Maybe I had the flashback because yesterday we went out to Palmdale to see Dad's memorial plaque. Mary had received a letter from the Office of Australian War Graves in Canberra several months ago, telling her that he was entitled to a war grave and asking if she wanted to take it up. The letter advised that official plaques are inscribed only with initials and surname and that it is not possible to add a religious emblem or personal message. Now they have written again to advise: 'Re the late Captain Brian N. James. The official memorial for the above veteran has been erected in the

Palmdale Native Gdn 10 Sec C Site 28. We hope that you are happy with the memorial which will now be maintained on your behalf.'

Palmdale is not far off the main north freeway. The narrow side road runs between small farms and orchards. One of them sported a hand-made sign advertising cow manure for sale. Dad would have stopped to buy a bag for his garden. He would have soaked it in the old tin bucket and poured the liquid over the plants regularly.

Several huge bunya pines stand sentinel at the main gates of a beautiful parkland, tinkling with bellbirds, on the edge of the dense green backdrop of Ourimbah State Forest. As it was a Sunday afternoon, families were visiting their loved ones. One group was sitting on a wide sweep of lawn around a newly placed plaque, a tableau in silence. The only one standing was an older man leaning on a walking frame.

Another group was wandering very slowly along a pathway through the native garden. The grandmother was stopping to read, aloud, the names and inscriptions, and to comment on them: 'Dearly loved, always remembered. That's nice. Sadly missed, gone to God. That's lovely.'

Two little children were toddling ahead, engaged in the intensity of some secret game. It was a relief to hear their high laughter break the deep resonant quiet of this settlement of souls. Boughs of crimson bottlebrush were nodding over the walkways and a small army of floral arrangements stood to attention in regulation vases across a vast sward of lawn.

We made very slow progress towards our destination. Mary seemed intent on reading every inscription too. She is unsteady on her feet now and, in her dark glasses, could have been mistaken for a Mafia dowager who'd had a stiffener or two to face a family funeral.

Wandering on ahead of her, I discovered a plaque: 'In Memory of Harry, husband of Ada and Molly'. I tried to imagine the family discussion that went into deciding that inscription. When eventually Mary caught up with me she was animated and seemed to be thoroughly enjoying herself.

'Some people take up a lot of room. That family have a whole garden plot to themselves!' She was outraged by the extravagance of the floral tributes and could not understand why anyone would bother with them.

'They'll be dead by tomorrow and then they'll look untidy and what's the point. It's unbelievable! And by the way I had no idea where you'd got to. I couldn't see you anywhere and I could easily fall over on these uneven pathways. You'd think they'd make them more even for people to walk on safely.'

I accepted the rebuke. She took my arm and we tottered onwards. 'Can you remember where on earth it is?'

The cedar tree was the landmark that led us to Dad's shiny new plaque. It's a small bronze square set into a rock decorated with lichen, in a row with others around the perimeter of a bush garden and inscribed, under the rising sun badge of the AIF, 'NX121935, Captain B.N. James, 114 General Transport Coy. 30-7-2000. Age 93.' The badge looks like a symbol of hope, a promise that there are those willing to give their lives so that others might live in peace. There were grevilleas in bloom nearby and small yellow native flowers I did not know, and lilli pilli and camellia sasanqua bushes beginning to make a spurt of growth. I had asked for the small slab of red river rock from Meroo Creek near Grattai to be part of the arrangement but they like to keep a uniform look and instead offered to bury the rock from Dad's home country beside his ashes. It seemed like a fair compromise.

As we stood arm in arm looking down at the plaque we said to each other that Dad would be pleased with it, that it was dignified, that it was in a good position, that the garden was indeed beautifully kept. Mary said, 'He liked things to be plain and simple,' and then there was no more to be said.

I could not contemplate that my father's body was reduced to ashes in a small container under that shiny plaque. As a wave of vertigo rose in my throat and my heart started racing, my mind slid away from the appalling idea. I swallowed the bitter gall and tried to focus, through my tears, on something mundane, something acceptable: the engraved symbol of the rising sun is the emblem of the Australian Imperial Forces. It stands for one concrete fact of Dad's story. He was an enlisted soldier. He answered the call to serve his country. He had a serial number. He held the rank of captain. That's all I can manage, at the moment, with a vivid memory of him, in khaki, coming home on leave to our cottage in Murrurundi, a handsome, rather intimidating stranger who brought me a luxurious bottle of lemonade and made wooden toys for me.

As I looked at his memorial plaque, his presence was strong. He could have been there with us, making some acerbic comment on the bastards awarding him the honour of a soldier's grave, in death, when they had denied him the status of a returned soldier in life. Because, in spite of his many requests, they had not posted him to fight overseas, as he wished to do.

7 MARCH 2001

I woke up crying from a bad dream I can't remember and I'm no good at all today. It's all I can do to stand up, make the bed, get something to eat and have a shower. The phone rings and I let the machine answer it. I haven't got the heart to talk to anyone. I turn the radio on for the news. It's part of my morning ritual but I don't take in the meaning of the news items. The bulletin finishes with the weather forecast but, as soon as it's given, I realise I haven't heard it.

It's seven months now since Dad died.

It's a strange, disorientating experience to lose someone who's been with you all your life. You think you're getting over it but it comes back, often first thing when you wake up. For a second or two you're alright, then you remember what you don't want to. Someone who has always been there is not there any more. How are we supposed to tolerate that, as though it's just a normal part of life? Why are we given the capacity to love with such intensity, to take responsibility for each other and to persevere with challenging relationships, if it all ends like this? As Mary would say, 'What's the point?'

The Blue Triangle butterfly I discovered six weeks ago on the windowsill is still there, still lovely and mysterious. The colour has not faded; the black fringe around the cerulean blue triangle on each wing remains bright and velvety.

Yesterday I looked it up at the library and read that it should have rusty red markings underneath the wings. Not until today when I turned it gently upside down to look, did I see that most of its body has gone—eaten away by one of the huge cockroaches which come up from the waterfront and in through the balcony. Only the butterfly's thorax and head remain. It was like a cruel joke. It gave me an awful sense of defeat. I looked at it for a while and then I turned it over carefully so that, once again, I could see the apparently entire perfection of the butterfly. I wondered where to put it for safekeeping but there is nowhere secure from cockroaches. They are as natural, inevitable and voracious as death itself.

9 MARCH 2001

The petunias are completely still on another breathless, humid evening, cascading over the rims of the pots on the balcony. Their fragrance hangs in the heavy air. Some purple ones have appeared now among the predominant crop of bright pink trumpets with white throats. Six small lettuces display crisp leaves in another pot and the cherry tomato bush has produced a few more vivid fruits.

My home is my refuge. My living room is quiet but for a subdued chorus of crickets. An occasional slow-moving party boat trails its music across the molten reflections of the bay.

On the piano Dad's photograph is surrounded by all the cards people sent and I have lit a saffron-coloured candle inscribed with one of Mary MacKillop's exhortations from 1871: 'Lean on God'.

One of the cards was given to me soon after Dad died by a woman at church whom I know only slightly. It is hand-made of purple paper flecked with silver and she has threaded it with a heavy satin ribbon in matching colours, its ends cut into V-shapes to prevent fraying. Pasted onto the card are three pictures cut out of a magazine. Two are large irises and one is of a glorious stained-glass, rose window. And she has written in gold letters: 'The Lord is our Shepherd through Life's Sorrow and Joy'.

I think about her making this card, assembling the pieces of it, looking for the appropriate pictures, pasting them on, working out how to thread such a thick ribbon without tearing the paper. I think about the kindness and the patience of it. If I could feel anything I know that it would be deep gratitude.

Here's one which reads, 'Dear Caroline, For the repose of the soul of your dear father, the holy sacrifice of the Mass will be offered, with the sincere wishes of B and D. Mass will be said by Fr Joe Dooley SJ.' What a touching connection. Fr Dooley is one of that family which owned the big general store in Murrurundi, where I accompanied Granny Pountney to do her shopping, when I was a child.

'Always the right change at Dooley's,' she proclaimed as though daring anyone to disagree. The Dooleys were Roman Catholic and Granny was Presbyterian originally but went to the Church of England. Apparently shopping could cross the sectarian divide, still very real at that time, although I never heard evidence of it in our home.

Another card from a dear friend, Pat Boland, reads: 'My dear Caroline, may your deep faith in God be a comfort to you at this time. The Holy Sacrifice of the Mass will be offered for the repose of the soul of your dear Dad at St Patrick's East Gosford ...' On the facing page, a verse from the Book of Wisdom 3:1: 'The souls of the just are in the hands of God'. These are printed cards with lines left vacant for the personal handwritten messages of sympathy.

I have received dozens of such beautiful cards and they give me the solace of knowing that even when I cannot pray, even when I feel uncertain about God and my faith, someone else will keep praying for Dad. These are perfect acts of compassion.

Wednesday, 14 March 2001

He was standing next to me at the sandwich counter today—a thin 'senior' in an old-fashioned straw hat with a strap under the chin. When the girl put his sandwich and coffee in front of him he gave exactly the right coins. With a shy, grateful smile, he told her that he was really going to enjoy his lunch today. When he carried it carefully to a table, I asked if I might join him. We were in the 'food court' of a shopping centre, disorientating with its artificial yellow light, massed potted palms and that soulless piped music that makes you want to give up. But he was happy and I hoped that he might tell me why.

'Well, this is my four hours of respite. I care for my wife full-time at home. I can do everything for her but, each fortnight, someone comes for these four hours, to give her a break from me.' As we talked, I discovered that he felt neither over-burdened nor resentful. He wanted to keep caring for her as long as he was able. He seemed proud of his achievement.

Was this outing his only respite? Well, yes. She could go to day care but she seldom chose that option. She preferred to stay at home with him. I asked what sustained him in this demanding responsibility. He replied that he had made a commitment to love her, 'in sickness or in health, 'till death us do part'. It must have been easy enough to make that promise sixty years ago when he was young and in love. How could he have imagined that it would turn out like this?

To me his life seemed difficult. Yet he was at peace, and delighted with this simple pleasure of having lunch out, in the shopping centre. Acceptance and faithful, loving service had produced serenity and gratitude for a small blessing. What more do I need to learn? Why can't I just accept and be grateful, as he is?

SATURDAY, 24 MARCH 2001

Mary has just turned eighty-eight. She has grown more frail in the last few months, especially since her last bout in hospital. She is on the waiting list now at a local retirement village which appears to be a good one. In the meantime her home support works pretty well and I stay with her as often as I can. Today, after lunch out and a drive, we were sitting by the bay. The warmth of the sun on her back is one of her favourite comforts and this is the outing she likes best: watching the boats at anchor; and people taking to the water in motor launches; youngsters girding themselves with lifejackets for a race in their sailing skiffs; seagulls screaming for sandwich crusts on the edge of family picnics on the grass. She tells me several times that she and Dad used to sit here after they'd done their shopping.

When she sees a small child tottering on newly discovered legs her face lights up and she laughs out loud. She can watch little children indefinitely with a rare, unguarded expression of delight. Maybe they recall her teaching days, or reach into the recesses of her uncertain memory to evoke some happy time of her own childhood.

There's plenty for us to watch. Suddenly she says, with a note of yearning, that it must be lovely to go for a spin on the water. I ask her how long ago she'd been in a boat but she can't remember ever going. Beside the jetty, two solid young men are hiring out small launches and dinghies. Business is not booming now that autumn is here. I walk over to explore the possibilities.

'How many of you, love?'

'Just the two but that's my companion over there. She's elderly and I'm not too confident about driving the boat.'

'Not a problem, love. If you can get her over to the end of the wharf, I'll come round and get you.'

It takes us quite a while to walk the short distance. She's very unsteady on her feet now and her head bends forward from the hump of osteoporosis. I can't imagine how we will bridge the gap between jetty and low water level, to get down into the boat. But, now that we've introduced ourselves, Darren and Stuart say there are 'No worries, not a problem'.

'You just hold on to me, love.'

She does and Darren virtually lifts her frail body safely down into the little launch, while Stuart holds it steady. Their kindness makes me want to cry.

Standing at the helm with legs planted like tree trunks, Darren inquires how fast we'd like to go and we're off.

There's nothing to hold on to and I soon realise that Mary can't sit upright without support. So I manoeuvre us into 'bookends' with my back making a brace for hers. It's lovely out on the water among the other boats—the world from a new perspective. Suddenly we are part of the weekend holiday instead of just observing it. There's a regular slap, slap as the thin skin of the boat hits the water with a steady rhythm and a bit of spray comes onto our faces. She's folded her cardigan tight across her chest.

We cruise along the waterfront looking at houses and receiving Darren's opinion of their probable real estate value. 'Top dollar,' he reckons. 'Just say the word when you've had enough.'

We say the word and he turns back up the bay. When we arrive, he puts his fingers between his teeth to whistle Stuart who, still with no other customers in sight, is reading the paper.

Disembarkation looks like a complete impossibility to me but the boys don't seem aware of any difficulty or risk of litigation. And strong arms come to the rescue once again.

Back on dry land, trying ineffectually to tidy our electrified hair, we thank them very much and get ready to pay. But Darren seems put out at the mention of money.

'It'll be a crook day when I can't take a couple of chicks out for a spin in me boat.'

And that's it. There's no room for argument. I realise then that we must look a sad case but his generosity brings tears to my eyes again. It's not the sort of thing you expect these days, in our 'user pays' society—more like an echo of the old Australia. We say thank you again and tell him we had a lovely time.

'No worries. Not a problem. Take care. Catch you later,' and he wheels the launch out from the jetty, loud and fast, raising a tight, curving wake of froth on the glassy water.

That evening, as I watched television, Darren's kindness came back to me, a little bit of evidence to set against the pain, and indifference to suffering portrayed in the news bulletin.

MONDAY, 26 MARCH 2001

Someone asked me today why I still go to Mass. It was a provocative question. When I was received into the church sixteen years ago I found that I could make sense of my life within the template of the Christian story, that it gave me a big story in which to situate my own individual experience. It felt like a homecoming, to a place I had known before and to people who seemed familiar, even in their wide range of human experience and frailty ... from the most privileged to the least. It's a story that calls the fallible, the broken, the unworthy, anyone who's struggling; a story offering forgiveness and hope. And I want that story still. It's just that I can't hear it now with the same significance. I sit in church and listen intently, waiting for it to gather me in, as it used to, to interpret for me the meaning of what's happened in the last nine months; waiting for it to put me together again, as it has done before.

I watch the people around me carefully; I see that faith seems real for them and I want to catch it again, by sitting there among them, by entering with them into the sacrament of communion with Christ: 'This is my body which will be given up for you ...'

It was the cross of Christ crucified which first gave me a way to think about suffering, even to make some sense of it. It was the cross, with its claim of 'not only death but also new life' which helped me to hope beyond the tormenting paradox of human existence: we are born, we live, we love, we suffer, we die, why?

Jesus Christ, son of God, champion of the poor, the afflicted, the sick, the marginalised, was indeed crucified but that was not the end of the story; suffering and death were the gateway to resurrection. He rose to new life, inviting all to follow. And his story has lifted people up and inspired them to lives of love and service for the past 2000 years. So why do I doubt it now? Why do I suspect it may be an illusion we choose to believe in because the alternative is chaos and despair? Since I first glimpsed its meaning, it has made sense to me; it has sustained me in both the small and large setbacks of my life. I have been able to discern that sometimes crisis does contain the seeds of opportunity, like the banksia seed germinating only after the ravaging heat of the bushfire. Of course this insight was available only in retrospect, when time had passed and I had somehow survived that particular problem. For the first time in my life I saw that suffering could have meaning, in that it calls forth our compassion. This was a revelation to me, giving me a way to think about suffering and to endure it with more trust and hope than before. But now I seem to be stuck in the crucifixion. Why do I still feel only the pain of loss? Why am I haunted by the suffering rather than illuminated by the kindness brought forth by that suffering?

My father's condition was pitiable yet it was his very woundedness that called forth the extraordinary skill and compassion of those who helped him. Their readiness to take responsibility for the survival of their patient was awe-inspiring. Could the kindness of strangers be the best evidence we're offered that there is a God of love? Perhaps it is, and perhaps it is enough.

I know that, for my father and the other patients, these men and women were the eyes and the hands and the heart of Jesus ('Inasmuch as you do it for one of these little ones, you do it for me', Matthew 25:40). Therefore I can accept that Jesus, through his own suffering, kept us company in our plight. And perhaps that's the most we can hope for; that we will not be abandoned in our suffering; that there will always be someone to watch with us, to stay with us, in our times of trial.

Companionship is the only thing I could honestly have faith in now. And we were given that, by all the staff, in Dad's last eight weeks in hospital—and by the chaplains who came, and by friends who rang, wrote and prayed. Perhaps I need to reimagine God as faithful companion, rather than demanding omnipotence, and raging against its absence.

As to my own role, I feel that I was a faithful companion for Dad, with only one important reservation: after he became conscious but still on the ventilator, unable to communicate, swallow, eat or drink, did I interpret all his speechless pleas for help and make strong enough demands to get him help, or to get him released, instead of accepting the doctors' assurance that staying on the ventilator was essential? That question is my place of crucifixion now.

And there must be others in church in that same place. There are people here with terrible problems and I can relate to them, just as I can to the many, many who write to me about their difficulties, in sadness or in anger or incomprehension at what life brings. They are the right company for me now, better than the ones who find themselves peaceful and prospering. Not that I envy them because their turn will come. It's just that we have little in common at present.

So I come to Mass for the company and to be open to the sustenance of Jesus Christ and to offer up my suffering and struggle to God, along with all the other people here who know crucifixion, and all those who are heavy-laden and who, like me, are needing an arm to lean on.

And I receive the sacraments and sing the hymns and listen intently to hear anything that will help me to survive my dislocation and my weariness. Today we sang that encouraging hymn by Deirdre Browne:

Come as you are, that's how I want you.
Come as you are, feel quite at home.
Close to my heart, loved and forgiven:
come as you are, why stand alone?
I came to call sinners, not just the virtuous.
I came to bring peace, not to condemn.
Each time you fail to live by my promise,
why do you think I'd love you the less?[8]

1 APRIL 2001, GOSFORD

I like housework at the moment. It's practical and tangible and I can see some result for my effort. It's a distraction from thinking. Mary will probably move in the next few months and decisions will be needed about what goes with her and what is to be sold or given away. I've also been restoring the leather of a writing compendium that Dad made for my mother many years ago. It's a folder, with two inside pockets to hold notepaper and envelopes and even two small compartments for postage stamps. It closes with two fine plaited leather thongs, long enough to tie in a bow. He raised her initials NRJ in capital letters on the front and decorated it with a stamped design. It's one of my treasures now; I keep in it letters of special significance. Over the years the leather has dried out and it needs some restoration.

Dad's boot-cleaning department in the garage is an old, rectangular tin with a hinged lid, containing a variety of fine brushes kept in a striped seersucker drawstring bag made by my mother, with tins of Kiwi polish and old soft cloths. When I opened the lid to find the Dubbin leather softener, the smell evoked my father's presence instantly. All my life, he cleaned the family shoes on his workbench. It was one of his morning jobs. He kept separate brushes for brown and black shoes. With his left hand pushed into the shoe, he applied the polish with a cloth in his right. He would put the first shoe aside while he prepared all the others. The next step for each shoe was a vigorous removal of the polish with a brush and a final flourishing buff with a soft cloth. You could almost see your face in them when he'd finished.

It's comforting to touch everything in the shoe tin that he used each day. And satisfying to see his handiwork regain its original glow as the writing case soaks up the restoring polish and softens into suppleness.

Next I wash a lot of curtains and hang them out to dry in the sun and then do some gardening. I like to get physically tired because it might induce sleep tonight and an escape from feelings.

In the afternoon, I lie on Dad's bed to have a rest and read for a while. I find his room a comfortable, peaceful place to be. It's full of his memory in a companionable way.

It's a simple, Spartan room, small, with a narrow single bed. Beside the bed a home-made set of shelves for his books, a torch, a phone, a hand-printed list of emergency phone numbers and an old fluorescent reading lamp. The lowboy is very old too, painted white—hanging space on the left; drawers and shelves on the right. It's empty now since my trip to Gethsemane. There's also another built-in wardrobe which I'm still working through. The only other furniture is a rocking chair where he sat to put his shoes on.

Last visit I gathered all the unused medications to return to the pharmacy. First I blacked out his name on all the labels. He was particular that nothing be thrown out with their names on it. I also took his many X-rays back to the radiologist. It was strange announcing my errand to the receptionist, a prosaic explanation for a momentous event in my life which meant nothing to her. Apparently X-rays can be used again in some way.

I don't mind doing these jobs because they are necessary and practical and they are just what Dad would do. He has left his affairs and belongings so well organised that it's no trouble to complete the task for him. He would describe it as creating order out of chaos, abbreviated to 'O out of C', as, in preparing to do the washing-up, he would say 'Let's create a bit of O out of C'. He was fond of describing himself as the best kitchenman in York Street. And Mary let him get away with it.

As I lie on the bed, looking out the window, a wattlebird is diving from branch to branch inside the tall camellia sasanqua bushes, making its rusty call and feeding on nectar from the mass of fragile pink flowers with centres like silky golden eyelashes. There are a few new flowers on the frangipani. Not nearly enough, according to Mary, who says we must have given it too much water—or not enough.

It's humbling to lie on your back and gaze at the wide sky. You see an unusual perspective, becoming aware of your own tiny place in the scheme of things. Today it seems an intimation of defeat which I have no energy to resist. The sky conjures infinity and opens a void of mystery but is silent in answer to all the questions it raises. I watch wispy clouds stirring and eddying in the thermal currents of the blue expanse, and the familiar, poignant longing for my mother and father fills my chest, as though I were a child, not an adult. I feel foolish weeping in the middle of the day, as I do when it happens on the bus or in the shops, but I'm used to it now—this lack of authority over my sadness. I get up and return to the practicality of the housework.

A big cardboard box came in the post yesterday, decorated with a pattern of black-eyed yellow daisies. I felt the usual resignation at perhaps another unsolicited manuscript to read, a heartfelt telling of someone's life that would deserve my full engagement. But inside there was a lot of shredded paper protecting four packages. I unwrapped the first, to discover a hand-painted, square, ceramic plate. The design is full of vitality—a dove in flight across the purple orb of Earth, surrounded by a swirl of new moon, stars and comets, a sunflower fully opened, and leaves and fishes in motion. In its luminous glaze and the spiral movement of the pattern, it's an evocation of the chaotic moment of creation, with the dove holding a still centre.

Turning it upside down, in curiosity, I saw that the artist, in her exuberance, had not been able to resist trailing the comet tail onto the back of the plate. In bright yellow, it framed her signature and the inscription: 'For Caroline with love'.

The other three packages contained an elegant cup, saucer and plate painted with fat pink, yellow-centred daisies on a mauve background, with leaf-green edges and raised scarlet dots. Louisa has spent hours making them for me. I love them on sight—because she made them, and for their beauty. They lift my spirits and console me and become instant treasures. With a husband and three children, how does she make time for this artwork? The parcel contains, as well, a photograph of her daughter, my goddaughter, on her birthday. She is sitting on the back lawn of their home, looking like a pavlova, in a froth of white tulle fairy skirt with a halo of flowers round her head and a doubtful expression on her two-year-old face. She looks tiny and ephemeral and, in my disordered thinking, all I can see is her extreme vulnerability in an unpredictable world, and my love for her turns to anxiety.

I put the little photograph up on the kitchen cupboard door among the photos of my other goddaughters and their children. They are so lovely and carefree: Sam holding up a proud fish; Jack as a swaddled newborn; Ziggy swimming in his father's embrace and another of him flinging food happily from his high chair; Emma, Georgia and Scarlett on a picnic in autumn. And my beloved Katie. All I feel for them is love and apprehension.

I know it's wrong; this is an aberration, the paranoia of grief, in which nothing seems safe any more. I pray that it will pass and I wonder to whom I am praying. I should exercise more willpower, most likely, keep busier, get out and see who else needs some help.

I wonder if writing all this down is keeping me stuck in grief rather than moving me through it. Perhaps I am wallowing, rather than striving to get back to some sort of normal life, whatever that may be. Is normality that state when everything is going smoothly, when not too much is happening at all? Dad didn't analyse and agonise. Not to me, anyway. Or perhaps he did, in the silence of the night when he couldn't sleep. How do I know what he thought about then? Yet when he had examined all avenues and made a decision, or a gamble, he seemed to accept the consequences without complaint. But you can be with someone all your life and still not know all about them. His apparent acceptance may have been bluff. He played a very good game of poker. In the last few years I sometimes changed his books at the library. At first I chose philosophical works about the spirituality of growing old and reflections on the meaning of life. He soon put me straight.

'I've done my thinking about all that. Just bring me something to make me laugh!'

7 A P R I L 2 0 0 1

Today I have been to a spirit medium. What would Dad think of that? Not to mention my mother. In their presence, any talk of a medium would have produced jibes, in a mock-foreign accent, and gestures of mists swirling in a crystal ball. 'I see a tall, dark, handsome stranger …' They were both intelligent sceptics with a sense of humour.

Sue's consulting room (is that what you call it?) is modest. She lives in a small flat in one of those densely populated home unit blocks that spill down the western hillside of suburban Lane Cove. She had left the front door open to welcome me. Peaceful music was playing when I arrived. The atmosphere was domestic and ordinary.

What a curious thing to be doing at 1.30 on a Saturday afternoon. Everyone else is at the beach or watching football or meeting for coffee after shopping or breaking into houses to steal money for drugs, or renewing their books at the library up the road.

If the faith I have professed for the past sixteen years was authentic I should not need to come here. After all, Christianity promises us life after death, that the soul goes on to eternal life with God. We recite it in the Creed: 'We look for the resurrection of the dead and the life of the world to come'. I have been happy to subscribe to this communal belief, which has sustained people down the centuries, as an acceptable mystery, rather than a problem to be solved. Of course, no one knows but, like Pascal, I gamble on its probability. It gives some meaning to life and death.

Our great poet Les Murray says, 'The harder it gets to believe, the happier I am with it',[9] meaning, I think, that he doesn't want to subscribe to a belief that mere humans can measure with our limited understanding. But when the worst happens, when the beloved parent or child or partner suffers and dies, what then, when trusted beliefs are torn from their moorings to float away on the tide like flotsam?

I know there's no proof to be had yet, childishly, I want some evidence, some hint, something more personal, warmer than the Creed, usually recited so fast that you can't think about what it means. I would be grateful just to hear someone say, with conviction, that suffering ends with death and that there is a new, richer life of the spirit awaiting us. I don't even know why some stranger's testimony should make any difference. I don't take opinions at face value. I'm always asking questions. But argument and reason are not answering my need in this loss.

On the walls of the small room where I sat in a comfortable armchair, there were pictures of several spiritual teachers and of American Indians in full headdress; and crystals of many colours on the windowsill, refracting the afternoon light. This decor reinforced my scepticism yet, in her manner, Sue could have been a doctor or a counsellor or a manicurist or a financial adviser. She was calm, detached, thoughtful, and she gave me her full attention.

She explained how she 'worked' and said that she was required by law to tell me that the 'reading' she would do for me was guidance only. She said that everyone has a psychic capacity for awareness of the spiritual dimension but few of us employ it. She claimed no special powers and said that she had studied the subject for twenty years since her own distress at the loss of her father. She told me the story.

Having been raised as a strict Catholic by her mother, she was frightened when her father died that, as a non-Catholic, he would go to hell. In a panic, she was hastening in her car to arrange with a priest for her father's body to be baptised before burial when, waiting at traffic lights, she heard a voice say: 'There is no need. Don't worry. Your father is safely here with us.'

That incident was startling and utterly convincing, she said, and set her on a path of inquiry. I did not doubt her sincerity but still I maintained my scepticism as she closed her eyes and appeared to wait. Then she started to speak as though she was listening to someone and relaying what she heard. There was nothing ghostly about it—no pretence of visions or ectoplasm—and she used her normal voice. And, instead of bringing me any ethereal messages, she began to enunciate a succinct analysis of a major problem in my everyday life, quite apart from grief. What she said was acutely perceptive and it was essentially personal, something I had not discussed in public. And it was coming, ostensibly via Sue, from 'Spirit' who apparently are plural since she said, 'Spirit are telling me that …' and asked if I knew what they were referring to. I knew exactly. To me this matter is a real dilemma, although it was not on my mind today. 'They' spoke of it pragmatically as being a lesson I needed to learn. Suddenly I was startled out of my unspoken doubts about the flakiness of the scenario. 'Spirit' had identified quite accurately the difficulty I have had since childhood in finding a harmonious poise between giving and receiving.

Fortunately, 'they' had a practical solution to offer which involved a need for discernment and a capacity to say 'No' when necessary. They even gave me a specific and gracious way in which to express it. I was also offered a meditation to practise for psychological reinforcement. Meditation is something I respect but have neglected, to my cost, for years.

I was given three stones for healing, including some haematite and a rose crystal, for which Sue would not accept payment. She said they were given to her and they were to hand on, where needed.

By this time my eyes were wide open and Spirit had my full attention.

But being the quintessential doubting Thomas, I was still waiting to detect some sort of trickery. It crossed my mind that this might be a symptom of the personal failing identified so accurately in the opening salvo. It used to be called 'looking a gift horse in the teeth'. It has probably come down to me through my ancestors—a long line of Isles and Highland Scots, south-of-England yeoman farmers and convicts—and it's no bad thing, as long as you know a gift horse with sound teeth when you see one.

I had to file this for later reflection because, after a pause, 'Spirit' had something more to communicate.

'Now your mother's here. She's telling me that …'

It was all plausible, the sort of things my mother would say, expressed in her idiom, using some of her vocabulary and describing the central element of our relationship. It was very moving and I was in tears at somehow being in touch with my mother again and sensing that she was alright. Yet I still felt doubtful. After years of yearning, one is not assuaged in an instant. How could it be possible—and if it is—if they are so close by, so accessible, why have we not known about it, been taught about it? I felt cheated; either I was sitting with a charlatan playing some clever, intuitive guessing game with my thoughts and feelings, or it was real, and I had spent years of sadness missing my mother when she was so near.

Sue said that it's all much more simple than we imagine, this capacity to contact a spirit. It's something we once knew, have devalued and then lost or forgotten. In Shakespeare's time none of this would have surprised even an educated person. The Enlightenment had not yet split the spiritual from the rational way of knowing. Science had not yet relegated the religious, the intuitive, the imaginative instincts in favour of only that which is material, tangible and able to be categorised, measured, dissected and demonstrated many times over. Before my mother 'left', Sue 'saw' her gathering lavender. I was disappointed. My mother's love of flowers was characteristic but lavender had no special significance for us. It's not a favourite of mine.

It was not until later in the day I noticed that, over the years, I have unconsciously arranged a corner of my home to contain the following: a small, old, white-painted wooden desk from my mother's house; on the wall above the desk four pen-sketches with wash, by artists my mother admired—Judy Cassab, Francis Lymburner and Unk White. The works are originals which I have acquired since her death. There are also two beautiful drawings of my mother by K. Day. Only one is dated, November 1936.

Among the framed sketches, I have hung a little wall plaque which I made as a child under my mother's supervision. I remember us pouring the wet plaster of Paris into a saucer with a loop of black velvet inset to hang it by. When the plaster dried, you could paste a small round picture in the indentation for the base of the teacup. This one has a little watercolour of a jug of roses. There are also two gold plaster angels of my mother's; two very fine plaster masks of my face, made by an artist friend, which bear a strong resemblance to my mother as well; two green ceramic plates in the shape of violet leaves, gifts from me to my mother.

The desk has one drawer. It's years since I've opened it. Inside I found packets of letters and photographs from long ago, the sort of things you can't bear to throw away; and a box of my mother's simple treasures: an acorn, a silver penknife, a small leather Florentine purse, a whistle and a pair of painted doves which roll on ball bearings if you rest them on a sloping surface.

Over the years I had gradually, unconsciously, created a shrine of poignant associations with my mother.

I stood back to gain a wider perspective and saw that I had hung, among the pictures, a bronze icon of the Holy Spirit depicted as a dove of peace by the Melbourne sculptor, Mimovic, given to me when I was received into the Church.

And finally, on the top shelf of the desk, in a pretty ceramic jug, given to me by someone else who loved my mother, a little bunch of lavender tied with a purple ribbon. It has been there for several years and yet it still retains its colour and a faint perfume. There are other mementos of my mother around the house but this appealing corner could well have been arranged by her. It is much more resolved and artistic than I usually achieve and it is very attractive to me and very familiar.

Sue was quiet for a minute, waiting, her eyes closed.

'Now I'm getting your father. I don't see him but he has a beautiful voice and he's telling me to say that he had something very wrong with his right leg, in childhood, so you can identify him.

In Sue's normal voice, 'Spirit' explained that Dad was in what they term the halls of healing. He described it—a beautiful place, peaceful, neither fully indoors nor out. There was a creek, a waterfall, a rainbow, a guardian angel radiating care and love and a 'chaise longue' (a term Dad used humorously for his cane lounge on the verandah), on which he was resting and recovering because he was so terribly tired. Suddenly believing it, I was relieved to hear that he was in the fresh air he had longed for. Later he would embark on a big peace-making mission for which there would be great need, according to Spirit. This was five months before 11 September 2001.

He said that I would find him and his love for me always in my heart. It was exactly what I was hoping to hear and half of me believed it gladly. The other half thought it was Sue creating a kind and reassuring picture for a person in grief or else exercising an ability to read my thoughts. And I'll never be sure. It will depend which side of me is in operation at any given time, whether I will take comfort from it or remain sceptical and anxious about my parents' destination, their proximity, their accessibility, their peace and the possibility of our reunion.

I seem to be as agnostic about this consultation with Spirit as I have become about God. I wonder what it would take to satisfy me, to bring back faith and hope. Am I now chronically disbelieving? Perhaps that's the human condition—not to know, not to be sure, but to yearn and search and sometimes believe that any testing may have some point to it: the opportunity for spiritual maturing, through acceptance and courage. Must I trust God, regardless of how difficult life gets, for me or those I love? The God of the Old Testament promises to be steadfast to us. Jesus in the New Testament promises to be with us now and always. What does this mean? How does it help? I may have to keep reimagining who God is, for me, over and over, as I grow older in experience and, hopefully, wiser in understanding. Maybe God has been here today at Sue's place.

As I left, with her gift of the little 'healing' stones in my palm, I felt as you do after crying. I felt as though I had been to a matinee at the pictures, into another dimension which I was reluctant to leave. But here was the reality of daylight and uncertainty again. Sue charged only a modest fee and asked me if I could manage it. If not, she would reduce it. She had made no claims, only purporting to be a messenger. She put no pressure on me to come back.

SUNDAY, 8 APRIL 2001

I felt a shift in my orientation today as though the kaleidoscope has turned slightly. All the same pieces are there but they have been rearranged with that curious, soft click-clack sound, into a new pattern. I had a feeling of lightness that I have not known for many months. I don't trust it but it was nice to meet it again, even if it doesn't stay.

In the weekend papers, I took in very little of the news, my concentration fleeting, sliding from one item to another without satisfaction. But three photos almost leapt off the pages at me, images that spoke to my state of mind. The first, taken by David Hancock, showed an Aboriginal park ranger holding a huge speckled cane toad. The caption read: 'Menace to native fauna …

the dreaded cane toad is spreading through Kakadu National Park'. The toad looked glum and ugly but the ranger gazed down at it with something like compassion. Her drab green uniform, sun-bleached hair and burnished skin seem to grow directly out of the fringe of casuarinas reflected in the khaki river behind her, the tangle of bullrushes in the foreground and the overhanging gum leaves. In the background, another ranger, a stolid, young, white woman was holding open a bag in plastic-gloved hands. This girl was slightly off-balance, uncertain, waiting for a lead from her black colleague.

I'm not sure why I found the image so arresting. On reflection it gives me a sense that I have felt before, in the presence of Aboriginal people. It's an intimation that they understand important things about life—how it all works, how things connect—and somehow I am reassured by their unspoken knowledge. It is good that someone can look at it all without terror. Like the young ranger in the background, I can only watch, listen, and wait for it to make sense to me. The photo suggested that nothing would happen quickly. Except perhaps that the toad might suddenly galvanise the powerful muscles of its great hind legs and escape to continue propagating its menace of the indigenous fauna.[10]

The second image was also in colour, startling amidst the newsprint. Distributed by AFP, it was a picture taken by the Hubble Space Telescope of Whirlpool Galaxy M51. It was a glorious catherine wheel vortex of Prussian blue studded with brilliant scarlet and silver stars whirling in two spirals out of a molten sun at the centre—like a Van Gogh night sky, vertiginous, ecstatic. It was a potent image of pattern exploding out of chaos; violent, cataclysmic and utterly indifferent to anything human.[11]

Why are we so sceptical of religious metaphors while accepting without question the claims of science which also stretch credulity to breaking point? The caption on this photograph read: 'Despite being 15 million light years away … reveals the complexity of its spiral arms and dust clouds, where stars are being born …' Perhaps science, too, seeks a way to propitiate the sacred, mysterious realm which it measures and categorises but can only describe in arcane language invented for the purpose.

The third photo, by Rick Stevens, was a direct invitation to the soul, in black and white: two hands stretching forward, holding a fairy penguin an inch above the water, in the act of releasing it back into the harbour. The text explained that the penguin had been found tangled in abandoned fishing lines, with a hook through its flipper. After a period of recovery at Sydney's Taronga Zoo wildlife clinic, it was ready to be returned to its element. It had been wounded but not overcome by its wounding. Clearly its enthusiasm for life had not been dampened. Every ounce of its little body was straining with intention to be freed into the water. One flipper had just clipped the surface, skipping up a few droplets. Wings vertical, neck stretching forward, eye intent, beak pointing, ready to dive, it was in the last second before reunion with the ocean from which it had been separated. I could intuit the urgency of the plump, muscled, downy body as it launched itself purposefully and in utter abandonment towards the deep. There was no doubt about it; the little penguin was going home, and nothing now would prevent it. The hands were disembodied. They held the wild creature firmly but carefully, guiding its determined trajectory forward with no hint of restraint.[12]

I have cut the photograph from the newspaper, with the other two, and kept it near me. It is a liberating image, full of promise. It suggests, more eloquently than any words, that there may be some meaning to existence, some hope of destination. A psychologist friend has explained to me why it's not easy for a human to be like the penguin. Our difference is the gift of consciousness, memory for the past and imagination of the future. Our dilemma is to use these gifts to good purpose, yet major losses can turn them to burdens which afflict us with sad memories and rob us of the capacity to imagine a new life without the presence of what or whomever we have lost.

HOLY THURSDAY, 12 APRIL 2001

I went to the Mass of the Last Supper tonight at the Chapel of Mary MacKillop in North Sydney. For me it is the most poignant night in the church calendar, not yet the stark horror of the crucifixion to come on Good Friday but the evening of parting. Jesus is preparing his friends for the fearful events of tomorrow and celebrating with them. At this Passover meal he gives them the sign by which he will remain with them for all time—in the breaking of the bread and the sharing of the wine. Like a servant, he moves from one to the next, washing their feet, to demonstrate yet again what he had been trying to teach them for the past three years as they tramped the dusty roads from Galilee and Samaria up to Judea: 'By this will all men know that you are my disciples, that you have love, one for another', John 13:34.

Then comes the unthinkable betrayal by Judas, son of Simon Iscariot. The long night of anguished waiting, before the arrest and trial, was spent in the Garden of Gethsemane where Jesus asked the disciples to watch with him but they fell asleep. In church we mark this by watching in silence for two hours in a garden of repose. This year the garden is exquisite. I thought it must have been done, as usual, by Sr Vincent, but when I asked her later, she said that a Polish lady, who is not a Catholic, had asked to do it this year. Instead of using flowers, she had draped the Lady Chapel in white and pinned to the back drapes five sparse fans of the filigree leaves of nandina, dark green shading into burgundy. On the floor was a scatter of large, curling, dried leaves, the size of dinner plates, turning to autumn yellow and brown. She had gathered them from under the plane trees in the street outside.

After the priest washed the feet of twelve of the congregation, he celebrated the Mass of the Last Supper and, donning a white robe, carried the Blessed Sacrament in a lidded gold vessel to the garden of repose where it was incensed. It stayed there for the next two hours, lit by four white candles in the darkened chapel, while people prayed in silence to accompany Jesus Christ in his lonely vigil.

As I knelt there, the ordeal of Jesus intertwined with my own experience. I remembered the gnarled ancient olive trees I had seen among bright flowers in the Garden of Gethsemane in Jerusalem in 1989, tended and fiercely guarded by the Franciscan friars. I thought about Jesus sweating blood, feeling abandoned and asking his Father, if it were possible, to let this ordeal pass him by but it was not to be and he submitted. 'Not my will but thy will be done', Luke 22:42. There would be no resurrection without crucifixion. Does that imply acceptance of suffering as a gateway to new life?

I thought of the long hours of my father's ordeal, his hands restrained, and wondered if he, too, unable to make any sound, cried silently: 'My God, my God, why have you abandoned me?', Matthew 27:46. And then, by some grace, or in defeat, accepted the end. And I thought of my stepmother, Mary, old and uncertain of her future, with her memory slipping away. I thought of my own long vigils with each of them. Why does God want us broken on the rack before we can go to Paradise? Or if he does not want it, why does he allow it, or can he not prevent it? The appalling questions recur and the only solace is that Jesus, too, begged the question. He, too, knew the suffering and therefore can accompany us in our hour of trial. Perhaps that's the only meaning to be won from this terrible story—that we should not run away, that we must endure this hardest penalty of love—to stay with one another in our pain. Is it to show each other that we really mean something when we say those easy, seductive words, 'I love you'?

Or perhaps God has no place in it at all. Maybe it's just an inherent human characteristic, this love which brings us both the height of joy and the anguish of pain and loss. Is that what the job of life is? To do this loving as nobly, as faithfully, as unselfishly as we can? We're stuck with love. It's in our nature. It's not an optional. It happens, it's real. We're in its thrall, in all its different forms. My thinking is going in circles again. I like the scientific approach to knowledge. I am prepared to follow it a long way. I like its order, its insistence on evidence and its discipline. But, in extremis, it lets me down. It has no answer to the question of meaning.

So I turn, reluctantly, back to God. God is love, we are told. Does that mean that God is pain and grief as well as joy and beauty, tenderness, familiarity and exaltation? That God is as helpless as we are? If that is who God is, I might as well be a humanist and I think, at the moment, I am. It's all I can find to believe in: the humility, the patience, courage and dignity of those who suffer; and the ingenuity, loyalty and service of those who care for the suffering, at war, in poverty, in hospitals, at home, in boarding houses, on the street. These qualities are evidence, not of anything supernatural but of a humanity that perseveres in the appalling impasse in which it finds itself, without escape or protection.

That is something to celebrate. That is real. That is making the best of a very bad deal. It suggests that we are much more than science describes and perhaps more than religion wants us to be. Because surely we do these things, not for some pie-in-the-sky reward, but because we are faced with them and, at our best, we respond with nobility. If God is in that human nobility, then I still believe in him. I hope God still believes in me.

Daoud rang from Bethlehem to wish me a Happy Easter. Very few pilgrims have come and he has no work. He sounds desperate: 'The situation now is going worst than anytime so I am asking you if it is possible to find me work in your country so I can support my family, we are suffering too much.' I must explore the practicalities for him.

17 APRIL 2001

Today I went to the shops, feeling almost steady, almost normal, almost as though I might be starting to regain strength after a long illness. It was pleasant to be feeling nothing much, just to be doing something unremarkable, the shopping.

Driving home I looked up to enjoy the sky. I saw a flight of birds, high up. They were wheeling in unison, as though one entity. I watched them until they turned away to the north, out of sight behind the trees. And suddenly I was bereaved all over again, left behind. They had gone on without me. My apparent recovery was just a mirage.

Each acute episode of grief has its own authenticity. I sometimes wonder if it acts as a cautery, burning away more of the wound in order to heal. But that sounds too logical. In any case, an effort of will is needed, in its aftermath, to strive for a return to reason and equilibrium. I presume that should be the objective. I could choose to celebrate the beauty of the birds in flight and resist the melancholy of their disappearance. At least I could try. I also have the intention to remember that my tragedies are not isolated or unusual. It is the human condition to suffer as well as to know joy. I don't imagine anyone escapes it.

I am reflecting on the need for communal rituals to remind us of this and to see us through it. Even now, when I am aware only of the suffering of people, and so uncertain of the place of God in it, I am steadied by the reiteration, in the Mass, of the journey on which we are all embarked, as human beings; the pattern of crisis, change, loss and hope that recurs in everyone's life; the dying and the rising of every day; and the corporate nature of the whole endeavour. As a competitive individual enterprise, it makes no sense to me at all and is terrifying. I need to huddle together with others for shelter in the storm and subscribe to some communal view of existence which gives me courage and company. For this reason alone, I am in little danger of leaving the Catholic Church. I may be still in the process of reimagining the place of God in suffering but I need companions on the journey. And I need the history: people down the centuries have endured the grief of loss and the pain of seeing their loved ones suffer. There is nothing new about it. And those same people have found solace and meaning through their hope in God, as a community of faith. I felt it myself until recently. And I suspect it is still there although presently obscured by grief. What is not in doubt for me is a sense of solidarity with other suffering people and with ancestors, whatever their faith or lack of it. There is nothing mystical about it, in my mind, nor even spiritual, necessarily. It's more to do with that earthy stoicism of my parents' and grandparents' generations, knocked about by two world wars and a depression, but making the best of things with modest acceptance and little complaint.

Peter Kocan has captured it well in his poem 'Blackout':

… I need not fear, need not be lonely, lost,
I am not abandoned in the dark
While there is something links me with a vast
And silent congregation stretching back—
All those anonymous men and women
Whose times and trials are forgotten now,
But who with unsung gallantry held on
And kept their vigil in a frail glow.
I can see them, ages before my birth,
Gathered around the one wick of truth.[13]

As far as I can tell, God does not have a place in this poem. Its encouragement lies in kinship with all those 'who fought and laboured for us long ago', so that we might have life today, as he puts it, in another poem 'Standing with Friends'. In this verse, he refers to:

All those who had the courage and the drive
To do their duty as they understood.
And many more whose contribution lay
In simply being human in their day …[14]

I take strength from the hand-tinted photograph portraits of the ancestors on my bedroom wall. Great-grandmother and father on Dad's side of the family. Granny and Grandpa and great-grandmother from my mother's side. Granny is young, wistful, beautiful. Grandpa is young and handsome. And his mother I can easily recognise as a relation. None of them are smiling. Apparently it was a serious matter to be photographed. I think of them as guardian angels and try to draw courage from their lives and steadiness from their characters.

April 2001

Last night I dreamed but could not remember, when I woke too early, what I had dreamed. Only the emotion of it remained—uneasy, disturbing. I still felt tired, hot and sweaty. My first, clear waking thought was that I no longer expected to be happy, as though happiness were a right or the only satisfactory condition in life. Happiness might come at times but it is only one of many states of mind. Its presence is welcome but may be rare and is not essential. Sorrow too is a legitimate condition, not to be evaded, or to require treatment.

The prevailing view is that people need to achieve something termed 'closure' after a loss, so that they can 'move on'. It may be true for some but need not, I think, be the only prescribed response and should not be expected to happen too quickly. Surely it would be inhuman, insensitive, unnatural not to feel deep sadness in the face of suffering or in bereavement? Joy, sorrow and the whole gamut of emotions might be felt quite authentically in the course of a day or a year. We need not be required to strive for happiness at all costs as though any other condition of being were a failure.

I am finding that it's good to acknowledge what I am feeling, whatever it may be, and not to regret the absence of tranquillity or be defeated by an evening of wistfulness.

A wise friend has reminded me of the healing properties of patience and waiting—that nothing important should ever be rushed, including recovery from major losses. Although life seems very pressured, I need to be respectful of time, to be aware of the present moment and to savour it, because hope may grow in the ability to keep an open mind and heart right now, always attentive to what goodness might be present in the moment, as a sign that our life is sacred and meaningful, even when the meaning is not clear.

In this sense, hope can be seen as the ability not to be overwhelmed by sorrow or other negatives of the past, and not to be fearful of an uncertain future, but to trust in the present moment. Patience and waiting may seem passive but I am finding that they yield an unexpected reward, when I can manage to surrender to them.

Sunday, 29 April 2001

Last night I went to a fund-raising dinner for a charity, the Ryder-Cheshire Foundation. The conversation was satisfying because it focussed on real and compassionate objectives. The speeches were rewarding too—personal accounts by the generous volunteers who work to provide homes and education for the poorest of the poor—the lepers, the disabled, the mentally ill, in a number of countries. There was real joy in their shared endeavour and our support of it. No doubt it is in giving that we come nearest to finding fulfilment.

I was glad to be there yet there was a terrible moment when this happy evening transformed, in my imagination, into the grim pageant of the medieval Dance of Death. Suddenly all flesh melted away, shining hair vanished, and all that remained was the clatter of our teeth grimacing in smiles and talk across tables decorated with withered flowers, smoking candles and plates of bare chicken bones. This hallucination must be one of the several alarming symptoms of post-traumatic shock.

When, after an instant, the scene returned to its former vitality, it had lost nothing of its richness.

30 APRIL 2001

Over the years, on radio and television, and in the course of my country travels, I have been given the wisdom of so many people's stories—their real-life struggles through setbacks and tragedies. I have broadcast them on the radio; I have published them in books; I have committed them to memory and treasured them in my heart.

Why are they not sustaining me now? There is nothing at fault in the stories. It must be something lacking in me, a lack of gratitude, a fatal forgetfulness just when I most need to remember. I suppose that is why I am expected not to grieve, or to recover quickly, because I have been the privileged listener, for so many years, the recipient of the stories of my countrymen and women, telling of struggle and overcoming, of trials and hope.

I thought that all the stories were safely embedded in my consciousness, gleaming like opals in the rock face, ready to be mined when I needed them. I go back to them now and they still ring true; they offer their sustenance. I still believe in them and see that they are precious. It's just that I cannot take them in as I long to do, to be nourished by them, to be reassured. It seems tragic to be deaf just when I most need to hear. This is a case of 'Physician, heal thyself', Luke 4:23. I think more willpower is needed, more attention to helping someone in need. That always lifts the sorrow.

16 MAY 2001

I had a bad start. Woke with a headache and relentless sadness. My most constant friend, Val, brought me some soup and casserole and urged me to get some treatment, to ask for a drug to lift my spirit. I feel resistant to the idea. It seems to me that you need to go through what you're going through, rather than avoid it. Sadness is real. If it is anaesthetised, won't it remain in existence somewhere in me and assume another form to express itself eventually—maybe in illness? Or some counselling perhaps? But surely I should be able to help myself, keep busy and aware of the needs of others?

I answer some more of the many letters waiting. One from a man who's been searching for his vocation and purpose. He's done a lot of hard jobs in industry and finally been retrenched, with two young children to support. He has drawn and painted the whole struggle in eloquent images of suffering, ugliness and hope, a real work of the soul. He writes that he thought I might be interested. Of course I am. I suppose people still send me these sacred passages of their lives because, through the *Search for Meaning* radio series and now *Australian Story*, I have apparently retained the mantle of listener. It's a burden sometimes but a gift as well because, as always, when I give my attention to someone else, it is healing for me.

Midday Mass at Mary MacKillop Chapel. My eyes rove from the statue of St Joseph, slowly across the stained glass windows and down to the red lamp flickering as a sign of the presence of the Blessed Sacrament. I can see that it's all beautiful, but it does not reach me. Or is it that I will not let it in? I watch the other people arriving. A lot of them are from offices in North Sydney: men and women in suits, in their lunch hour. I watch them for clues. I feel numb but if it's important to them to come out of their pressured professional lives to Holy Communion, then it could turn out to be important to me once again, some day.

(I recall the fable of some children who lived within a boundary fence, until a well-meaning person removed the fence, to free them. But the children huddled together because they did not feel secure without the boundary.) Or maybe the business people come to enjoy the calm atmosphere, the silence, the beauty and terror of the ritual of bread and wine. (Is there any other faith which consumes its saviour?)

The Gospel is John 15:5: 'I am the vine, you are the branches'. It's a sustaining metaphor, promising more than connection with the divine. The imagery suggests the closest intertwining with God, the same sap running in the veins; growing out of one root in the earth; supported by the same trellis. I visualise it as the grapevine that grew over the porch out the back of Gran's cottage in Mayne Street, Murrurundi, under which she taught me to read and write. I suppose a vine might also be vulnerable through its branches, dependent on them to find something to grow on, extend and prosper and bear fruit, muscatels and small, round Isabellas, almost black, exquisitely sweet.

This sort of musing is what I do now in my search for meaning. There's no passion in it and it's probably an avoidance of the invitation at the heart of the Gospels—to become immersed in relationship with Jesus Christ, utterly in love, dependent and trusting. I wonder if my experiences of loss have made me incapable of the surrender needed? Fortunately the priest, Paul Coleman SJ, includes malingerers and doubters like me in his homily. He says that we are here, at Mass, because we want to come closer to God. At the same time, we can each allow or achieve that nearness only to a certain degree. We waver and flicker in our faith, according to what's happening in our lives. What an insight. Is he saying it's up to us how close we get to God—not up to God? I think of him as a man whose faith would never be shaken. He's seventy-four and he lives a life of striking example. Sleeves rolled up, a man for others, a man who always says 'Yes', instinctively, in response to the endless demands made on him. And it makes him happy. He seems always to be just suppressing joyful exuberance. That's the most attractive thing about his practical Christianity. He spends himself for others and he enjoys life to the full.

But I'm grateful he knows that some of us aren't up to it and he accepts that. It's validating to hear him say: 'Sometimes all you can manage is just to get here, just to be here, as you've made the effort to do today. You've got worries and problems and you can't see your way out of them, but you've come here anyway. So you can just say, "Here I am, Lord. I've come along. Please feel my pulse, listen to my heartbeat. I'm here, that's about all."' It's such an accurate description that maybe he does know this condition sometimes himself. This compassionate understanding of our frailty is almost certainly what keeps this chapel full. You can be accepted here, even when your faith is in tatters.

On the way home I called in to the shop. I go there nearly every day. I wanted to get some fennel and Pink Lady apples which have just come into season again. As I arrived, Paula was unloading the back of the van, hauling out great bunches of yellow and orange lilies wrapped in rustling cellophane. And sienna and white chrysanthemums left over from Mother's Day, and pots of early daffodils and purple hyacinths. She lingers over them, rearranging them until the display at the front of the shop pleases her. Every day she gives us another glorious, heartlifting flower show on the footpath. She was up at 4.30 a.m. to get to the market. 'Must be there early to get best flowers.' By afternoon she was almost asleep. She will work through now until 7 p.m. when the shop closes and then another hour cleaning, ready for tomorrow.

In the doorway, between the snow peas and the sweet corn, I met Dianna, one of the young nursing sisters who cared for Dad in the Intensive Care Unit. Although she lives locally I had not seen her since then. Her eyes filled with tears as she greeted me. Her arms were full of shopping and her children were swinging on her skirt, but she said there was something she'd always wanted to tell me.

'The morning your father died, I was on duty, not in the Cardiac Ward, but along the corridor in the ICU where he spent such a long time with us. It was a Sunday morning. It was very busy, we had several emergencies. Suddenly the doctor on duty came in to tell us that he had just left your father and that your father had died. Of course everyone in ICU had nursed him, over the weeks, and, as the word passed around quietly among the staff, so the patients could not hear, we all stopped and the strongest feeling of peace came over the place. We all said we felt it.'

I asked what she made of it. She didn't know, but said that his room had never been the same since he left it to graduate to the ward, and that they had all been fond of him. I asked her why, but she couldn't find many words. She looked over my shoulder, with her eyes brimming, as she tried: 'He was so patient and accepting and brave ... and funny'. If she said anything else, I can't remember, but the sense of it was that they respected him and honoured him for his grand effort to respond to their care and their encouragement to recover, against all the odds. She had wanted to write to me. She'd even chosen the words to say but somehow she just hadn't done it. I could well understand. She has little children and her nursing shifts and, in her life, every minute is accounted for.

Our encounter had a calming effect on me, reassuring, like a visit from an angel to say that all is well. Is it really possible that, immediately after he died, Dad went the short distance along the corridor to the ICU to give them all a sign of peace, and to say thank you and goodbye? Whatever you make of it, my meeting with Dianna was a grace and a blessing for me.

11 SEPTEMBER 2001

In the United States, civilian aeroplanes fly into the twin towers of the World Trade Center in New York, and into the Pentagon building in Washington.

5 NOVEMBER 2001

Thank goodness the days are warm again. I have been in some sort of emotional hibernation all winter.

There was a gecko on the kitchen floor last night. At first I thought it was a brown gum leaf and was about to sweep it up. The gecko looked prehistoric and I felt in awe of it, a mysterious visitor. It kept completely still, pretending not to be there. It must have climbed in through the wall cavity as the lizards do, or under one of the doors, venturing far beyond its usual environment in search of coolness or water. I set a saucer beside it, turned out the light and left it in the dark, cool kitchen. Half an hour later it had vanished.

I went to bed early, wearied by a long episode of tachycardia. I have been assured that it doesn't do much harm yet it is alarming to have your heart beat fast and violently, as though it is trying to escape your chest.

It's a beautiful day, restful and consoling. There is a light mist, promising rain, over the river, and the jacarandas are now fully saturated with colour in great umbrellas of mauve among the gum trees. The new white daisies are flowering profusely, entirely happy in their sunny position beyond the long, high bank of hydrangeas, now dotted with many flower clusters, still green.

Two small magpies wearing the pale, fluffy plumage of youth, are pecking at imaginary worms and insects as they learn slowly to hunt for themselves, encouraged by parents who must be tiring of loud demand-feeding after all these weeks.

I went for a massage with Lee today. She has healing hands which bestow solace and also dig in to loosen the knots of tension. Her presence is serene and trustworthy. If I do not talk, neither does she. If I talk, she listens. She asked me how I was feeling and, in response, gave me a Bach flower remedy containing gentian for sorrow, and Star of Bethlehem to bring tranquillity. She diluted the flower essences carefully in brandy and water and gave me the small brown bottle as 'an early birthday present'.

As I left, the front gate in the picket fence closed with a soft metallic click of the latch. Exactly the same as our front gate at Murrurundi. Instantly I pictured the short pathway leading to the bull-nosed front verandah of the cottage with its corrugated iron roof on which you could hear the rain drumming; the cane chairs half-hidden behind the thick yellow-flowering vine, tall crimson hollyhocks against the cream weatherboard walls. I could feel the buffalo grass on the soles of my bare feet and then the cool, flat, brass binding on the hall runner. Gran, Aunt Beryl or my mother could not be far away because there was the comforting smell of biscuits baking in the oven of the fuel stove. I would like to have opened and shut the gate with the clicking latch a few more times to keep the vivid memory longer but there was another client approaching.

10 November 2001

At dancing school they have asked me to present a tango routine with my teacher at the April ball which will be a showcase for a number of students. The routines will range from waltz to jive to foxtrot, rumba and other Latin dances. It's an opportunity to dress up and perform what we've learned. Three minutes in the limelight, each looking our best, with the professional dancers who are our teachers. It's nerve-racking, but very exciting and satisfying, especially when it's all over.

My first response was to say 'No'. But then I could see the good psychology and kindliness behind the suggestion and, on consideration, I've agreed to it. It will mean several months of concentrated preparation to learn what my teacher has choreographed for me. In the last two years I've become increasingly fascinated by the Argentine tango, a complicated dance that began in the bars and brothels of Buenos Aires in the late nineteenth century. In contrast to the solo disco dancing that's been popular since the 1960s, Argentine tango is a dance for couples. The partners' heads and bodies are in a close embrace, while the legs intertwine or move fast, almost in conflict, with accurately placed kicks and flicks and foot pushes. It's an intense, intricate and dangerous dance which takes all your attention if you're to sense and follow a lead indicated only through your partner's body.

The music is melancholy, lyrical, growling, sensual—expressive of the longings of life, the contradictions of love and the ever-present knowledge of death. For some reason it speaks to my temperament exactly and allows me to dance with deep feeling. So this will be engrossing to work on.

One of the characteristic sounds of tango music comes from the bandoneon, a larger version of the accordion, which arrived in Argentina with German immigrants in the early twentieth century. The tango was improvised music of the people, street music. In the 1920s classical musicians took it up and tango songs produced famous singers like Carlos Gardel who became a national hero. In the 1930s the tango took on a big-band sound. In the years of military dictatorship in Argentina it was forbidden for groups of more than three to gather. Still the tango stayed alive underground and now it has become an international hit for theatrical performance, and a craze in many places from Berlin to Tokyo. It was made even more popular by two films, *Shall We Dance* and *The Tango Lesson*. Devotees of tango take conducted tours to Buenos Aires to experience the real thing and compositions by modern composers like Astor Piazzola have brought the tango to concert hall audiences in Australia.

THURSDAY, 22 NOVEMBER 2001

Last night I took three friends to see a revival of Ron Blair's marvellous play *The Christian Brother* with Peter Carroll in the title role. He was brilliant, as he was in the original production. Perhaps his maturity brought even more depth to the performance this time. It was completely satisfying—especially evocative for my companions who were all members of religious orders at the time in which the play is set. A perfect evening at the theatre with just the right company. How blessed I am in my friends.

Another letter from Daoud. The contrast between our lives is surreal, mine so very privileged, his so difficult. Yet he is the one who maintains his steadfast faith. We have discovered that Australia does not provide humanitarian visas for people in his situation, and he has decided himself that it is too difficult at this stage of life to leave his country and his family.

Typically he turns this setback into a generous invitation: 'Me and my wife Ibtisam, Fadi and Lina never forget your help and kindness to us. We always remember you in our prayers. We are looking forward to you be our guest one day here in Bethlehem, Jesus Town. Thanks be to God.'

Sunday, 25 November 2001

The long slender trumpets of November lilies are pale against their deep green lustrous leaves. There are five tall vases overflowing with them in the sandstone niches behind the altar, on the red-carpeted expanse of the sanctuary. A white candle gleams on either side of each vase. Overhead fans stir the air lazily and it's pleasantly cool in the high-vaulted cavern of the old church. The rows of wooden pews with their dark sheen are filling gradually. By custom many people sit in exactly the same places each week. Familiar faces, middle-aged or older. This time of the morning suits them. The first Mass was at 7 a.m. The 9.30 a.m. Family Mass has just finished. We'll sing the old favourite hymns: 'Be Thou My Vision', 'Praise My Soul the King of Heaven'. I know the words by heart from my Anglican childhood.

Carmen plays the organ beautifully and sings in a clear, true voice, harmonising with her son. Michael's on the parish staff. He's young and modern and looks as though he could break into a soft-shoe shuffle and a chorus from *Chicago* at any moment. Among many other duties, he decorates the church. Today on the Feast of Christ the King he's suspended three sweeping red panels of something that looks like silk to soar above our heads the length of the nave. They draw the eye upwards and lift the spirit. Two old-fashioned white plaster angels with long robes are flying high on the pillars either side of the sanctuary. I wonder how they escaped the enthusiastic modernisation of the church after Vatican II. I'm glad they are still there.

All through November we pray for all our departed loved ones, a month of prayers which started on All Souls Day, 2 November. I still can't get through Mass without crying but I keep it quiet. I regret putting mascara on my eyelashes. I'll end up with 'panda' eyes.

I light a candle and pray for the repose of the souls of my father, my mother, my family and all my ancestors down through the centuries. I pray for my deepest heart's desire—to be reunited with my mother and father in the world to come, if there is such a place. If only I believed that promise, but I still have only the fragile threads of hope and faith and a terrible doubt.

After Mass I sit for a while in the side pews to talk with two friends. Olive lost her mother at the same time as Dad died. It's a bond between us. We can talk about how much we miss them and understand each other. Heather still has her father. At ninety-two, he lives with her and drives her to work each day. She's very proud of him. We compare notes about the ordeal of the yearly driving test for over–85-year-old people and agree that we would probably not pass such a test ourselves. Our conversation is reassuring. We meet on the common ground of single women who know the challenge of caring for elderly parents and the heartache of seeing them suffer.

Now a christening party is gathering around the altar. A young couple with their precious new baby in a long white dress, surrounded by excited family members. Grandmothers with new handbags and youngsters with shining ponytails, best-dressed for this joyful rite of passage. Everyone is smiling. The mother is smiling and she is crying too, as she places her baby carefully into the arms of his godmother.

More than ever now I love to see people happy, like this little group celebrating the continuity of life, pledging to support their newborn boy on his journey, welcoming him into a community of faith, giving him the light of Christ to accompany him on his uncertain journey into the new century.

Just inside the door of the great church, I dip my fingers into the cool holy water and make the sign of the cross on my forehead, heart, left shoulder and then right and kneel down to genuflect. I wonder if they'll decide one day that this, too, is optional, like kneeling for prayers. For me the ritual is significant, an echo of the baptism which brought me into the Church and a blessing to protect me as I venture out again on the pilgrim's way.

Outside the heat is like a blow to the head and shoulders and the glare is startling. Summer has come early. The plumbago hedge has sprung into bloom at the foot of the sandstone stairs. Its mass of blue flowers takes me back instantly to Dad's little back garden where he grew them, intertwined with a luminous deep pink geranium. In the mornings, after completing his jobs, he would sit out the back on a canvas chair in his white cloth hat, shirt and khaki shorts and riding boots, to give his gnarled, bruised legs a bit of sun. And I would take him a glass of water and sit with him. We would hear the gentle sound of the doves and we wouldn't need to talk.

17 DECEMBER 2001

A unit has become available at the retirement village and Mary has decided to take it. Val came up from Sydney to help me pack all the things from the old home which are to furnish the new apartment at Yallambee Lodge, part of the RSL Retirement Village.

First I made a floor plan of the new place and marked it with accurate measurements of each of the rooms. Then I could start to juggle what will fit and where. I've been consulting with Mary on each decision but she's not really engaged with the project. I am also worried that she will not remember the decisions she has approved. She's been in hospital again for the last two weeks. Perhaps it's just as well, as she will not have the upheaval of moving but will just walk in to a new, smaller home which looks as much like the old one as I can make it. And it's given me time to repaint her bed and tables and chairs and do a lot of sorting and cleaning. We labelled each packing case with its contents to help us tomorrow at the destination. It was a big job. I could never have done it alone. Val's presence was a blessing. By seven o'clock we'd finished packing and labelling the last box and went to the RSL club for something to eat.

18 DECEMBER 2001

Up early, ready for the removalist. I'm thankful Mary is missing this. It would be distressing for her to see her life packed up into cardboard boxes, her bed dismantled, her lamps and furniture standing exposed in the driveway to be loaded into the back of a van.

At Yallambee Lodge we arrange everything according to the floor plan. My measurements are pretty right and everything fits in without the place seeming cluttered. After a few hours work it looks very attractive. With the help of Yallambee's maintenance man, Alan, we've got Mary's pictures up on the walls, family photos on display, the bookshelves stacked, her little writing desk in place. Her clothes are hanging in the convenient walk-in wardrobe and neatly packed into chests of drawers. The table is set with her favourite cloth and a vase of flowers. The bedroom is the most successful of all. The measurements were almost identical and I've been able to reproduce it exactly in the new setting. The contents of each little drawer in her dressing table are just as they were. Packing and unpacking them was a fiddly job. The bed is made up and her familiar bedroom curtains hung in place. The pencil sketch of Dad is on her bedside bookshelf, with her little gold travelling clock. Her radio is in its usual place. The living and dining area opens onto a level patio and small garden, then into a wider, enclosed courtyard for the use of all residents. I can do more with the garden, over the coming weeks.

Altogether I am thrilled with it. It's just like her home, only more compact, bright, clean, safe, convenient and welcoming. There are emergency call buttons in bedroom and bathroom and friendly members of staff put their heads round the door to see how we're going and to admire our efforts. This will surely be so much better for Mary than living alone. The atmosphere is cheerful and organised.

At the end of our work we're tired but very satisfied. It has made all the difference having Val's help, turning a tough project into fun.

19 December 2001

It's always a lengthy process discharging Mary from hospital. She moves slowly and looks very frail, her stoop more pronounced than before. I am tired and apprehensive about her reaction to her new home. We go first to our favourite cafe for lunch to help her orientate back into the outside world. She recovers a bit of spirit to comment, 'The coffee cups here are rather small, you'll see'.

When we finally arrive at Yallambee the manager welcomes Mary, takes her arm and accompanies us to the apartment. I keep back and say nothing.

When she opens the door Mary is overwhelmed at seeing this translation of her life into a new setting. The first thing she focusses on is her mother's framed photo on the bookshelf and she starts to cry but quickly controls herself. She stands still for a few minutes in the doorway, just taking it all in, saying nothing.

The manager is a nursing sister, a tactful woman who has negotiated this vulnerable moment many times before. She does not hurry Mary nor put any pressure on her for a reaction. Gradually Mary moves into the room and sits down. She's going to defer any further exploration for a while. She says nothing.

As the afternoon goes on, I show her where I have put everything and she begins some tentative, detached inspection. It's impossible to know what she is thinking, as usual. One of her regular community care visitors comes and is enthusiastic, which is a help. Mary remains noncommittal and chooses to focus on filing her fingernails.

Before leaving I make sure that someone will come to collect her to go to the dining room for the first time. When I say goodbye I promise that I will bring her to the old home tomorrow. I'm trying to keep everything matter-of-fact and undramatic. I'm emotionally exhausted with the effort but I am very relieved that she has made this move to a more secure environment with constant care and company. I'm happy with everything I've been able to find out about Yallambee, having researched every other retirement place in the district. Arranging her entry has been complicated but all the paperwork is done and the financial side of it is manageable, thanks to Heather and Frank.

I know it's the right move but still I feel like a traitor leaving her in a new place. I know that I will hate leaving my home when the time comes. I wonder if Mary feels as I did when Mum and Dad left me at boarding school.

When I say goodbye she looks very small in her big armchair and doesn't smile. I have no idea what she is thinking and I'm sure that's the way she wants it.

2 JANUARY 2002

Val invited us for Christmas at Putney. We drove down the F3 before it got too hot. We have spent Christmas Day together for many years. As usual, we all ate too much of a very good lunch.

It was still hot when we set off on the drive back to Gosford in the evening through the red haze of bushfires on the outskirts of the city. Mary seems to be getting used to her new home. She refers to it as 'where I am now' and has never told me what she thinks of it.

The fires have been ravaging during these days of relentless dry heat: weather forecasts holding out no hope of rain, urgent radio news broadcasts, terrifying images of inferno each evening on television, the mythic figures of our firefighters, and the sad faces and drooping bodies of shocked people standing in the ruins of their homes. 'Her beauty and her terror, the wide brown land for me', as Dorothea Mackellar described Australia in her classic poem.

Just as certain native species need fire to initiate germination, the terror of natural disaster seems to release the grace of human generosity. Men and women got up from their Christmas dinner tables to report to their local brigade or emergency services HQ. Some even caught planes and buses long distances to risk their lives saving the homes of people they had never met. Such acts of sacrifice and compassion are repeated every season but they never become commonplace, nor lose their capacity to startle and inspire—and no one's looking for glory. When a fire captain with a sooty face is reluctantly interviewed on television, during a rest break, propped up on one elbow with a mug of tea, any suggestion of heroism is neatly deflected with a weary smile and a pragmatic comment about the hopes of a wind change.

On Boxing Day I drove through a shocking, blackened landscape to a district where the homes of seventeen families had been burned out and the threat of fire from flying embers was still present. Throughout the baking day and into evening, the sun remained an angry red. The birds were silent as people began to drive up and park under the trees for Mass in the old weatherboard church. I was surprised how clean everyone looked after their ordeal.

As they gathered, out came the stories of narrow escapes, of how the fire had come to within yards of the house. It was the first chance to account for everyone, to know who the newly homeless were staying with, how they were coping. Beside the church, the semi-retired priest's cottage had been burned out while he was fighting spot fires around and under his church. Eyewitnesses had to tell the story over and over as each new family arrived.

Inside the old church, the air was still and people were restless, uneasy. At the end of Mass, Fr John Evans spoke about what had happened to him. When fire engulfed his home, he had wanted to save things that had belonged to his mother and father, their wedding gifts from 1910, but it was too late. He lost a chalice containing his mother's diamond ring, and the stand his father had made as an apprentice carpenter and joiner. Everything he owned that was valuable and familiar had gone.

'I don't own a thing now except the clothes I'm standing up in.'

Yet he went on to say that, while material things are precious, life is more precious. He thanked those who had helped him. He praised the people for the wonderful way they had helped each other in the last two terrible days. He said he was ready to start again, from scratch, and you could have cried for him, and cheered him too.

In the days to come, many Australians must have been encouraged to hear him put his loss wisely into perspective, as he was interviewed on television in the ruins of his home, an elderly man in poor health but calm and grateful still to have his life, and the care of friends in the district he had served for thirty-two years.

The clothes Father stood up in were a shirt and a pair of shorts and sandals. After Mass he stood outside with a white plastic bag containing his worldly goods in one hand, talking to us all, as we slapped the mosquitoes off our ankles and conjectured where the fire would strike next. Some of the farmers were angry about bureaucratic restrictions on regular back-burning and maintenance of firebreaks.

In the red glow of twilight people carried big boxes of donated goods into the church, to be distributed. The children were fossicking in the blackened remains of the old cottage. After a while they came running over proudly to offer Father what they had found in the ashes of his home—a few charred pages from a book, a little vase, broken, a spoon.

On the long drive back, through the burned-out forest and grasslands, I saw a rough, handwritten sign on a farm gate, 'Fireys are angels, thankyou'.

Home again, I opened the front door on my familiar surroundings with fresh appreciation.

Summer 2002

A full tide again this morning at the baths, the water heaving gently, lapping the white duckboards rising and falling with every swell. I swim a length, then hang by hands and feet from the softly bucking board, green seaweed squelching between my toes, before I set off again. Tim, the caretaker, scrubs the weed off every few days but it's soon there again; you can even feel it on the ropes he's rigged to mark a couple of lanes. I heard him telling someone that he dives each day to check for holes in the shark net.

It is twenty-three degrees this morning but the water is cold because the nor'easter, which has been blowing for days, pushes the surface water before it and cold water rises from the deep to replace it. So I was told.

Swimming backstroke slowly, I watch the magnificent pattern of clouds: two layers, one high—a great mackerel skeleton speared across the blue; and, below that, a weightless, broiling tumult of grey and cream that I can almost touch with each stroke.

There are swallows darting swiftly across the surface of water and, a little more distant, the cooing of doves which will always mean eternity to me now. When I am in the baths the veil between this reality and whatever else there is seems almost sheer. I am as much spirit as body—insubstantial, as though the water could easily dissolve me into infinity. Perhaps because of my weightlessness and the lack of any clear horizon between swelling tide and sky, I merge with it all. Maybe as I swim I am slipping into and out of that other dimension without being aware of it. The water is my skin as I slide through it, unaware of any boundary.

The sense of separateness returns in a shock with the clammy touch of a jellyfish on my shoulder and another rolling off my shin. Suddenly feeling the cold, or fear, I swim ashore.

There's a small sandy beach under a big, old Moreton Bay fig tree with purple agapanthus nodding top-heavy out of the banked garden beds, and yellow canna lilies upright among them. Collapsible plastic lounges in many bright colours are stacked into a sandy club sandwich under the big tree. Lying on one, I can gaze slowly along the city skyline across the harbour. Centrepoint Tower and other tall, landmark buildings rise in a familiar cityscape punctuated by giant cranes not yet in motion.

I watch the ferry sail past Goat Island and call in briefly at Longnose Point before it bustles, like a green and yellow water beetle, into our wharf, with pennants fluttering, right near the baths. Gliding past, faster and silent, are the sleek Rivercats on the way upriver to Parramatta to fetch reluctant workers into the city.

The dressing shed is open to the sky, concrete, with green, slatted wooden benches. There are rows of wooden pegs to hang your hat and towel while you try to peel off your damp costume, clinging like a second skin—and push your unwilling, sandy feet into sandals which seem to be a size too small. Some people have a shower but I like to feel the dried salt on my body and in my hair. I find some consolation in it, perhaps because it evokes an old memory.

In the shocked, sorrowful weeks following my mother's death in 1969, I drove from Sydney to Gosford each Saturday after my week's work on *This Day Tonight*. I went to keep Dad company in the aching house and to cook him some meals for the week ahead. I was also hoping that there had been a mistake and that she would still be there, after all.

On Sunday mornings we'd go to the beach for a surf and return home with a parcel of fresh prawns in white paper, to have with a beer. We did not speak about what had happened but it was a short time of distraction and respite from the grief which sat at the table with us in silence.

And that's what these hours at the baths are like for me now, an opportunity for the bruised psyche to rest and the mind and body to be bathed and soothed in the buoyant salt water. Finding solace in beauty does not eliminate the inevitable return of grief but surely it is part of a slow healing of the soul?

I took a case of peaches to the staff room at Yallambee. It's difficult to find adequate ways to show appreciation for their kindness and care for Mary. She seems to be settling in but she has said nothing about her new home and I still do not know what she thinks.

There's a lot to do at the old home, deciding what's to be sold or given away. Mary likes to come over from Yallambee and roam through the rooms. I hope these visits give her an opportunity to say goodbye. We talk about Dad and remember things that have happened over the years. I keep the memories positive.

The Salvation Army came one morning to collect, the Smith Family the next, and one night I made about twelve trips down to the front footpath to stack things for a council clean-up collection. During the night vandals went through it all, stabbed the big plastic bags and scattered my neat arrangement up and down the road. The council truck didn't come so I had to reassemble it all with the endless traffic whizzing past only a metre away from me, creating a constant wind tunnel.

We gave Dad's tools to the lady gardener who's been helping Mary. It's so hard to see them go but she will appreciate them.

A contract cleaner came to give a quote. The auctioneer wandered through the house with a shrewd dealer's eye, telling me what he would and would not take. Gradually the dear old home is giving up all its memories. The real estate agent inspected and predicted a likely price. If he's right, it will leave Mary with a good nest egg to invest after paying for her new home.

Back in Sydney I saw *Monsoon Wedding* with Val and met two ladies who had won morning tea with me in a charity raffle. A new experience.

F E B R U A R Y   2 0 0 2

We have started the *Australian Story* year strongly, with a program, produced by Vanessa Gorman, on actor Gary McDonald, who is candid about his struggle with depression. It included an interview with Ruth Cracknell, his co-star in *Mother and Son*, recorded before she became ill. On Thursday 14 February, the Governor-General Peter Hollingworth appeared in an *Australian Story* produced by Helen Grasswill; it received a good deal of attention in the days following.

This week I introduced an intriguing story featuring Kirsty Sword Gusmao, an Australian who played a role in East Timor's resistance and is now married to the new nation's president. Produced by Ben Cheshire, it was shot by Quentin Davis, with sound recording by Ross Byrnes. On Wednesday I guided a day of reflection for staff at Royal Rehabilitation Centre which went well.

We are making progress with the tango routine and I enjoy the concentration of learning the choreography. It's by far the most difficult thing I've done at the school. I hope I will get to the stage where I can visualise the complete routine in my imagination and then just relax into dancing it with feeling, rather than worrying about the order of the intricate steps. I'm not there yet but I'm fascinated by the challenge.

L A T E   S U M M E R   2 0 0 2

The storm bird has been crying its insistent, mournful call all day. At mid-afternoon it ceased. In the hush, three big drops of water splashed onto my balcony. And then several more. At last it's raining. What an unusual, welcome sound. It's falling steadily now, straight down, drumming gently on the leaves. A streak of lightning in the west, followed quickly by a whipcrack of thunder. The storm is close; there may not be much rain in it.

But it's a relief, after these parched months. If only they're getting it out in the country over the Divide, where it's really needed—across the desolated western division, up in the north-west and down the Riverina. If they are, parents and teachers will have to explain what it is to little children who know their families have been desperate for rain but who've never actually seen it.

The magpies are carolling, the gutters are running, spilling over. I can't see to the other side of the river through the downpour. Car tyres are splashing on the roadway. The petunias have lifted their drooping heads and are glowing almost luminous in the semi-gloom, pink and deep, velvet purple; the birdbath is full. The huge spines of the aloes are glistening wet. A fresh earth smell is beginning to rise from the sodden mulch of leaves fallen under the trees on the slope below the balcony; this is what we've been waiting for. Kookaburras some distance away have launched into a round of hysteria that goes unrestrained for minutes. Raindrops hang like a string of pearls under the iron balcony railing.

Friday afternoon. It will be bedlam on the roads. People are ringing the radio stations to report where it's raining. The rain is news. It's pouring at Penrith, pelting down at Emu Plains, Windsor, Wollongong. One caller is laughing. He says it's wonderful … he's going to get out of his car and stand in it.

Australia is subject to drought. It's a fact of life in a vast, dry continent. Yet the farmers cling on year after year, with little or no income, forced to shoot starving animals, hand-feeding the rest, trying at any cost to save their precious breeding stock, waiting, waiting for relief. We see them on television, grim faces eroded into crevasses of worry, like the dry paddocks in which they're filmed. One heartbreaking story follows another.

This year there was so little grain to load that it took just one man and his wife to manage the railway junction silo. Just the two of them. Other years they'd need fifteen men to do the job. In many districts it looks hopeless as the north-west winds blow away the topsoil in choking red dust storms to dump it out at sea.

Yet they stay on. Is that real faith in life or are they trapped, with no way out? Some don't make it. Some men and teenage boys take their own lives. Some walk off their land and head for towns where there are too few jobs already. They hold a final, humiliating auction sale where their homely possessions are displayed outside in the yard for anyone to see, private things being appraised by strangers who cannot know their meaning.

APRIL 2002

We've done the tango routine. Everything went beautifully, from the dress rehearsal last week to the ball last night. I was alarmed to see that I had been placed as the last routine for the evening, which seemed to raise expectations of a grand finale. I could have done without the pressure. But the dance was there, in my head.

Dianne did my hair in the afternoon, pulled back into a large knot on the back of the neck. It was just right and got me into character, as did the fish-net stockings and the fitted, black dress onto which I had sewn a long silk fringe and some red roses.

It's an unusually situated ballroom, overlooking the ocean through the Norfolk pine trees at Manly. We walked out on to the floor and waited in position. Once the familiar dramatic music[15] began I danced with feeling, free of the self-consciousness that has made previous performances something of an ordeal.

I remember the scene in Sally Potter's film *The Tango Lesson*, where she danced on stage for the first time with her famous partner, Pablo

Veron, who castigated her later for getting in his way. My partner, my teacher, had the opportunity to play that role in the film. He is a star dancer, too, but unselfish, knowing how to bring out the best in his students, rather than draw attention to himself. I ended the evening feeling grateful to him and to his dancer wife, for their years of encouragement and understanding of my desire to dance. I'm glad I agreed to do the routine. I put a lot into it and I was rewarded by feeling alive and happy.

I hope it lasts.

JUNE 2002

A relief to hear from Daoud as it has been difficult to get him on the phone for some time. He has received something that I sent two months ago. Amazing, considering the situation. He writes: 'We were under siege for days, the Israeli soldiers open fire everywhere, some people died, others were injured, they shelled our houses and destroyed many. They shot even our water tanks and pipes, and crushed cars. We were hidden in the kitchen, and we got out only in a miracle.'

The cycle of violence brings misery for the innocent on both sides, the victims of the suicide bombers in Israel, and those Palestinians longing only for peace and stability, like so many of their Jewish neighbours.

None of it shakes Daoud's steadfast faith. 'Thanks God and our Lord Jesus Christ. We went to stay for eleven days at Beit Sahour (Shepherds' Fields) at the house of my wife's sister. We thank Our Lord to be alive.'

PART FOUR

Seeds of Consolation

December 2003 – January 2005

It's three and a half years since Dad died. I wish I could say that time heals but that's not exactly my experience. Grief takes its own time and cannot be hurried. It has changed me in that it has become part of me, and there is some gain in that. And time does allow a wider perspective.

In the eighteen months since I have written in this journal it has dawned on me, slowly, that there has been some arrogance in my unhappiness and in my doubt. I have seen other people bear their suffering and their losses with grace and courage, as my father did, and with no sense that they have been singled out for special treatment. I have seen the spiritual dignity of people living in deprivation or afflicted by natural disaster. Why then should I expect some personal revelation of the meaning of suffering in life?

Fr Tom O'Donovan SJ has been an inspiration to me as a man of steadfast faith expressed simply and directly, a man for others, all his life. Countless people must have been lifted up by his example and his encouragement.[1] He says that, in the face of whatever happens to you, the best thing is just to keep on going. At the moment, this makes great sense to me and I find it liberating. Just keep on going, accept what happens with humility, reflect on it, try to find some lesson in it, some growth for the soul. My journalistic training rebels sometimes and I am still discerning where acceptance is the wisest response and where questioning is more appropriate. But I have an idea that to keep on going establishes a steady rhythm which may allow acceptance and healing to take place below the surface of everyday life. I have been cultivating the habit of gratitude so that I am inclined to notice the positive aspect of a situation rather than the negative. Even if other people find this aggravating, it's coming naturally to me now. And I try to be open to help someone else, even by just listening. That usually helps me to feel better too.

Working at my desk this morning, I saw that the thicket of trees outside the window has become more dense, shading the blue and white plumbago bushes which have finally come into flower. And a ginger plant, which I thought was dead or hibernating, has put up a tall, dramatic head of orange and yellow flowers with red tendrils like a cluster of vivid spiders.

In one of the nearby branches a young magpie warbled for two hours with hardly a pause. He must have been scaling three octaves with an astonishing variety of liquid sounds, head thrown back, beak pointing to the sky and his whole body vibrating with gentle, inventive carolling and the occasional louder high note, as if to express a creative joy he could not contain. I suppose a biologist would describe this as a reflex action, hard-wired into the bird's neurones. Maybe, yet his song is far beyond the characteristic repetitive call range of most birds. And it's unpredictable. It sounds like composition but how has he gathered such a repertoire? Is this a fantasia based on all the sounds he has heard in recent times, adorned with his own flourishes? How does he remember all these sounds and arrange them into a certain order? And why does he produce such glorious song? There's no demand in it and I hear no answering call. Perhaps it's a song of gratitude to my neighbour Joan who feeds the magpies daily with generous morsels. Or even to me, for the bowl of water, always filled, on my balcony. Or could it be a spontaneous response to being alive, without thought or motive? 'I am, therefore I sing.' It's consoling to listen and wonder.

But suddenly, another flashback to Intensive Care and Dad's terrible restraint. The flashbacks still come vividly, although less frequently. Each time it happens my heart starts jumping in my chest with agitation. But deliberately now I choose a different thought: that horror is not happening now; it is finished; choose a positive memory. Taking the initiative gives me a sense of control.

So I think of Dad free, recovered, in his garden. I picture him laughing, cleaning Mary's shoes, pouring a whisky, drop-kicking his darned socks down the stairs. Perhaps he is in another close dimension, nearby … he has sent the magpie as a messenger of beauty, reassurance, familiarity—a messenger I will surely recognise because of his affinity with magpies.

Waiting for a few minutes in the post office this afternoon I saw a display of 'Pocket Inspiration' cards. One caught my attention. It was entitled 'I will be there'.

And if I go, while you're still here …
Know that I live on, vibrating to a different measure—
You will not see me, so you must have faith.
I wait for the time when we can soar together again—
both aware of each other.
Until then, live your life to its fullest.
And when you need me,
Just whisper my name in your heart … I will be there.

It's close to what the Church teaches: that we live in hope that our beloved, departed in faith, have joined the communion of saints and that they watch over us and help us, awaiting eventual resurrection and reunion. I ask people about this, to see if it is their experience, and many have told me that it is.

Interesting, because I have seen this verse before, in the booklet at various funerals, and found it sentimental. It seemed like glib, wishful thinking. But with the passage of time, I understand it differently. I do now have a strong sense of the benevolent presence of my parents in my everyday life. In place of the unfocussed yearning of the early period of grief, I am consciously aware now of their guidance in my decision-making. I imagine this is partly because of their influence while they were alive: inevitably I was shaped by their values, their preferences, their approach to life.

As well, there are many times when I fancy they help me in ways so obvious as to be almost comical: against all odds, a reference book opens at exactly the page I need … or I find something which I thought lost … I am able to balance my cash book much more easily than usual … out of the blue, I meet someone who can help me or direct me … I am guided to good healthcare practitioners … I am offered interesting work. When I see something beautiful or endearing, I sense that I am enjoying it, not alone, but in appreciative company.

The consequence is that instead of longing for reunion with my parents in another place, somewhere in the future, I treasure what I take to be their companionship in the present. I cannot explain it rationally but it is real enough to be comforting and reassuring. It contains the crucial seeds of hope needed to fend off the raw loss of grief and the fear that death means permanent parting.

Since Dad died, I've spent more and more time in the garden.

I feel their spiritual company there. Both my mother and father were gardeners. My mother never bought plants. She liked to collect cuttings from other people's gardens, not necessarily with their permission. I also like the earthiness of the garden. I move out of my mind into my body. I get dirt under my fingernails. Tying tomatoes to stakes, pruning, planting seedlings, weeding and watering bring me close to the earth and awaken my senses of smell and touch and seeing and hearing. I become fully focussed on what requires doing. I pay attention to details: does this pot of orchids need separating? The compost could do with a good stir. The white star jasmine is flowering at last, after struggling to gain a foothold in not much soil. These things give me satisfaction, even joy. I am absorbed in them. There is no room for worry, sadness or doubt. It's a relief and there's a feeling of rightness about spending time in the garden.

DECEMBER 2003

Today there was another of those king tides we have had lately. The harbour was brimming full. I waded in from the sandy shore and plunged into the high water. I floated on my back and felt my ears fill and ring to the timpani of water on my eardrums. I looked up into the trees at the water's edge and slowly explored the gardens of the waterfront mansions with my gaze.

The towy-haired teenager minding the pool fetched a green net and began dreamily scooping leaves from the pool's surface. I had no doubt that, if I got into difficulty, he would dive in and rescue me.

The ferries were at eye level and each one sent a wash which arrived a minute after its passing. With no effort on my part I was lifted and rocked and lifted again.

I swam backstroke in slow motion across the pool under the huge, vacant morning sky. My chest relaxed and expanded to let in more air and I felt that I had been holding my breath, or breathing shallow, for a long time … even for years.

With toes and fingers beside each other, I gripped the bucking pontoon board anchoring the net walls of the baths and rode the swell. Then I plunged backwards, arching into the water and propelled myself by kicking hard without breaking the surface of the water. Small transparent jellyfish brushed against my trailing arms. Suddenly I realised that the shroud of dread I had worn for so long had lifted. I remembered what it was to feel alive and even peaceful, almost exuberant.

It didn't last the morning but it reminded me that it is possible.

And so it is now with my faith. I have recovered it, or perhaps re-awakened to it but with a new understanding: I have received so many blessings in my life that it would be absurd for me not to have faith in a gracious God, who accompanies me. Still, when challenged by shock or suffering, my faith is shaken by doubt. But I am realising now something that seems very important: that the two conditions need not exclude each other. If I allow them to co-exist, sometimes faith predominant, at other times doubt, then I can spare myself the stress of over-vigilance and just accept that this is so.

I have an idea that I lost a sense of God during Dad's illness because I panicked and believed that I alone must deal with this crisis. The confronting physical reality did not seem to have a spiritual dimension to it. My mind was full of anxiety and I was deaf to anything else. I could not surrender myself and my father into God's care. He was already in the care of doctors and they were doing things I did not like to keep him alive, to aid his recovery. I thought they were good people, but I did not approve of their process. If I could have handed over to God, it would have been easier for me.

I know now that it is important for me not to wrestle with such a situation on my own. I could have been more frank with my prayer group about what was happening. We meet once a fortnight in each other's homes. We reflect in silence on a passage from the Gospels and then talk about where we have been finding God in our lives or failing to find God, as the case may be. Bringing real-life challenges out into the open and seeing them in a spiritual context adds depth and enlightenment to our discussions. We may not solve each other's problems or our own, but we do benefit from the variety of our life experiences and from a deep companionship that builds up in the course of a long friendship. Our discussion does not centre on dogma or fine points of theology but rather on the events of our lives that may be the source of rejoicing or struggle. Over the years we have built up a climate of trust in which we enjoy the freedom of being honest with each other. We have a sense of shared vision and purpose drawn from our faith. We explore the meaning of our lives, our relationships and our work, in the light of this. We strive to be people of hope who try to bring alive the love of God in how we conduct ourselves in daily life. Sometimes we succeed, sometimes we fail, but a consequence of this practice of faith is a deep gratitude for the gift of life and an appreciation of the gift of free will. Our meetings offer the opportunity to ponder how our lives are unfolding, and of contributing in a positive way to the lives of others in our orbit.

The personal rewards of our meetings are determined by the depth at which we are prepared to share our experiences. And that sometimes challenges me: I hesitate to take up too much time or to draw attention to myself. I have spent much of my life working things out on my own. This has a value as it develops personal responsibility and each soul has to make its unique spiritual journey essentially alone. But, when I really enter into it, I find that my community of faith, whether in the Church as a whole or in our small group, gives me an additional spiritual strength and point of reference for the way I live my life.

I have also found it valuable to read rich and consoling books like John O'Donohue's classic *Anam Cara: Spiritual Wisdom From the Celtic World*.[2] In this book he offers the Celtic understanding of life as an imaginative and unifying gift for the 'sore and tormented separation' of our times. He suggests that the Celtic mind was not given to argument, opinion, discussion, measurement and systems but rather to 'lyrical speculation' which brought the sublime unity of life and experience to expression. 'The Celtic imagination articulated the inner friendship which embraces nature, divinity, underworld and human world as one. The dualism which separates the visible from the invisible, time from eternity, the human from the divine, was totally alien to them.'[3]

Perhaps these ideas satisfy me because I am descended from the ancient Celtic people of the Highlands and islands of Scotland: or perhaps he is tapping into a universal wisdom which is familiar at some level, to all people. At any rate, his writing reminds me of the existence of the soul as a place of sanctuary, a place in which to encounter the sacred. He encourages me not to live 'merely according to the visible or possessible within the material reality of life' but to become aware of the 'treasures that are hidden in the invisible side' of my life. 'We are always on a journey from darkness into light … your body and your face were formed first in the kind darkness of your mother's womb. Your birth was a first journey from darkness to light …'[4]

Imagine if you could talk to a baby in the womb and explain its unity with the mother. How this cord of belonging gives it life. If you could then tell the baby this was about to end. It was going to be expelled … pushed through a very narrow passage finally to be dropped out into vacant, open light. The cord which held it to this mother-womb was going to be cut and that it was going to be on its own for ever more … For the baby within the womb, being born would seem like death. Our difficulty with these great questions is that we are only able to see them from one side … Therefore we cannot actually see the other half of the circle which death opens … I like to imagine that death is about rebirth. The soul is now free in a new world where there is no more separation or shadow or tears … the body was merely a covering and the soul is now freed for the eternal.[5]

'The life of each person is … a circle. We come out of the unknown. We appear on the earth, live here … and eventually return back into the unknown again. The oceans move in this rhythm too; the tide comes in, turns and goes back out again.'[6]

He writes of the eternity that is waiting to welcome us and of the dead being very, very near us. So he can write of death as being, not the end of everything, but rather a profound invitation. He writes of the rewards of harvesting the stored treasures of the memory, in old age—'the beauty of the inner harvest'.

The human eye adores gazing; it feasts on the wild beauty of new landscapes, the dignity of trees, the tenderness of a human face or the white sphere of the moon blessing the earth in a circle of light. The eye … finds some deep consolation and sense of home in special shapes. Deep within the human mind, there is a fascination with the circle because it satisfies some longing within us. It is one of the most universal and ancient shapes in the universe. Reality often seems to express itself in this form. The earth is a circle; and even time itself seems to have a circular nature. The Celtic world was always fascinated with circles; they are prevalent in so much of its art work; the Celts even transfigured the Cross by surrounding it with a circle. The Celtic Cross is a beautiful symbol; the circle around the beams of the Cross rescues the loneliness where the two lines of pain intersect; it seems to calm and console their forsaken linearity.[7]

I find a solace in this image which is beyond words but which finds a resonance in the language of the soul.

In his writing, John O'Donohue draws on the great religious traditions as well as on his exploration of the Celtic imagination, and these enrich what he has to offer. Such writing does not contain explicit answers to the questions of suffering and grief with which I have been struggling. Rather it liberates me into another perspective, just as the slight turn of a kaleidoscope reveals a new prism for contemplation. His insights free me from the limited treadmill of literal, argumentative thinking into a much wider sphere of imagination; it is like being reminded of a truth known long ago but half-forgotten, like meeting again an old and beloved friend. Such writing is a crucial source of relief, consolation, faith and fresh hope, a sort of deliverance from that rational frustration which is a signpost only to desolation.

DECEMBER 2003

Mary has had three falls in the space of a week. The third fall was at 3 a.m. When the hostel's night sister came on her hourly round, she found Mary on the floor of her little sitting room with a badly broken right wrist. Thank goodness she was not still living alone.

The ambulance angels brought her to the district hospital. By the time I arrived from the city a few hours later, she was still waiting for attention. She was in pain, pale and exhausted. She looked very small in the high Emergency bed. Seeing me, she reached out her good hand and started to cry quietly, but only for a few moments. She's very brave and was determined to stay in control of herself. I wondered how they had managed to get the drip needle into her frail little bloodless hand.

The hours went by. Eventually one of the overworked doctors anaesthetised Mary's arm and set her wrist in plaster. But the X-ray, taken an hour later, showed that it was not in place. She was scheduled for theatre the next day, where an orthopaedic surgeon would do it again.

More hours in the Holding Ward and eventually, late at night, she was admitted to a ward.

Now she's in rehabilitation in the convalescent hospital, being helped to regain confidence. She's sharing a room with Sophia, a wraith of ninety-four, who's recovering from a broken knee and hip. They are both deaf so conversation is difficult but they've made a connection. On my daily visits, I'm the go-between. When I brush Mary's hair, she directs me, 'Ask Sophia if she'd like her hair brushed'. When I pack up her clothes to take home for washing, she says, 'See if Sophia needs her clothes done'. But Sophia says that her son, who is seventy-seven, does it for her. It is pitiable to see two such vulnerable old ladies suffering. As Sophia says, she's really too old for it now. But somehow they endure in their gentle, stoic way.

The nursing varies in quality. One day I arrived to find Mary sitting miserably in a chair, with bare legs in slippers, trying to support the heavy weight of her arm in plaster. Yet, today, she's perfectly arranged, fully dressed in matching clothes, showered, with her teeth cleaned, smiling. Her arm is suspended in a sling to support its weight and drain the painful swelling. 'I'm so cosy and comfortable,' she says.

I thanked the sister on duty who is fifty-ish, brisk, capable, with a family of her own. She says it's not that difficult, really; you just have to care for them with love. With a sly smile, she adds that she didn't need to go to university to learn that. She's a registered nurse, one of the old brigade, who learned her nursing on the ward.

My daily round trip takes almost three hours, plenty of time to think. I wonder how well I'll manage when my turn comes to be humbled, helpless, dependent on a stranger to take me to the toilet.

The young doctor in charge of rehabilitation is a bit tired, being a new father, but he is patient and respectful with Mary as he encourages her to stand up shakily, to take one tentative step, then another.

Some days, eight-year-old Ryan visits Sophia, with his mother. Probably her great-grandson? Only when he's there do the elderly ladies smile with joy, to see a child so beautiful, carefree and playful, at the beginning of the journey they are now completing. They offer him the little buckets of ice cream from their lunch trays and watch, with delight, as he eats. Ryan is their Christmas present. What could be more precious than the gift of a child into their world of weariness and suffering?

D ECEMBER 2003

Today, on the way home from visiting Mary in hospital, I called in to the shop for some salad but once I got in there I couldn't decide what to buy. Suddenly the abundance of Tony's display of fruit and vegetables filled my eyes to overflowing. Which lettuce to choose— a crinkly mignonette, leaves blushed with russet, or a long crisp cos, or one of those loose bundles of delicate green frills that melt in your mouth? So many different shades of green. It was like being out in the bush: without the distraction of vivid colour, you have to refine your focus, maybe even narrow your eyes, to distinguish between grey-green and blue-green eucalyptus leaves and all the other subtle variations in tone. How do we manage with only one word for so many greens? I believe the Japanese response to this is *shibui*—the practice of planting, in their classical gardens, a range of greens and achieving subtle distinction and harmony through differences in height, shape and texture.

Tony's sensibility is more extrovert: heaped behind the lettuces are bunches of rocket tied with string, scarlet radishes, creamy-green leeks and spinach in a red bucket; celery, fennel, fat buds of chicory and cabbages cut into quarters to expose their tightly packed curly leaves in cross-section. On a raked shelf of pragmatic oranges, yellow pears in purple paper jackets and five varieties of apples, he's placed the seduction of an opened box of ripe figs.

Figs! My imagination reels back into the Song of Solomon, detours via the Sufi poets and alights on Corfu, among a group of elderly men wearing caps and moustaches, worrying their beads and gossiping in the shade of spreading branches softening the glare of lime-washed walls. The hooves of a little donkey clip-clop on cobblestones.

Tony has cut the butternut pumpkins into halves so that their bright orange flesh glows against the dark, lustrous skins of the Queensland blues, among which they nestle. Ever so casually, he's spilled a pile of tiny acid-red chillies beside the purple eggplants; and quite illogically, huge cut wedges of watermelon, studded with seeds, gleam in a cascading shelter of dill, coriander and basil.

I wonder if anyone else is drunk on the dazzle of this cornucopia. But the customer next to me looks determined and fully sober.

She presses her thumb into the black rind of an avocado and finds it wanting. He sees her out of the corner of his eye. She knows it. She also knows he won't say a word. The customer is always right. He smiles to himself and glances away. She does the same test on the Shanghai peaches, heaped in a pink and cream mound and the velvet skin gives way to her insistent touch. Her face is expressionless as she fills a bag. She reveals no anticipation of the exquisite taste to come but I am already suffused with it. In my mind's eye, the juice is running down my chin as I bite slowly into the pale, fragrant flesh with my eyes closed, their hunger satisfied at last.

Calm in conquest—he is so used to it—Tony supervises the lad packing my purchases into two bags. He explains to me how to chop the tops of the leeks 'in pezzi, cosi', to cook them in a little oil, for an omelette 'deliciosissima'! He joins his thumb and forefinger and kisses them with a flourish. Then, with the authority of a Caesar commanding legions, he orders the lad to carry my parcels to the car.

'Ci vediamo, Carolina.' He is solicitous in farewell, just as he was yesterday and will be again, tomorrow.

With all my senses enlivened by this encounter, I felt lighter in spirit, as I do, more and more often, these days.

26 DECEMBER 2003

Christmas again. Mary and I shared it with Val. And now Boxing Day. For me, the celebration highlights the absence of loved ones no longer here, but that's the blessing of friends.

I went to Arrupe House to watch the cricket on television with Fr Cecil. Third Test, Australia v India at the MCG. It's Steve Waugh's last series, his last Test at the MCG.

Fr Cecil was in excellent form, as usual. He's eighty-five, in a wheelchair, patched with bandages on both forearms, both thighs and his face. They're removing a number of melanomas, and grafting skin onto the wounds.

'Oh, it's nothing,' he says and tells a couple of amusing stories about his most recent of many visits to hospital. His long run of ill-health began with a stroke. He looks a bit pale and, when I enquire, says that the diabetes got away from him this morning but he's increased his self-administered injection of insulin and it's alright now. Father is the complete lesson in how to deal with suffering. He laughs at it. It's a healing joy to be in his company.

Ponting and Hayden have taken root at the wicket and the Indians look dispirited as they try every variation of their bowling attack, to no avail. Having won the last Test in Adelaide, they were beginning to look as though they could challenge Australia, for once, but now Ponting's on his way to a double century, with Hayden on 98. It's a pushover, so we're yarning as much as watching.

Father demonstrates his method of transferring from the wheelchair to the bed, without assistance. He's a big man and his chance of accomplishing this feat unaided seems unrealistic. There's a moment of extreme peril in the middle of the manoeuvre when he must balance on his one remaining foot and swivel through 180 degrees, with fingertip control only, on bedside cabinet and wheelchair arm. Achieving the turn, he falls heavily onto the bed with a triumphant laugh. After a brief recovery period, he performs the process in reverse. Another precarious success.

His description of how he has a shower, on his own, with one leg and a recently broken shoulder and wrist, is both alarming and entertaining. He apologises for talking too much and says it's probably compensation because he has lost a leg. Until recently he was chaplain to Year 7 boys at Saint Ignatius' College, Riverview. When the little boys asked him about his missing leg, he would tell them that unfortunately he'd lost it somewhere and send them off to see if they could find it for him.

When the cricketers adjourn for afternoon tea, so do we. Around to the dining room where several other retired priests in residence are already gathered. I've made a date loaf. I left the sugar out of the recipe because of Fr Cecil's diabetes but it tastes good anyway and receives over-generous praise. We want to be back to the room in time to see Fr Carlson feeding the birds at 4.30 p.m.

First come top-knot pigeons, then pink and grey galahs, and third, wheeling and swooping on wide white wings, the sulphur-crested cockatoos, screeching ravenously. Landed, their waddling gait is a parody of their grace in flight. They all feed close outside Fr Cecil's glass doors.

The afternoon passes quickly and enjoyably. Father is a cricket coach of many years and I can ask him to explain fine points of the game which elude me. It reminds me of summer afternoons watching sport with my father, but I do not mention that, in case it should make this occasion seem only a substitute. It is not. They are separate experiences, each with its own value. Fr Cecil is very good company and I learn from spending time with him. He has not a scrap of pity for himself. He sees each new experience, good or bad, as being interesting. He says he inherited optimism from his wonderful mother. His faith is so much part of him that it doesn't need mentioning. As I grow old and vulnerable, I hope I will always remember his example, as well as Dad's, and do my best to emulate them, with courage and humour.

5 JANUARY 2004

It was still thirty degrees at nine o'clock tonight as we walked slowly around Circular Quay. A still evening, cloudless, with another day of dry heat promised. It seems as though the drought will never break. Jenny and I met to see a film together. It was a shock to come out of the cool, subterranean cinema into a balmy Sydney summer night. People were strolling languidly or sitting at outdoor cafe tables.

Later, when we caught the last ferry home, it was still hot. We sat out on deck, relieved to feel the movement of air on our faces, as the boat pulled backwards out of the Quay. The amphitheatre of city lights widened around and above us, reminiscent of the big cinema screen, slowly revealed, as the curtains slide back. Past the glowing shells of the Opera House and the whole sweep of the eastern harbour opening up into a John Olsen mural—scribbles of light from Pinchgut and Garden Island shimmering into an expanse of ultramarine.

Steaming under the Harbour Bridge we craned our necks to watch the last groups of night-climbers, each holding a twinkle of light, edging slowly up the great arches. First stop Luna Park, brightly lit but regulated silent, devoid of revellers. Next wharf McMahons Point, with late diners at Sails, gazing out smugly from their coveted, expensive window tables.

An acceleration of the throbbing engines propels us west across darker waters, past Goat Island, where they film *Water Rats* for television. The city lights are hidden now by the great Walsh Bay wharves, Observatory Hill and the harbourmaster's tower.

Jenny got off at Darling Street and I watched her fair head under lamplight climbing the hill until the ferry had drawn too far away, heading across to the mooring dolphins off Birchgrove, flashing their green starboard warning beacons.

Suddenly there was a prawn trawler right alongside, in our wash, baffles out wide to spread the net dragging in the water behind her, two crewmen taking it easy before the action to come. A cigarette glowed in the dark. I felt ecstatic to be sitting outside on the shiny red-slatted bench of MV *Supply* with the warm north wind in my face and my head swimming with the salt spray. No one has captured the mood of the harbour at night like Ken Slessor in 'Five Bells':

… the Harbour floats
In air, the Cross hangs upside-down in water.

It's a poem about a friend's drowning which Slessor is seeking to understand. It's not primarily about the beauty of the harbour, yet that is what he has captured, in a way that has never been surpassed—perhaps because he was concentrated on his main theme and glimpsed the images obliquely, out of the corner of his eye?

I looked out of my window in the dark
At waves with diamond quills and combs of light
that arched their mackerel-backs and smacked the sand
In the moon's drench, that straight enormous glaze,
And ships far off asleep, and Harbour-buoys
Tossing their firebells wearily each to each …[8]

Long Nose Point, Birchgrove, next stop Greenwich. I could hardly bear to disembark. I was feeling exhilaration again. It was like meeting a beloved friend after too long an absence. I stood reluctantly on the wharf and watched the lighted craft growing smaller as it bustled across to Valentia Street wharf at Hunters

Hill, where I was born, and where my father caught the ferry to work in the 1930s. At last I turned away, with a sigh that released something, and climbed the ten stone steps slowly, intoxicated by the pungent smell of the brackish river as the tide began to run out. There's a waning moon tonight. In a few days time, during the dark of the moon, the boats will be out in numbers as the prawns rise on the slack and ebb tides.

It's Dad's birthday. He would have been ninety-seven. I feel he's not far away.

S u m m e r 2 0 0 4

I am content in my home on these bright, hot, summer days. The first of the white agapanthus have opened fully into flowerheads. They're as tall as I am, a joy after months of waiting. These are the ones that Joanne and Peter gave me when they were dividing their long, densely packed beds. They came originally from the hundred-year-old garden of her friend Noel, so they are heirlooms. There's a new, vivid, pink geranium in behind them. I struck it as a cutting from Dad's garden. Above, brilliant scarlet, yellow and orange portulacas bloom each morning in the shallow ledges of soil running across the sandstone wall. I don't know how they manage to take root there, let alone prosper, yet they are a delight, day after day. At the top of the wall, seaside daisies I put in last summer have now established themselves, spraying out in a long, thick, springing fringe, intertwined with a cerise, hanging geranium. A friend has a poster in her office showing a field of thousands of small daisies, with the caption 'Bloom where you're planted'.

I am finding consolation in beauty once again. I take it as a significant sign of healing. And the seasons of the garden remind me of the cycle of all life, including my own.

S UMMER 2004

The Skin Cancer Clinic waiting room is festooned with patients. Most of us are middle-aged or older with fair Anglo-Celtic skin that has suffered from too much exposure to the sun in our ignorant youth. When I was young we did not realise that sunburn would cause skin cancer and melanoma later in life. We spent hours unprotected in the sun and even aided the tanning process by basting our skin with oil. It's unthinkable today. A bad case of sunburn would be salved by your mother rubbing half a tomato over the tight, red skin of your back, face, arms, legs and agonising insteps. Or she might dab all the burned areas with cotton wool soaked in cold tea to ease the pain. In a few days the top layer of ruined skin could be peeled off in long, papery streamers. Soon we'd be out on the beach ready to repeat the whole ridiculous process.

All this foolishness in order to achieve tanned skin which, for some reason, was desirable in the 1950s and 1960s. At that time, Aboriginal people, who had beautiful, natural brown skin, were not even recognised as citizens of Australia. That did not come until the historic, long-overdue referendum of 1967. An Aboriginal friend told me, hesitantly, for fear of offending, that she felt rather sorry for us in our sunbaking ignorance and misunderstanding of our environment.

The man waiting next to me looked like an elderly lizard, as most of us did, with our leathery necks and faces. And the backs of our hands freckled and blotched from years of unprotected gardening, fishing and driving with no knowledge of what we were in for later: this annual pilgrimage to have our emerging cancers burned off or removed surgically. All we had to look at, while waiting, were tattered popular magazines or, on the walls, terrifying posters in several bright colours and graphic detail, illustrating what we're suffering from. Altogether too much information. My companion said that he only wished he had shares in this thriving clinic as it was so obviously booming.

Six more patients from outer Sydney and four from the country gave their personal details to the receptionist. The room was too small for privacy of disclosure, so we learned a good deal about each other. Another victim told me that this would make a good *Australian Story*, just to let me know I was not getting away with anonymity while he was around. I could only agree with him.

As each of the fourteen doctors came out, in turn, to see off their last patient and claim the next, we noticed that almost every medico, whether male or female, was a young Asian with beautiful, unblemished olive skin never damaged by the sun. Except my practitioner who was, like me, Anglo, fair and freckled. But she was young and the sun cancer education campaign of recent years had saved her from undue exposure. She told me she doesn't even bother to produce a tan by any of the artificial means available now. She's quite happy to be her pale self. We agreed that Nicole Kidman had made pale not only acceptable but thoroughly cool. Good on you, Nicole, but alas too late for me.

I stood in my underwear, arms outspread like a cormorant drying its wings, while the doctor examined me all over with a large magnifying glass and a bright light. Not too bad at all this time, she decided. Last time I had had a basal cell carcinoma removed surgically from my face. She sprayed the icy burn of nitrogen onto a dozen or so areas on the backs of my hands and then put several small, stinging injections of anaesthetic into my back. After a few minutes she excised an enlarged mole and repaired the wound. The mole goes to pathology and she will ring me with a result. The cost to me of the whole procedure is only fifty dollars, which I can claim on Medicare. Any additional costs are bulk-billed. It's a wonderful service and just as well because clearly it's a growth industry in my age group.

~

All through summer I've been aware of the shade of trees. What a grace it is to walk out of hot, glaring sunlight into a verdant haven of shelter—a cool, pleasant relief from the heat of midday. I imagine a world without trees. Terrible. Living in a city, I treasure the trees which grow astonishingly out of asphalt footpaths, softening the sharp edges of office blocks, and lifting the spirits with a wistful reminder of distant, green countryside. The tree I know best has a powerful presence, impossible to ignore. It spreads its dense branches onto my westerly balcony, offering gracious protection from the relentless afternoon sun. At dusk, if a southerly buster sneaks round the corner of the building, the tree rattles its leaves boisterously against my windows with a sound uncannily like laughter.

Yet, as summer subsides into autumn, this exuberant tree changes personality completely. Gradually, as it loses its extravagant foliage, it falls silent. Its slim branches reach in bare candelabra towards the sky, admitting the welcome warmth of winter sunlight. Not until September does it produce the first pale buds of its spring resurgence. It's a perfect companion for all seasons.

There's another summer tree I have been enjoying in a friend's garden. She invited me to pick her flowers while she's away travelling. Several times I've gathered sweet bunches of yellow nasturtiums, white daisies and purple penstemons and lavender for a friend in hospital. He's very ill and he finds some pleasure in these homely cottage flowers.

As I gather them, slowly, a soft peal of liquid notes ripples from a wind chime in the tree casting a lovely shade over the back lawn. The tree has cascades of leaves the shape of lozenges, falling in elaborate, serried fans of luminescent yellow-green, filtering the light as stained glass windows do. In the afternoon garden, throbbing with cicadas, time dissolves. Little wonder that many people, when asked for their sacred place, recall a place of trees as a natural cathedral.

That great Methodist churchman and preacher, Rev. Alan Walker, told me a tree story which was an epiphany in his life. In 1953, he was appointed to lead the Mission to the Nation, the largest evangelical undertaking of any church, at that time. Overwhelmed by the responsibility of the task ahead, he lay, one evening, on the warm grass under two big gum trees, trying to pray. He recalled Jesus explaining to Nicodemus the mystery of the Holy Spirit (John 3:8).

Jesus showed Nicodemus an olive tree blowing in the wind. He said that you couldn't see the wind, where it came from or where it was going. What you could see was the movement of it in the trees. And suddenly Alan Walker heard the wind rustling in the leaves above him. A phrase sprang to his mind: 'The wind is in the gum trees … the wind is in the gum trees … the Holy Spirit is going to blow across Australia!' He said that the experience transfigured his ministry.[9]

I suppose many people have a special tree, one they climbed for adventure or for a hiding place, as a child; or, which brought them hope or solace; or a tree which filled them with awe. My friend Peter Solness spent several years photographing Australians with their favourite trees. Complete strangers opened up to him with their tree stories linked to deep associations with identity, landscape or ancestry. Peter thinks the tree is as vital a national symbol as the outback or the beach.[10]

FEBRUARY 2004

The renewal of an invitation to facilitate some twilight retreats for the staff at two of our major city hospitals, to give them an opportunity for some peace at the end of another busy day caring for sick people. Yes, this is work for which I feel some energy and enthusiasm again. I feel excited at the prospect of the meeting next week at which I will collaborate with the hospital staff to design what is needed. Work has been an essential element in the process of my recovery, especially work which is purposeful and congruent with my gifts and experience, based in listening and facilitating the sharing of personal life stories. Such work is meaningful and rewarding.

20 FEBRUARY 2004

We've started the year well with *Australian Story*. This week's program was an inspiration. Dr Michael Holt, the head of Orthopaedic Surgery at a Brisbane hospital, walked out into the street one day and a car hit him. His injuries were terrible, mostly to his head, including the loss of one eye. Our story followed his dogged determination, not only to recover, but to regain the same high standard of surgery he had achieved before the accident. It seemed impossible but he did it, with the support of his family and in spite of some serious bureaucratic opposition. It was fascinating to see a doctor become a patient; and to hear a colleague describe how the rather arrogant, demanding surgeon has become more human as a result of what he's been through. The program was made over an extended period by producer Claire Forster with our Brisbane crew, Anthony Sines and Marc Smith. Michael Holt even wanted to do his own 'stunt' work in the re-enactment of the accident.

AUTUMN 2004

I brought Mary home from hospital a few days ago and she is settling in. She has just rung to let me know that the first flowers have appeared on her lasiandra bush and that they are bright purple. She sounds very pleased and surprised, as though she has never seen them before, even though the same thing happened this time last year and the year before, when we bought the shrub together at the nursery and planted it, to provide a burst of autumn colour.

I've planned her little garden to produce something colourful in every season but she seems astonished each time something blooms. I think she can't remember very much at all in the recent past. She will tell me the same story three times in one day. I don't tell her she's repeating herself as I can't see how that would be helpful. I trust that difficult events are also forgotten, especially my own moments of impatience with her. The main thing is she's enjoying the lasiandra now, today. Because I've planted densely in the small space, the shrubs have formed a thicket, attractive to little birds, and sometimes blue wrens and willy wagtails come, to dart from the leafy shelter out to the birdbath and swiftly back again. Then Mary's face is transformed with the joyful smile of a child.

And that teaches me something important: I have not discovered any easy answers for the pain of grief, yet increasingly I find hope and sustenance in paying attention to such moments of consequence[11] in everyday life. In some magical way, they restore perspective and equilibrium.

MARCH 2004

There's an evocative photograph[12] by Kate Geraghty in the *Sydney Morning Herald* today. It shows a man sculpting a swan from an old tyre outside his shed at Rylstone, New South Wales, fifty kilometres from Mudgee, with two teenage boys watching intently. This traditional Australian art is back-breaking work. According to the accompanying story, Mr Michael Keating marks the tyre with chalk before cutting. Then he uses a chainsaw to create a beak, a back and the swan's neck. The most difficult task is to turn the tyre back to create the body of the swan. Then he'll probably paint it white. The paper reports there will be a competition held tomorrow in a bid to revive this dying craft, so that the rubber swan will not disappear forever from Australian gardens. Splendid.

A U G U S T 2 0 0 4

When I arrived to visit Mary today she was standing in front of her bedroom mirror, a small, very stooped figure, peering at her reflection in dismay. She stayed there, quite still, for a few minutes. Then, with one hand on the dressing table for balance, she lifted the other hand to her short white hair.

As she had not heard me, I went out and came in again, calling a greeting. She turned and, steering the walker slowly towards me, she smiled wistfully and announced: 'I think that finally I've turned into an old lady. I can't understand it. It's unbelievable. It's only just happened. I used to go for a long walk every morning. And now ...'

She shook her head in disbelief and then turned her attention to my basket.

'What on earth have you got there?' Very disapproving, as though I might have brought her a death adder.

'Lisianthus, your favourites.'

'Well, I don't know anything about them. And they make such as mess when they die. They're quite unnecessary.'

I filled two vases with water and, while she arranged the flowers, went out into her garden and planted three pots of impatiens:

bright burgundy, pink and white. The garden is beautiful. When I filled the birdbath, two blue wrens hopped out of the shelter of the azalea bushes, thick with scarlet blooms. They were planted by the daughter of the previous resident. I called Mary and she wheeled her way tentatively to the open doorway. Her face relaxed into a look of unguarded pleasure as she watched them. Apart from practicalities, I think the best I can do for her now is to draw her attention to beauty.

We go for a drive to Pearl Beach. Mary has always enjoyed it in the past but today she has no recall of it, so she is pleased to be going to a 'new' destination.

'Something different, for a change.'

I bring a couple of cushions from the car so she will be high enough on the cafe chair. Unusually, the meal is a success and her face breaks into a sweet smile when someone brings a small dog to the next table. The coffee arrives in a high, glass beaker.

'What on earth do they serve it like that for? It's unbelievable. I can't possibly drink all that. Nobody could drink all that!'

We watch the guests arrive for a wedding reception at a beachfront restaurant over the road. Mary notices the informality of their clothes.

'Unbelievable!'

She is certainly enjoying herself.

On the drive home, we stop at a scenic lookout, where Mary is outraged by graffiti and some scattered litter. Friends we have not seen for a long time pull up beside us. They ask Mary if she likes where she is living now.

'No, I certainly do not.'

I must remember that I cannot make her happy. As we drive on, she holds her handbag up as a shield against the westerly sun. Even on a cushion, she is too low to benefit from the sun visor.

As we come through the front door of Yallambee Lodge, Wendy, one of the evening staff, meets us with a friendly greeting. Although I know her quite well, Mary introduces me, obliquely, as usual. (Once a teacher, always a teacher?)

'Do you know who this is?'

'Yes, it's Caroline.'

'It's Caroline Jones. She's my stepdaughter.'

I realise suddenly, and with surprise, that Mary is quite proud of me. As we make our slow progress to her door, she pauses at the staff photographs on the wall near the office and points out to me all the carers and nurses she likes best and comments on their idiosyncrasies and some of their hairstyles.

'Do you tell them what you think of their hairstyles?'

'I most certainly do. Some of them are unbelievable!'

She offered to buy one member of staff a new set of teeth but I understand the offer was declined, although the carer was touched by the thought.

As she settles into her big, comfortable, recliner chair, I put a layer of mulch on the garden. Wendy puts her head round the door to see if Mary would like a tea tray in her room so she can watch *As Time Goes By* on television. Mary accedes to this suggestion with the air of a duchess granting a favour.

'It's what they call dinner. At this hour! Of course, I won't be able to eat it.'

Wendy rolls her eyes, smiles and winks.

When Mary was last in hospital but ready to get up on her feet again, Wendy packed Mary's walker into the boot of her car and, at the end of a long day's shift, drove to the hospital and delivered it to Mary's ward, with her name on it. Mary has forgotten this but I haven't.

When I'm leaving, Mary gives me a little cake of chocolate and explains in detail how to remove the wrapper.

An hour and a half later, when I get home, I give her three rings on the phone as my customary signal of safe arrival. She never hears it. A bit later in the evening she will ring to ask if I'm home yet.

'You didn't remember to give me the three rings. I was so worried.'

'I did actually, maybe you didn't hear.'

'I can't hear you if you mumble.'

'I did ring. Maybe you were watching television.'

I have bought her a high quality set of comfortable headphones and she hears the television sound very clearly.

'I wouldn't have been watching television. I'm far too busy.'

'Did you see *As Time Goes By*?'

'I can't hear you.'

'*As Time Goes By*. Did you watch it after I left?'

'When's it on?'

'It's just finished.'

'Yes, I saw it. I think it's gone off lately. You know, your father and I always used to watch it. I'm sorry but I'll just have to go now. I've got so much to do. I hope I might see you again some time. But don't bring any more flowers. They make such a mess. Thank you for ringing.'

SEPTEMBER 2004

There is a hint of warmth and the perfume of jasmine in the air. This year I can enjoy it. Much of the news from overseas is appalling and I marvel again at how fortunate we are to live in

Australia. Most of us. To our disgrace, there are still asylum seekers and acknowledged refugees in Australian detention centres, after several years—people whose stories we are not allowed to know or to tell. Mary is outraged by this and so am I. Now that the plight of Africa is in the news again after years of neglect, I saw on television a report about the lost boys. In the mid-1980s, a big group of young teenage boys, orphaned by war, walked out of Sudan on a long, long march into Ethiopia. There they stayed for four years, surviving on their wits until once again war forced them to take to the road. Their destination this time was a wretched refugee camp, where they took every opportunity for education. Finally, aged eighteen and nineteen, some were selected to come to Australia. Beautifully spoken, magnificent-looking, one of the young immigrants said: 'I hope I would be very good for Australia'.

Arrived here, they were completely amazed by their freedom as they were welcomed to a country town. Their most urgent concern was their schooling. It was touching to see their wide-eyed appreciation of things we take for granted every day. As they came through the immigration check at the airport, a laconic Australian official, wearing shorts and long socks, was interviewed. He summed up the situation perfectly in a few words and his response said it all: 'Sudan's loss. Our gain.'

Our Australia as it should be … Dad would have approved. He told me that in the immediate post-war years, prime minister Ben Chifley, with Immigration Minister Arthur Calwell, brought more refugees to Australia, per capita, than any other country at the time.

Monday, 26 November 2004

The campaign of fear has succeeded. The Howard government has been returned. Enough voters have been persuaded to reject the asylum seekers arriving by boat, described by government ministers as 'these people', 'these queue-jumpers', who would even 'throw their children into the water' to gain entry to Australia. The word 'Muslim' is unspoken but implicit. The events of 9/11 in the United States have prepared the way for our political leaders to appeal to the worst in us. Mary is appalled: 'I just can't understand why people have voted that man back in. It's unbelievable. What would your father have said?'

(He probably would have said, 'Those awful bastards!')

She was very distressed by the plight of the asylum seekers rescued by the Norwegian vessel *Tampa*, and then by the prospect of families being held in detention centres, with Christmas coming.

'I didn't know we had detention centres in Australia. We never used to have detention centres!'

Has she forgotten that Australia did intern Italians and Germans during World War II? In any case, as an ex-servicewoman, she is incensed by the Australian government's policy and feels betrayed by it. This is not the Australia for which she served as a WAAAF flying officer and radar operator in World War II.

JANUARY 2005

This morning there are five cormorants at the baths. Not fishing but resting, each on top of one of the posts that support the shark net. I've never been so close to a cormorant before, only seen them fishing at a distance, and always thought they were jet black. This morning they are still, giving only an occasional sudden elastic twist of the long, serpentine neck to inspect the surroundings with eyes like black beads. Sometimes I've seen them sitting on rocks with wide wings outstretched to dry. Not this morning. They are dry and as I float beneath them and close to them I see that their black wings are softly dappled with grey. I thought they would be alarmed when I came so near but they stayed and it is moving to be accepted as no threat by these wild, free creatures.

I am later than usual, to take advantage of a king tide at 9.30. High water is almost lapping the top of the net when the mothers and children start to drift slowly down the steps, through the turnstile and onto the sand, still dreamy, trailing a paraphernalia of floaties, towels and sea toys in their wake. Gradually they establish their beachheads, the mothers yawning and greeting each other to exchange news of the night before: who has slept well, who has been awake with a teething baby, asleep now under a net in its capsule.

Little noses are smeared absentmindedly with sun cream; pink and purple caps pulled down front and back over faces and necks; floaties attached to wriggling bodies squirming to escape to the water's edge to begin the concentrated business of digging holes and mounding sand into castles and squealing as the little waves undermine them.

Two new mothers sit together in their bright sarongs and straw hats, sleepily breastfeeding their babies in companionable silence. Tim the caretaker's little daughter slowly and deliberately buries her patient dog Astro Boy up to the neck in sand as he lies quite relaxed and unprotesting. This intriguing procedure attracts some new playmates, as she had hoped.

Little boys challenge each other to made-up games of 'jumping in'. Little girls interfere with their smaller brothers' attempts to float unaided on long foam snakes or boogie boards.

The high children's voices mix into a harmonious chorus with the mothers' lower-pitched murmured conversations.

Two grandparents, swathed in protective sunclothes, are

dunking an over-dressed, plump infant up and down in the water. Adoringly they pass him to each other, responding to his every gurgle with delighted, silly sounds of their own which would be absurd in any other situation. Standing waist-deep in water, they are gloriously, extravagantly fulfilled.

Imperceptibly, as the morning draws on, the tide ebbs, leaving a few seashells and glossy green fig leaves stranded at the water's edge. The junior engineers are lured further down the glistening sand to risk the thrill of building their castles in the pathway of inevitable flooding. They are utterly focussed on the task they have set themselves, crouched on their knees, scooping holes in the heavy, wet sand—piling it up, watching danger approach through squinting eyes, mad with mock fear, and then delirious in the climax of annihilation, rolling about to get maximum pleasure from the moment. And then doing it all over again, absorbed in their glorious endeavour, deaf to any adult voice until the words 'ice cream' break through and the waterfront is deserted in a stampede on quick sandpiper legs to the kiosk.

If I stay long enough, here at the baths, I am gradually surrounded and integrated into the family scene, like an honorary nanna with children playing around my feet and conversation seeping into my consciousness and dissolving.

It would be easy to while away the whole day on the sand until the tide turned again.

Epilogue

It's seven years since Dad died.

I have not written in this diary for two and a half years because I have been waiting to gain more clarity on what has happened in these past seven years. I have also been uncertain if writing it down, as honestly as possible, was essentially a therapeutic process for me, or if its publication may have any benefit for a reader experiencing loss and grief.

In the late 1970s, through a period of personal counselling, I first discovered the healing value of disclosing a difficult passage of my life to another person who listened carefully and accepted what I was telling, without judgement. Several years later, a similar opportunity was presented by the processes of preparation to come into the Catholic Church.

These were both deeply healing, life-changing experiences, so I am confident that recording the events of the past seven years has been an important step for me towards recovery from the traumatic reaction I had to my father's illness and death.

But before deciding to publish, I needed to put my individual story into the context of a wider perspective that could be illuminating and hopeful for anyone else challenged by the powerful human experiences of love, suffering, struggle, grief, loss of faith and aloneness. To achieve this, I have been reading, and talking to people who have reflected deeply on these questions and who have insights into them.

In her book, *Scarred by Struggle, Transformed by Hope*, Joan Chittister writes that

struggle is an unavoidable part of life. It comes with birth and it takes its toll at every stage of development We tussle between the dark and the daylight moments of the soul … So how are we to think of struggle? Is it loss or is it gain?

Life itself is the answer. If no one can escape struggle, then it must serve some purpose in life. It is a function of the spirit. It is an organic part of the adventure of development that comes only through the soul-stretching process of struggle. No other process in life requires so much so deeply of us. Struggle bores down into the deepest part of the human soul … bringing new life, contravening old truisms.[1]

Such an approach begins to give some meaning to suffering and I found myself ready to reflect on the claim that suffering is a function of the spirit.

Today is the anniversary of my mother's death in 1969. Dad's anniversary was two days ago. He died on 30 July 2000.

August is the cruellest month yet it is an exquisite evening, piercing in its beauty. In the western prospect from my window, the high, cerulean sky is streaked extravagantly with streaming pink and golden clouds. The colours heighten to a luminous glory and then begin to fade quite quickly. Paradise lost again, as it is each evening. But with the promise of morning to come.

I have come to understand that suffering is a universal human experience and an integral part of being alive. The challenge is to find a meaningful response so that I am not defeated by it and can live through it with trust and hope; and know that it is normal to be changed by it.

I recall the wisdom of writer Barbara Blackman, telling me in a *Search for Meaning* interview, that there isn't necessarily a solution to every problem.

We, of course, in our so-called scientific age, are conditioned to think that there is. Yet the ancient wisdom points out that the tree cannot grow through the rock. The tree roots grow round the rock. Very often you don't solve the problems, you transcend them. By accepting both sides of the problem, the conflict, you move beyond it … So I find that when I come up against a problem I cannot solve, I do nothing. I just lie there and wait. I've always trusted the Unknown and It has never let me down. Something you cannot, for the life of you, imagine or plan for, happens.[2]

The concept of 'not either/or, but both/and' occurs in a number of the Eastern spiritual traditions. To hold apparent contradictions in balance does not come easily to the Western mind, trained to seek the resolution of opposites. Yet, once grasped, it does open a way beyond the dilemma.

The well-known writer of detective novels, Agatha Christie, understood this when she said, of her personal life, that she had, at times, been racked with despairing sorrow—yet, through it all, she knew quite certainly, that just to be alive was a grand thing.

And so it is with grief. In my experience, there is no easy cure for it and no end to it. You carry it with you, in varying degrees of consciousness and intensity. It becomes part of you and it changes you. Yet, as time goes on, grief is not all that there is. At its worst, it is disabling. But, as I've grown through it, I believe I have gained a more profound perspective on life, a new depth of spiritual maturity and an altered image of God which I hope will sustain me in future crises.

I hope that my own painful experience has nourished my capacity for compassion and will enable me to be with others more authentically in their time of loss or pain. The way forward, for me, is somehow to hold the joy and the suffering of life in equilibrium, or in ebb and flow; the contradictions not seeking reconciliation but each suffusing, permeating and giving meaning to the other. I hope that I will be able to do it.

I used to wonder why Dad enjoyed reading the newspaper from back to front. As he browsed the death notices, he would murmur: 'Well, well, old so-and-so has finally put down his knife and fork'. When I asked him why he always turned first to the obituary columns, he replied: 'Just to make sure that I'm still here myself'. Then, with a sigh—of gratitude perhaps—and a poker face: 'I suppose that means I can't get out of the washing-up this morning, yet again. A kitchenman's work is never done.'

I'm quite sure he would want me to leave you with a smile.

Appendices

Carmel Ross has been a colleague for some years and we have often discussed the bigger and deeper issues of life. Her experience is in the areas of counselling and organisational psychology, including recent work in trauma recovery within an organisational setting. Carmel has also undertaken studies in theology and spirituality, including some Summer Institute courses at Boston College, a Jesuit university in the United States.

Reinforcing the fact that telling the story is a crucial step in recovery, I found it very moving and healing that Carmel read my account so thoughtfully, accepting the validity of my experience and responding generously with insights into the questions I had been struggling with. For instance, it has been a great relief to discover that after a traumatic experience you are a changed person, and that this is normal. Normality is not a state to recover but a new place, psychologically and spiritually. It was a relief, too, to be told that my traditional image of God limited my capacity to maintain my faith during a crisis, and that I could choose to change this.

Carmel has placed my story into a wider human context, identifying major themes she believes emerge strongly in it. This is an edited version of her summary. It has been illuminating for me and I hope that it may be for others also.

Caroline, a strong underlying theme of your book is the issue of how medical decision-making happens. You have provided a detailed chronicle about the events post-surgery, including your father's and your own struggles and anger at the traumatic impact of what happened.

Despite living in the era of 'informed consent', it's hard to tell if this was really the case for your father. You indicate in various ways that while he agreed to have the surgery, perhaps he might not have adequately understood what complications might occur, so the issue arises of how thoroughly was he able to inform himself of all possible outcomes in order to come to a well-informed decision.

There is also the question of your father's age, ninety-three years. Much as medical intervention should never be denied on the basis of age, a body of that age is likely to struggle more with recovery. In decision-making for major medical treatments, part of what we weigh up is the issue of 'How long might I receive benefit from this?' In that sense, is it worth a great deal of pain and discomfort because I'll live another ten years?

You raise this in various ways, but I often felt this initial decision, and how carefully it was taken, was the basis of much of your own rage about what happened post-surgery. I guess what would have been very hard to reconcile was that you had hesitation about this right from the start yet decided to fully support your father's decision; most close relatives and friends would do exactly this, not wishing to override or unduly influence the right of the patient to come to their own decision.

Related to this, the reality is that once the surgery has happened in a very elderly patient, what happens next may become a rollercoaster ride of one organ in trouble after another. Even with the care and considerable effort of the medical staff, your father's age and state of health, and the limitations of medical capability, made these issues more likely to happen yet less able to be remedied. As a result, our fundamental human right to freedom of will or choice vanishes because the juggernaut simply spins out of control, and saying 'No' is not really an option.

The impact of this on you is something you refer to often, as a situation where you realised neither you nor he had any real control over how events were unfolding. Helplessness in the presence of a desperate need to protect either yourself or others from harm can be the trigger of a reaction of trauma—we have virtually no ability to influence what is happening, yet experience a desperate need to do so. If we hold the view that the trauma could have been avoided, the inevitable reaction is one of anger—the sense of 'How could they do this to him?' If that experience of helplessness continues unabated over time, then the sense of watching life 'through a pane of glass' is a reaction very like being in shock—the sense of suspended animation when time happens differently and you feel more like an observer than a participant in the events around you.

You also mention what you perceived as a change of some kind within your father, that he seemed not quite to be the person he was pre-surgery. One of the possible effects of heart attacks, major surgery and any other sudden substantial onslaught on the body is that the mind at least temporarily stops laying down new memories, and may forget some of the recent past (such as giving permission for the surgery, the previous angiogram, and so on). Psychologically, there is a normal, constant process by which we unconsciously filter what we gather in short-term memory and move the important items into long-term memory. For people in your father's situation, this process seems to stop happening—this is quite a common occurrence. The drugs would not help either, but the phenomenon is more than just the drugs.

There is also the issue of your role as a relative and supporter of the patient. For you and others who find themselves supporting someone who is critically ill, how do you juggle the hope that they will achieve recovery to a point where life is worth living; or at some point come to the view that the prospect of recovery and/ or the quality of life afterwards would be so abysmal that scaling down treatment and allowing death to occur earlier would be the better option? This is a distressing position to be in because we are conditioned to believe, as are the medical staff, that life should always be preserved. How do you avoid guilt when you reach the point of thinking life might be too hard to continue yet not betray the patient in holding this view? This situation is exacerbated by your father being in an acute medical care facility, that is, a hospital Intensive Care Unit. Most people of his age with failing health would be living in an aged-care nursing home or hospice, where the understanding is that death will come naturally to the very elderly, and care should be delivered with this and the resident's wishes in mind. This would perhaps result in a different mindset among medical staff about how much medical intervention to undertake that is aimed at prolonging life.

One important aspect of this is the issue of how we see death. Again, for the most part our society avoids death and therefore often avoids those for whom death might not be too many years away. Yet, death is a natural part of life, the final step. I think part of your anguish for your father was that clearly by his age he would have had a limited number of years left to live, yet the outcome of the heart surgery was that the process of dying became unnatural, driven by one medical decision after another, and with a plethora of medical equipment and medications keeping him alive. This seems to have abated a little once he was moved to the cardiac unit, but the overwhelming impression, from reading your diary accounts of the time, is that of the unnaturalness of it all. If death is meant to occur, how does it occur naturally and with dignity when so much technology is present? In the midst of all this technology, how well are we able to remain aware of the sacredness of life and the dignity of the person who inhabits the body being treated?

It is fortunate that the practice of the hospital was to encourage you to sit with your father's body after his death, and that you were able and willing to do so. Our society is still uneasy about the naturalness of death, and many people would not want to be with a loved one after death. Yet to do so provides a chance to soak in the reality of the death, reflect somewhat on the life that has just concluded and on the effect this particular death might have in your own life.

Caroline, one other theme in the book that is strong for you and your father is that of aloneness. There is a paradox in life in the fact that we need to rely on each other in myriad ways whether for friendship or more practical matters, yet on the other hand the biggest things in life go on inside us, which is where we are alone. We can share these things with others, and indeed need to do so, but they remain our personal struggles, and they are the most personal, distinctive things about each of us as a human being. For example, no one else has my thoughts, my history, my reactions, my needs, or my hopes, and these are all things that reside deep within me—true for everyone on the planet.

In the section of the book that covers the final two months of your father's life, this is a strong theme: you regularly comment on what you can't know about his thoughts while he is unconscious or heavily sedated, and you also often write about your personal experience of aloneness. In time this in some ways is lessened by the regular presence of Sr Monica and Fr Robert and others, but your comments that you wish you had a brother or sister pick up this experience of the basic aloneness of life. I'm also conscious in those reflections that you are a single woman who has no children. In this sense, the death of your father heralds your new-found aloneness as the only member of your family, and this is important in defining your current identity. In terms of ongoing grief, when the death of a close loved one happens, we can feel that a part of ourselves has died with them. It's as though we have a sense of wholeness when they are alive and part of our life, so when they have died we then have a sense of incompleteness, of something vital missing.

A related and important matter is that the final words we exchange with anyone, at the time of death or any other final parting, are absolutely critical to our subsequent wellbeing with respect to how we see that relationship. That's why unresolved conflict can be so destructive to people, whether in marriage, parent–child, or any other significant relationship where either death or estrangement ends the relationship. You were fortunate that your last two conversations with your father were warm and positive, giving you a peaceful memory of the end point of that relationship.

For those who become parents, in most cases they more easily return to a focus on the future after the death of their own parents because of the presence of their children, who hopefully will outlive them and be part of their legacy for the future. The reality of this becomes evident when a son or daughter pre-deceases a parent: there is a sense of this being against the natural order of life, that those younger are the future, those older will in time 'move on' and leave the world to those who follow. This is simply the cycle of life and is a reminder that we are part of the billions of people who at present or in the past have inhabited this planet, and equally that there are likely to be millions more who follow us in the near and distant future.

Once death has occurred, one of the ways our loved ones remain with us is by virtue of what they did during our shared time on earth to make us into the person we now are, especially how well they loved us—this means they will remain alive in our heart because of who we now are. With respect to hope, it increasingly seems to me that hope is a concept of the heart, not of the head. What the head comes up with by way of a positive future is better referred to as optimism, whereas hope is more fundamental and comes from an attitude of the heart, a trust in life itself—much harder to develop but such an exceptional gift when you meet people who have it.

You also raise the question of how we should regard the place of suffering as part of life. One of the reasons for so much research and development in medicine is our ardent wish as a society to alleviate suffering, especially physical suffering, and it's clear that much of your distress in the final two months of your father's life was watching the physical pain he endured. At a bigger level, our society will do anything and everything to avoid suffering or to pretend that it doesn't really happen, or needs to be fixed quickly if it does. Our dependence on alcohol and other drugs to dull the pain of life; our way of life that keeps us in perpetual motion so we don't become still long enough to realise we are in trouble spiritually or psychologically; our readiness to treat depression, stress and anxiety with drugs rather than look for the real cause and try to deal with it, are all signs of our rejection of suffering as part of being alive.

Yet, we do know at a deeper level that suffering is part of the human condition, and that it can be physical, psychological or spiritual. It is a natural, normal part of being alive, and when we deny it or fight it rather than live through it we create problems for later years, and difficulties sometimes for those close to us who have to live with our inappropriate responses. At issue is when it is appropriate to fight against suffering, to seek to alleviate its cause and restore wellbeing, as opposed to when do we live within the struggle, knowing and accepting that it is part of being alive. We will certainly not enjoy struggle and pain, but we need not fear them as much as our society tends to.

In one part of the book you make a similar observation with respect to happiness—that as with the avoidance of struggle, our society has an often mindless, unrelenting pursuit of a somewhat superficial kind of happiness, with a view that if you're not happy then something's wrong with you. Our society has some unhelpful views about what happiness actually is, including that we should always be happy or we're just not trying hard enough. Happiness and sorrow are both cycles in life, and in the normal process of living we move between them over and over again.

You quote your father's memory of his meeting with Ben Chifley in which there is an especially important reflection which he attributes to Stan McCauley. He cites McCauley's point that 'happiness comes from within', and then adds his own insight 'presumably from the heart and the mind'. This is one of life's hardest yet most important insights to gain mastery of (if we ever do), and it is generally counter-cultural to the perspective of our materialist and consumerist society that perpetually tells us happiness consists of our new car, our last holiday, our clothes, our expensive home, or our professional status. The message of the great world religions is as your father and Stan McCauley expressed—for the most part those religions would hold that our sense of divinity and our experience of it is a personal, interior experience, even though we also need communal ways to share that belief and experience.

Academic research on happiness (Seligman, 2002)[1] also makes it clear that happiness as an enduring characteristic of our being is by no means a fleeting or superficial experience or phenomenon. Seligman's research has found that a deeper, more satisfying experience of happiness comes from investing one's efforts in the wellbeing of someone or something beyond the self. In consequence, Seligman would argue that the very high levels of depression that beset most affluent Western societies are exacerbated by a misunderstanding of what happiness is; many people stay focussed on the pursuit of superficial and transient experiences of happiness, not realising the need to 'stretch' oneself by going beyond the self in order to tap into a deeper capacity for enduring meaning and happiness in life. Yet much of this is counter-cultural, so being open about the issue in your book is important as a way of helping to 'normalise' the pain of grief and other struggles for readers.

Carmel next addressed the question of spiritual perspectives on struggle in life. She referred to a book entitled The Way of the Wound *by Robert Grant,[2] an American, Catholic-raised psychotherapist whose work is in the area of trauma and recovery. His insight is that we miss the mark when we regard post-traumatic stress disorder and recovery as simply a psychological phenomenon. He believes that often it is also a spiritual phenomenon—that when something is deeply traumatic to us it is because it tears apart something of our fundamental belief systems about ourselves, others, life and God; about who and how we are as human beings. For the most part they are beliefs all of society holds, and we are conditioned to believe them quite early in life. Some examples are that 'Life is fair'; 'If we work hard we'll be fine'; 'Justice will always happen in the end'; 'Goodness is always rewarded'; and so on. And despite the overwhelming amount of evidence around us that none of this is consistently true (it will sometimes be the way things turn out, other times not so), we tend to adopt these kinds of beliefs as a life creed, and have the capacity from our earliest years to block out evidence that makes a mockery of them. Additionally, we seem to unconsciously hold the belief that if bad things happen they will happen to other people, not to us, so it dismays us when we are the one in trouble. Reflecting on Robert Grant's approach, Carmel continued:*

With this in mind, trauma hits us at two levels. One is the external event itself, which for you was the experience of watching the anguish of your father's last two months of life. The second is that we personally are hit at the core—a blow to our very psyche. From what you have written, this was not just that your father died, but that the final two months were a living nightmare for him, and for you. Some spiritual writers would refer to this experience as a 'spiritual wounding'.

For many, such a life-changing event is more likely to happen around their middle years (forties or fifties); some can face it very early, others very late. For journalist Gail Sheehy (*Passages*, 1974)[3] the event that catapulted her into trauma was the experience of standing next to and interviewing a young man in Northern Ireland when a bullet 'blew his face off'. While processing the terror of this she came to the shocking yet often true realisation that 'No-one is with me. No-one can keep me safe. There is no-one who won't ever leave me alone.' And so began her journey within to learn what life is and can be once you have faced this distressing fact. Her last sentence is questionable, though for some people the sad reality is that their suffering is borne in isolation; your father had the good fortune to have you journey alongside him throughout his final ordeal in life. However, Gail's other statements are true: regardless of our interdependence on each other as human beings, our own life is our own, and in living it we are alone, irrespective of family and friends. No one can live our life for us, be held accountable for what we are or do, set our values and priorities for us, and so on. For Gail, when she witnessed the shooting of someone standing beside her, life took an unexpected and unacceptable turn in another direction. Similarly, I think something similar happened to you when your father died in the circumstances he did. I think your experience of grief would have been very different had he 'simply' died of 'old age', with his heart or something else not working any more.

When we experience this level of trauma that shocks our wellbeing at a core level, we have experienced what can best be described as a life-changing event. Put simply, we will never be the same person again because what has happened will challenge and change our life views on the big issues of life. This journey is one that enables transformation to take place deep within us, but it requires a combination of courage, humility and a sizable dose of God's grace to make this journey. The problem, as Robert Grant sees it, is that most people seem to believe that the aim is for life to return to 'normal' as it was before the trauma occurred (and the word 'recovery' implies this too). Grant's insight is that following trauma, 'normal' is a new place psychologically and spiritually, and it takes quite a while to develop the new 'normal'. There is no possibility of returning to be exactly the person we were beforehand, and to attempt to do so would be to gloss over the impact of what has happened and deny ourselves the opportunity for growth.

Caroline, your book is full of questions about all of this. You question suffering, God, all manner of things, giving the impression that the beliefs you once held about all of these things have been tested, if not shredded, by the traumatic impact of your father's suffering and death, as well as the experience of aloneness, of having your second parent die. What is really important is that in the face of all of this you become a different person—*and that's normal*. Spiritual writers would say that during this period of transformation, if we can be open to it, God's spirit is working within us to remove those beliefs that are unhelpful to our spiritual journey, and steadily rebuild a more spiritually mature version of us. The feelings of emptiness you describe are consistent with this, as is the sense of disorientation over a longer period of time during the transition.

In the New Testament, one of the most powerful quotes of Jesus on this is in John's Gospel 21:18 (New Revised Standard Version): 'Very truly, I tell you, when you were younger, you used to fasten your own belt and to go wherever you wished. But when you grow old, you will stretch out your hands, and someone else will fasten a belt around you and take you where you do not wish to go.' This is said in a post-resurrection appearance of Jesus, and follows the exchange between Jesus and Peter in which Jesus asks Peter three times, 'Do you love me?' And when Peter persists in stressing that he does love Jesus, Jesus gives the instruction to Peter, 'Feed my sheep', John 21:15–17. It is considered to be a statement that a commitment to the will of God, rather than our own will, requires not just a love of God but also a 'death to self', as is attributed to Jesus in other passages of the Gospels. It is also a statement that the experience of death and resurrection is something we might all experience not just at the point of biological death, but during life, perhaps a number of times.

Another point Robert Grant makes in his writing is that the experience of trauma often brings us face to face with evil and/or true helplessness and lack of control for the first time in our lives. It will bring us closer to a deep insight into human limitation, human failing, and/or human sinfulness than we might have had before. It will often draw to our attention that we also are capable of behaving badly, and that the choice between good and evil sits alarmingly close to us every minute of every day, however small or large the issue before us. In your situation the issue of evil in the sense of deliberate harm to others is not an issue, but for those whose trauma is triggered by physical or psychological violence of any kind, it is.

To work our way through all of this requires a long journey of rethinking what we believe God to be (if God comes into our framework of meaning), what we believe life to be, and what we believe ourselves and our fellow human beings to be capable of. By way of how we conceive of God, I also find myself pondering the passage in Matthew's Gospel 5:45, that 'God makes his sun rise on the evil and on the good, and sends rain on the righteous and on the unrighteous'. The point of the death by crucifixion of Jesus was that his human perfection and goodness were not enough to preserve him from harm—indeed, it was exactly these qualities that threatened the authorities and led to his death by such ugly violence. Isaiah in the Old Testament captures this mystery of God's presence in our world and our incomprehension of it well: 'For my thoughts are not your thoughts, nor are your ways my ways, says the Lord', Isaiah 55. One of the ways in which we are called to humility before God is to accept this very reality—we will often not understand how God deals with us, others, or the rest of creation, but we are called to have faith and trust in God regardless. For many people, the task is to try to 'unlearn' the negatives and inaccuracies we've absorbed from any number of sources over the years and 'relearn' what God and life might really be about—I think this is a lifelong journey, with many potholes along the way.

Given my continuing experience of severe grief, I have been interested to read about recovery from trauma. There is quite a body of literature on the subject. The term 'trauma' is used to describe situations where people realise or believe they have little or no control over the situation, either for themselves or for others also involved in it.

The degree of impact of a distressing or traumatic event can be increased by any of the following three factors:

- *Being personally present when the traumatic event occurred, experiencing a period of distress, fear or terror while the event was happening*
- *Incurring significant personal loss, whether this involved injury or death of others, or major loss of possessions*
- *Continuing to live in a context in which the impact of the loss remains apparent over a lengthy period, including where the loss involved death or ongoing illness or injury.*

In her book Trauma and Recovery,[4] *Judith Herman states that the pathway to recovery is relatively consistent, regardless of the original event: illness, accident, natural disasters, violence, and so on. She identifies a series of essential phases towards recovery, and although ideally they should occur in the sequence listed below, there is a degree to which they may be concurrent:*

- *The establishment of psychological and physical safety*
- *The opportunity for the story of the experience to be shared with at least one other person, and the losses incurred to be mourned*
- *The re-establishment of a sense of personal agency, that one's own decisions and actions can have a causal effect on one's immediate environment*
- *The redefining of meaning and purpose in life and of core relationships.*

I was especially interested in the second and final phases and asked Carmel Ross to provide some professional insights.

The range of individual reactions to the experience of trauma and its aftermath varies enormously, not just due to the nature and degree of loss but simply because we are all unique and have different capacities for bouncing back, as well as having different resources to support us through that process. Therefore after any major life event, some people would be fine even if nothing was offered to support them, whereas others very much need every possible support, and may continue to need it for an extended period of time. It is important to note here the distinction between the event itself and the person's experience of trauma. The experience of trauma is within the person, separate to the event. An event I might find traumatic might not bother you at all; similarly, an event you might find traumatic may not unsettle me at all. We differ in our responses, and the message is not to judge the reactions of another person against yourself as a comparison.

The first step, especially the re-establishment of psychological safety, can be challenging to achieve, and the range of individual differences in what it would take for each of us to feel psychologically safe is extensive. The important element in this is whether we continue to feel psychologically vulnerable or exposed to more experiences of trauma from the same or a similar cause. Human beings are social by nature, and for most of us there are family and friends who contribute to our sense of psychological wellbeing. Because of this, psychological safety can often be regained through social conversations, counselling and other relationship-based activities, as we steadily assimilate what happened to us and around us and come to realise that life will steadily settle into a normal pattern.

The second step Judith Herman names as essential to rebuilding and recovery is that of having an opportunity to 'tell the story' of what happened, especially from the perspective of the experience of the person who experienced trauma. The story belongs to those involved, not to those in the audience, so there is a need for care in how these conversations take place. Sometimes well-meaning friends and family will hammer the person with a million questions, yet if the person is already feeling fragile this can add to their distress by taking even more control away from them—they can't even tell their story their way, and wind up with the feeling of not being really listened to or understood. For those who genuinely want to express care and support to sufferers of trauma, very gentle and patient listening is required to support the person who needs to share what happened with a non-judgemental listener, who simply accepts the account without evaluative comment. The psychological literature is clear that if trauma of any kind has been experienced, the effects will not dissipate until the sufferer has the chance to tell their story.

You may recall in some parts of the world that truth-telling commissions were set up after periods of civil or international war—their objective is to air the horror of what happened rather than ignore or even suppress it. Herman would argue strongly that such trauma kept within and never shared will stop recovery from happening. For example, one reason sufferers of sexual and other forms of abuse are often so psychologically damaged is not just that the experience occurred in the first place, but that they are often compelled not to tell anyone what happened, to keep the darkness of their experience locked up within them. Canadian oblate priest Ronald Rolheiser[5] makes this same point, that what we keep secret that should have been shared will become toxic within us—we can help ourselves to some extent, but we also must rely on others and share our own distressing experiences with at least one trusted other. For many, a spouse, family members or friendships will achieve this outcome, just in the natural flow of family life and social conversation. But for others more specific opportunities to share what has caused distress may be needed.

In this sharing of the experience with at least one other person, two objectives are achieved. First, the avoidance of isolation that can easily occur when a person believes their own experience was qualitatively different from everyone else's—sharing in conversation begins a normalisation process, where it starts to become apparent that others may also have experienced similar losses and reactions. The second is the opportunity to mourn the losses within a community, again taking away what can be crippling grief when a serious loss is held within rather than being shared with others who can extend care and sympathy.

The third step Judith Herman names is the regaining of a sense of personal agency in one's life—that you have the capacity to make decisions and take actions that make a difference at least within your own life. This is important because a central element of the experience of trauma is the sense during the event that one has virtually no control over what is happening, and perhaps cannot even attend to one's personal safety. Depending on the impact of the original event that led to trauma, this step might take quite a while, as confidence in oneself and the world is slowly rebuilt.

One of the hardest lessons from an experience that undermines our security is the realisation that we live under an illusion when we choose to believe that we do have full control of our life and fortunes. On a day-to-day basis we comfort and reassure ourselves that we are masters of our own destiny. We are not, and the foundation of our faith and hope is that we trust in the God who journeys with us that all has meaning, and, in ways often invisible to us, all will be well within God's time and plan.

The final step is a critical point in the recovery process—when a person comes to the view that life does go on, that life must go on, and that they are willing to take the risk of starting again or trying again. For many things we encounter in life, there are no guarantees. But *life* goes on, and it is the individual's decision and determination to try again that is a major step in the recovery and rebuilding period.

The decision to move with some confidence (however tentative) into life's next phase is an expression of our inner hope, as opposed to living in a state of enduring bitterness, anger or despair. Hope is multi-faceted, whether regarded from a religious or secular perspective, but among its elements is a fundamental trust in self, life, others and God (where there is a religious belief). Yet after an experience that is deeply traumatic, the shape of our hope may well be different. Gone might be the idealistic dreams of our earlier years. In their place is the knowledge and acceptance that life both wounds and blesses, and that that's okay. Life's blessings are of sufficient benefit that future exposure to difficult life situations is unlikely to cause us the same extent of trauma once we've crossed the bumpy terrain of revising and renewing our inner beliefs and expectations of life. We find ourselves more aware of what really matters to us in life, and for many people, an increased desire to live in a way that leaves a positive legacy for others emerges. Of course, many people reach a point of choosing a life of service to others without any traumatic experience inspiring that decision.

In our achievement-driven culture, such people might look like losers to others, yet they convey very well the sentiment in St Paul's second letter to the Corinthians: '[The Lord] said to me, "My grace is sufficient for you, for power is made perfect in weakness"', 2 Corinthians 12:9. A commitment to redefine life's meaning and reconnect with others through a focus on service may emerge from this more mature understanding of our human vulnerability and our mutual interdependence on each other.

We know that the inner transformations that move us towards wholeness are often the outcome of 'death and resurrection' experiences within and around us, as some of the certainties of life vanish before our eyes and in our vulnerability we become more open to inner growth and maturity. We also become more aware that we all experience the uncertainties of life from time to time, and the response we are called to make is to exercise compassion towards others journeying a similar path.

Faith, hope and love, along with courage, compassion and gratitude for the gift of life are somewhat resistant to being destroyed by any of the myriad kinds of traumatic experience that might be encountered, whether at a personal or community level. They are the enduring qualities we have to move us through the faith journey that human life is. For people beset by major life disasters, these will be the qualities that help achieve a successful transformation from death and loss to new life. Where these virtues and qualities are already present in large measure, the personal capacity to rebuild will be there, however slow that rebuilding process might turn out to be. Yet people will emerge as a slightly different version of their former selves, having experienced changes—seen and unseen—during their recovery and rebuilding period. But what really matters is that they do have these qualities underpinning their life, relationships and work, because it is these that will endure, deepen and strengthen as a result of lived experience post-trauma.

Carmel Ross

Appendix 2

The Head of Intensive Care at North Shore Private Hospital during my Dad's time there was Dr Ray Raper. He continued to take an interest in Dad's progress after he graduated to the Cardiac Ward, and was with him when he died. Because I found Dad's suffering, and some aspects of his treatment, so confronting, I asked Dr Raper to read my manuscript.

However, at the time of my request he became critically ill himself and required Intensive Care. Then, during his recovery, and with many other demands on his attention, he very graciously wrote a response; he has given permission for this edited version to become part of the book.

I am deeply grateful to Dr Raper for his care for my Dad in June and July 2000, and I equally appreciate his accessibility, humility and readiness to discuss the process of his specialty, Intensive Care, so openly. What he has written is clarifying for me; it has also taught me something valuable about my behaviour—the importance of expressing anger when you feel it. I hope I will be able to do so the next time the need arises.

Dear Ms Jones

Thank you very much for the opportunity to read your manuscript. It is a fascinating view of heathcare from a perspective I have not really encountered, except via imagination. I must say it has given me cause to think. I still have the correspondence you sent me when your dad died. With that preamble, may I offer the following observations?

You raise the very important issue of informed consent. I have long wondered about this; I am unsure that it is really possible. I guess it is for something like cosmetic surgery where the risks and benefits are known and quantifiable. But the many decisions that see people end up in an Intensive Care Unit relate to less quantifiable issues. And the focus then tends to be on mortality or survival, whereas the other scenario—prolonged capture somewhere between these two distinct states—is a very real possibility, and one that is difficult to relate to or appreciate.

One of my father's friends told me about his encounter with a young surgeon when he was diagnosed with oesophageal cancer. At the end of the rather gloomy, though accurate discussion led by the surgeon, he felt thoroughly demoralised and sought a second opinion. A more experienced surgeon provided a less detailed and more up-beat assessment and undertook the surgery without any major complications, much to the delight of the patient. The odds are that the younger surgeon would have delivered the same outcome, and so the lack of detail delivered by the second one would only have become relevant had relatively unlikely complications occurred. As a matter of interest, in *Rogers v Whitaker* (1992) 175 CLR 479 the patient won a judgment against the surgeon over a complication about which the surgeon had not forewarned the patient. (The complication has an estimated occurrence of 1:20,000 and does not relate to technique or expertise.) How can anyone factor that into a decision-making process that of necessity takes place before the event? It is a bit cheap, I believe, to say 'Had I known I wouldn't have gone ahead'.

I recently consented to surgery after discussion with the surgeon. I consider myself to be an informed consumer, but was fully aware that I was placing my faith in the surgeon's judgement. I accepted that something bad might happen in the endeavour and really couldn't factor in the percentages of this or that. I just knew that I could not continue to live as I was; I was more afraid of the pain than the possibility of something theoretically worse.

Do you really believe that your dad could have fully understood what eventually happened to him if it had been explained as one of several possible scenarios linked to statistical estimates? And could he have used the information to formulate a meaningful decision? I believe he was entitled to as much information as he wanted, but I am not sure whether anyone's best interests are served by forcing patients to listen to largely indigestible estimates and possibilities: they may well increase fear and impede rather than assist sound decision-making.

One of the fascinating themes in your manuscript is the notion of contained anger. In several places you talk about the anger, even rage, that you felt had to be suppressed. Who or what were you angry at, and why did you think you couldn't express it? We see angry people quite commonly. It doesn't affect the care we deliver to the patient. When I mentioned your anger to my colleagues, one expressed the opinion that you were a 'controlling' relative. I didn't agree, but on reflection wonder if he very sensitively perceived your careful self-control. So, perhaps not 'controlling' but 'controlled'. I wonder what damage such self-control might cause?

My bereavement guru, Mal McKissock, often talks about the impact of sad events and stories on those exposed to them. He describes the concept of 'taking it in and letting it out'; for counsellors this is essential for maintaining their mental health and avoiding burnout. For people like me, who go through a great deal of suffering with families, it is a fantastic concept. Relatives, too, need to find a way of 'letting it out'; perhaps this manuscript is your way of doing so? But I wonder if it might have been better for you to have 'vented your feelings' when your dad was going through his illness? I think we would have coped.

My guess is that you were actually angry at Fate more than anything else. Your dad received good advice and care. The decision to operate on not-so-young patients is not undertaken lightly. And it is very likely that the best chance, statistically speaking, for your dad to be alive in five years was surgery. If he had not had surgery the alternative was for him to live with perhaps very significant symptoms for an uncertain time.

I have long struggled, without satisfactory resolution, with the problem of a long-stay patient who ultimately dies. It is very hard to make sense of it. I find it most difficult with elderly patients who, in the end, die as much from old age as anything else. They just don't have the resilience to get over the initial and subsequent insults. In the public hospital we are frequently asked, in review of such patients, whether we could not have predicted the final outcome sooner and thus shortened the suffering: my unwavering response is, 'Not without a crystal ball'. We discuss all patients at a twice-weekly multi-disciplinary round that includes all available specialists; the propriety of continuing active therapy is often discussed. Where the patient is willing, and the possibility of recovery remains, active treatment seems most appropriate. Your dad's treatment was frequently discussed and reviewed in a less formal atmosphere; remember, he almost made it, and treatment was only stopped when he suffered yet another significant problem.

Finally, can I say that I still cannot reconcile the seemingly pointless travails of people like your dad. How does their suffering at the end of their lives make any sense or have any purpose? Nevertheless, I believe our processes are sound and that we should continue to do what we can, all the time questioning whether we should be doing it. I often tell young trainees that Intensive Care is actually a pretty easy specialty, with limited options. Knowing what to do is not so difficult; the real challenge is whether or not to do it.

I wish the book well. I am sure it will find an audience, and I hope it will help others who are going through the sorts of things you went through, and are possibly still enduring.

Ray Raper

Notes

ACKNOWLEDGEMENTS

1   M. McKissock, *Coping With Grief*, ABC Books, Sydney, 1985; D. & M. McKissock, *Coping With Grief In My Own Way*, ABC Books, Sydney, 1996; www.bereavementcare.com.au

p. xii David Rowbotham, 'The Gardener', *Selected Poems*, University of Queensland Press, St Lucia, 1975, p. 75.

RECLAIMING THE PAST

1   Caroline Jones, *An Authentic Life: Finding Meaning and Spirituality in Everyday Life*, ABC Books, Sydney, 1998, p. 290.

2   ibid., p. 285.

HOSPITAL DIARY

1   Les Murray, 'The Steel', first collected in *The People's Otherworld* and cited in Peter Alexander, *Les Murray: A Life in Progress*, Oxford University Press, Melbourne, 2000, p. 38.

2   Brian James, 'On Reflection' (abridged), *The NSW Doctor*, 1998, p. 22.

3   John O'Donohue, *Anam Cara: Spiritual Wisdom from the Celtic World*, Bantam Press, 1997.

4   *Photolanguage Australia*, with Manual for Facilitators, Catholic Education Office, Sydney, 1986.

5   Caroline Jones, *An Authentic Life*, ABC Books, Sydney, 1998, p. 201.

THROUGH A GLASS DARKLY

1   *The Words to Remember It: Memoirs of Child Holocaust Survivors*, Scribe, Melbourne, 2009.

2   Les Murray, 'Don't die, Dad—but they die …', 'The Last Hellos', *Subhuman Redneck Poems*, Duffy & Snellgrove, Sydney, 1996, p. 266.

3   Letter from Les Murray to Angela Smith, 3 March 1995, in Peter Alexander, *Les Murray: A Life in Progress*, Oxford University Press, Melbourne, 2000, p. 266.

4   Kenneth Slessor, 'Five Bells', *Selected Poems*, Angus & Robertson Modern Poets, Sydney, 1977, p. 121.

5   Ina Taylor, *The Edwardian Lady: The Story of Edith Holden*, Michael Joseph/Webb & Bower, London, 1980.

6   Edith Holden, *The Country Diary of an Edwardian Lady*, Michael Joseph/ Webb & Bower, London, 1977.

7   Peter Ustinov: 'Love is an act of endless forgiveness; a tender look which becomes a habit.'

8   Hymn 31, 'Come as You Are', Deirdre Browne, *As One Voice: Hymns to Celebrate Life*, vol. 1, Spectrum Publications, 1992.

9   Peter Alexander, *Les Murray: A Life in Progress*, Oxford University Press, Melbourne, 2000, p. 106.

10   *The Sydney Morning Herald*, 7 April 2001, photo David Hancock.

11   ibid., photo AFP.

12   ibid., photo Rick Stevens.

13   Peter Kocan, 'Blackout', *Standing with Friends*, William Heinemann, Melbourne, 1992, p. 1.

14   Peter Kocan, 'Standing with Friends', *Standing with Friends*, William Heinemann, Melbourne, 1992, p. 37.

15   *Nostalgias* by J.C. Cobian and E. Cadicamo, performed by Orlando Marconi and Juanjo Dominguez, from the film *Tango*, written by Carlos Saura, directed by Vittorio Storaro.

SEEDS OF CONSOLATION

1   Tom O'Donovan SJ, *In the Footsteps of Christ*, Delphian Books, Epping, NSW, 2006.

2   John O'Donohue, *Anam Cara: Spiritual Wisdom from the Celtic World*, Bantam Press, 1997.

3   ibid., pp. 15–16.

4   ibid., p. 24.

5   ibid., p. 269.

6   ibid., pp. 203–4.

7   ibid., p. 202.
8   Kenneth Slessor, 'Five Bells', *Selected Poems*, Angus & Robertson Modern Poets, Sydney, 1977, p. 121.
9   Caroline Jones, *An Authentic Life*, ABC Books, 1998, p. 153.
10 Peter Solness, *Tree Stories*, Chapter & Verse, Neutral Bay, NSW, 1999.
11 'Moments of consequence' is a term coined by Australian novelist Thea Astley.
12 *The Sydney Morning Herald*, Weekend Edition, 20–21 March 2004.

EPILOGUE
1   Joan Chittister, *Scarred by Struggle, Transformed by Hope*, Eerdmans, Michigan, 2003.
2   Barbara Blackman, in Caroline Jones, *The Search for Meaning Collection*, ABC Books/Dove, Sydney, 1995, p. 181.

APPENDIX 1
1   Martin E.P. Seligman, *Authentic Happiness*, Random House, Sydney, 2002.
2   Robert Grant, *The Way of the Wound*, Robert Grant, Oakland, CA, 1996.
3   Gail Sheehy, *Passages*, Bantam Books, New York, 1974.
4   Judith Herman, *Trauma and Recovery*, Pandora, London, 1992.
5   Ronald Rolheiser, www.ronrolheiser.com

Index

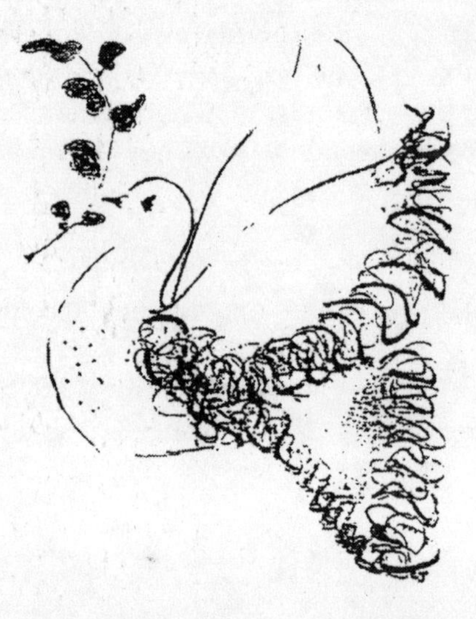